Better Left Unsaid

THE CULTURAL LIVES OF LAW
Edited by Austin Sarat

Better Left Unsaid

*Victorian Novels, Hays Code Films,
and the Benefits of Censorship*

Nora Gilbert

Stanford Law Books
An Imprint of Stanford University Press
Stanford, California

Stanford University Press
Stanford, California

Printed in the United States of America on acid-free, archival-quality paper

Library of Congress Cataloging-in-Publication Data

Gilbert, Nora, author.
  Better left unsaid : Victorian novels, Hays Code films, and the benefits of censorship / Nora Gilbert.
        pages cm. -- (The cultural lives of law)
  Includes bibliographical references and index.
  ISBN 978-0-8047-8420-7 (cloth : alk. paper)
  1. English fiction--19th century--Censorship. 2. Fiction--Censorship--Great Britain--History--19th century. 3. Motion pictures--Censorship--United States--History--20th century. 4. Literature and morals--Great Britain--History--19th century. 5. Motion pictures--Moral and ethical aspects--United States. 6. Censorship--Great Britain--History--19th century. 7. Censorship--United States--History--20th century. I. Title. II. Series: Cultural lives of law.
  PR878.C45G55 2012
  363.31'0941--dc23

                        2012030435

Typeset by Bruce Lundquist in 11/13.5 Adobe Garamond

For Scoop, for "humoring" me

Contents

Acknowledgments

BECAUSE THIS PROJECT was conceived and, for the most part, completed at the University of Southern California (USC), I must give the majority of my thanks to the people I met there along the way. Early independent studies with Jim Kincaid and Dana Polan first got me thinking about the role that censorship plays in literature and film, and my involvement with USC's invigoratingly interdisciplinary Center for Law, Humanities, and Culture helped me begin to shape those thoughts into more complex questions. I was fortunate enough to receive insightful feedback from Leo Braudy, Jim Kincaid, Tania Modleski, and Michael Renov, each of whom brought a valuably different perspective to the issues at hand. But it was Hilary Schor who guided me through the writing process the most, showering me with the warmest of praise when my efforts were successful, advising me with the frankest of candor when they were not. This project benefited equally from her praise and her candor (not to mention her friendship), and would not be what it is now without them.

I would also like to extend my thanks to the peer reviewers and editorial board members who commented upon an article based on this book's first chapter that appeared in *PMLA*; some of their suggestions helped me to clarify the goals and methods of this work. Even more, I would like to express my gratitude to Kate Wahl at Stanford University Press and series editor Austin Sarat for their generous and swiftly communicated support of this project from the start, Emily Smith for shepherding me through the production process, Kay Kodner for her careful copyediting, and outside readers Maria DiBattista and Ned Schantz for their thoughtful, nuanced, and enormously constructive remarks.

Archival work for this project was conducted at USC, the University of California, Los Angeles (UCLA), the British Library, and, most of all, at the Academy of Motion Picture Arts and Sciences' Margaret Herrick Library in Los Angeles. I am grateful for all the assistance I received from the staffs of those institutions. A publication grant from the Text and Academic Authors Association covered the costs of reproducing illustrations from *Vanity Fair* and *A Christmas Carol*; the illustrations from *Vanity Fair* are reprinted courtesy of University of Southern California Libraries, Special Collections, and the illustrations from *A Christmas Carol* are reprinted courtesy of the William Andrews Clark Memorial Library, University of California, Los Angeles. For helping me navigate my way through the book publication jungle, I thank James Penner. For proofreading services in the final flurried moments, I thank my meticulous aunt, Alys Washington. And for much-needed camaraderie and moral support throughout and since graduate school, I thank Natasha Alvandi Hunt, Ruth Blandon, Beth Callaghan, Jennifer Conary, Michael Cucher, Mariko Dawson Zare, Laura Fauteux, Tanya Heflin, Yetta Howard, Stacy Lettman, Alexis Lothian, Alicia Macias Garnica, Marci McMahon, Alvis Minor, Kevin Pinkham, Michael Robinson, Jeff Solomon, Kathryn Strong Hansen, and Erika Wright. It was through conversations with each of them that I maintained my sense of perspective and my sense of humor, which are perhaps the most essential writing tools of all.

On a more personal note, this project owes much of its impetus to the taste and influence of my parents, Arnold and Janice Dicke, from whom I may not have inherited my political views but certainly inherited my love of novels and films. On a more practical level, I am also deeply indebted to my parents-in-law, Fred and Judy Gilbert, for providing me not just with a room of my own but an entire house of my own in which I was able to burrow away from the interruptions and distractions of daily life. I am extremely lucky to have had so many friends and family members cheering me on throughout this process—most loudly and energetically of all, the four impossibly wonderful men of my life, Josh, Grady, Quinn, and Keaton. Words cannot express the love I feel in those quarters, but I'll try these: I could not have written a book on the subject of "joy" without you.

Better Left Unsaid

Introduction
The Joy of Censorship

THE BOOK THAT FOLLOWS is in the unseemly position of defending censorship from the central liberal allegations that are traditionally leveled against it: censorship leads to fewer and duller representations of human sexuality; censorship squelches political protest; censorship domesticates and disempowers women; censorship destroys art. The problem with this insistently destructive formulation is that it gives the censor both too much and too little credit—too much because it assumes that the censor is shrewdly omnipotent, controlling and restricting the artist's every move, too little because it assumes that the goals of the censor are necessarily at odds with the goals of the artist. The censor that I will be describing in this study is at times more fallible, at times more broad-minded than the phantom enemy of free expression so often evoked by the anticensorship cause. And the artist that I will be describing knows it. Less in contest than in collaboration, the censor and the artist of my account work together to create an allusive, subtextual style of storytelling that is, in many ways, precisely the style best suited to telling tales of sexually and socially subversive desire. To demonstrate this, I will focus my attention on the role that censorship played in the shaping of two narrative art forms that are often critiqued for their seeming acquiescence to the pressures of propriety: the mainstream Victorian novel and Production Code–era Hollywood film.

Although these genres are linked by neither time nor place nor medium, it is my contention that they were governed in very similar manners by very similar rules and regulations—with very similar artistic results. These regulations were primarily moral in nature, intended to prevent the highly popular art forms of the novel and the cinema from corrupting the "susceptible" minds of their young, lower-class, and female audiences. But they were also, importantly, extralegal; Hollywood filmmakers chose to embrace the directives of the Motion Picture Production Code of 1930 (also known as the Hays Code) in order to forestall legal battles at the state and Supreme Court levels, while Victorian novelists chose to censor themselves in order to appease moral reform groups and the conservative sector of their book-buying public. Both types of artists were, then, affected not by the political censorship of tyrannical governments but by the more insidious censorship of public opinion, of middle-class morality, of the marketplace. And, in response, both sets of artists could be seen to employ comparable strategies of censorship resistance. Rather than being ruined by censorship, the novels written in nineteenth-century England and the films produced under the Production Code were stirred and stimulated by the very forces meant to restrain them.

As much as I will argue what these two censorship histories have in common, one marked difference between them is the degree to which the rules of acceptability were spelled out for the artists who were expected to play by those rules. Starting in 1930 and continuing until the late 1960s, Hollywood filmmakers were provided with an ostentatiously formal list of verbal and visual requirements and prohibitions that dictated the way their films could treat everything from crime ("Revenge in modern times shall not be justified"), to sex ("Sexual perversion or any inference to it is forbidden"), to religion ("Ministers of religion should not be used as comic characters or as villains"), to particular locations ("The treatment of bedrooms must be governed by good taste and delicacy").[1] Victorian novelists received no such document. Theirs was a quieter, more intangible form of censorship, perceived by many to be all the more powerful because it went without saying. This intangibility was perhaps best described by Lord Thomas Macaulay who, in the course of writing his *History of England* in the mid-1850s, peevishly observed:

> During a hundred and sixty years the liberty of our press has been constantly becoming more and more entire; and during those hundred and sixty years

the restraint imposed on writers by the general feeling of readers has been constantly becoming more and more strict. At length even that class of works in which it was formerly thought that a voluptuous imagination was privileged to disport itself, love songs, comedies, novels, have become more decorous than the sermons of the seventeenth century. At this day foreigners, who dare not print a word reflecting on the government under which they live, are at a loss to understand how it happens that the freest press in Europe is the most prudish.[2]

Like the nineteenth-century foreigners who gazed with wonder at the gratuitous prudery of the Victorian press, contemporary critics have a difficult time discussing the Victorian novel in terms of its relationship to censorship. By studying the implicit injunctions of Victorian morality alongside the explicit edicts of Hollywood's Production Code, however, we can understand more about both versions of censorship. Because Code administrators were specifically trying to bring a more "Victorian" aesthetic to the morally depraved world of popular film, their meticulously preserved correspondence with studio heads and filmmakers provide us with a concrete language to describe and discuss the Victorian censorship practices that have eluded critical inquiry for so long.

I am not the first to identify a parallel between the Victorian novel and classical Hollywood film; scholars have, in fact, been remarking upon their resemblances ever since the 1944 publication of Sergei Eisenstein's seminal piece of comparative criticism, "Dickens, Griffith, and the Film Today."[3] In particular, many film historians who write about the studio era's intricate system of self-censorship point to its Victorian ancestry at some point in their analyses. Thomas Doherty, for example, argues that an "amalgam of Irish-Catholic Victorianism colors much of [the Code's] cloistered design," while Francis Couvares connects the Code's fear of "arousing strong desires and strong antipathies in an untrustworthy public" back to the concerns brought on by "the emergence of the dime novel, the penny press, and the popular theater in the nineteenth century."[4] But if the Code is Victorian in its paranoid priggishness, it is also Victorian according to the reconceptualization of the term that began with the work of Steven Marcus in the 1960s but that is more often associated with Michel Foucault's juggernaut of cultural genealogy, *The History of Sexuality*. False,

Foucault informs us, are the modern world's presumptions about its discourse-suppressing Victorian past; what the Victorians ought really to be credited with is the institutionalization of prurience. In the world of film, similar credit may be given to the creators and enforcers of the Production Code. For in sifting through the copious Production Code Administration (PCA) files that are now accessibly housed in the Academy of Motion Picture Arts and Sciences' Margaret Herrick Library in Los Angeles, one is struck not by the Code administrators' hegemonic smothering of all controversial content but rather by what Foucault describes as "a determination on the part of the agencies of power to hear [such content] spoken about, and to cause *it* to speak through explicit articulation and endlessly accumulated detail."[5] Censorship, in classical Hollywood as in Victorian England, paradoxically catalyzed the overt discussion of covert desires.

Acknowledging the paradoxical nature of prohibitive practices is the unifying feature of a specific branch of censorship study to which this work clearly belongs.[6] Yet in spite of the relative abundance of criticism that sees censorship as a productive force—insofar as it generates discourse as much as it inhibits it—there continues to be something of a critical taboo against viewing censorship as productive in a more pleasurable, beneficial sense. Even when such a view is hinted at, it tends to be presented as a qualification or subordinate point to the critic's larger argument and is often voiced in a hesitant or apologetic tone. This hesitancy is, of course, understandable, since extolling the benefits of censorship can come dangerously close to encouraging or excusing acts of oppression and silencing. Indeed, as Robert Post points out in his foreword to a collection of recent censorship essays, one of the primary pitfalls of this new scholarship is its tendency "to flatten variations among kinds of struggles, de-emphasizing the difference between, say, the agonism of poets and that of legal aid clients."[7] I would like, therefore, to emphasize at the outset that I do appreciate this difference, and to acknowledge that the majority of my claims about the "joy" of censorship in the Victorian novel and classical Hollywood cinema hold true only because nineteenth-century England and twentieth-century America had each established foundational levels of artistic and political freedom.

In England, this foundation is typically traced back to 1695, the year in which the House of Commons opted not to renew the Licensing Act that required books to be approved by the government before they were published. As Lord Macaulay's complaint about his nation's inexplicable reticence makes clear, however, the course of free expression in England never did run smooth. From the very beginning of the eighteenth century, the fear of Jacobite and other political insurrections resulted in a rash of sedition and libel suits, just as the battle against obscenity was declared by the various Societies for the Reformation of Manners that spread across the empire in an effort to fill the void left by the decline of the morality-monitoring church tribunals known as the "Bawdy Courts." By the end of the eighteenth century, the Evangelicals emerged as the most vociferous and influential of moral reform groups, eliciting from King George III in 1787 a "Proclamation for the Encouragement of Piety and Virtue, and for the Preventing and Punishing of Vice, Profaneness and Immorality," at which time the Proclamation Society (later renamed the Society for the Suppression of Vice) was born. Yet, as historian Edward Bristow has pointed out, "little of significance was accomplished [by the Society] until after 1789, when Britain's first pack of smuthounds were able to take advantage of a repressive climate in which invitations to sexual indiscipline were equated with invitations to political rebellion."[8] According to Bristow and many other recent scholars of English morality, it was in the wake of the French Revolution that the groundwork for the conservative Victorian era was originally laid.

In the United States, 1789 was an equally pivotal year in the history of moral censorship. It was the year that the Bill of Rights, with its First Amendment guaranteeing freedom of speech and freedom of the press, was submitted to the states for ratification. But it was only a matter of nine years before the authority of that amendment was to be limited by the Alien and Sedition Acts of 1798. As in England, civic and religious protest groups voiced their concerns about dirty words, images, and ideas throughout the nineteenth century, most famously under the pugnacious leadership of the turn-of-the-century moral watchdog Anthony Comstock. With the advent of motion pictures in the early twentieth century, an even greater sense of urgency was brought to the moral reform cause. Because the cinema was so appealing to young, lower-class, and (I will argue) female audiences, it served as a source of enormous anxiety for those who believed in the power of popular culture to corrupt susceptible, impressionable minds. Pressures to regulate film content mounted over the course of the 1910s and '20s until, in 1930, Hollywood struck upon a solution to its censorship problems in the form of a pseudolegal document that promised to disinfect the morally depraved world of film. The purpose of adhering to the dictates of this document, from the studios' perspective, was to keep the question of film censorship out of the courts as much as possible, just as the purpose of writing inoffensive literature in Victorian England had been, at least in part, to keep the novel "safe" from the law.

This is not to say that Victorian writers and Production Code–era filmmakers were wholly successful in their attempts to avoid legal confrontations. In the middle of the nineteenth century, for example, Parliament signed into law the Obscene Publications Act of 1857, which most legal scholars consider to be the first modern obscenity statute. In it, English magistrates were authorized to seize "works written for the single purpose of corrupting the morals of youth and of a nature calculated to shock the common feelings of decency in any well-regulated mind."[9] A decade later, the definition of obscenity was altered in a slight but important way. According to the verdict of *Regina v. Hicklin* (1868), the original "purpose" or "intent" of the material was no longer what mattered; instead, "The test of obscenity is whether the tendency of the matter charged as obscenity is to deprave and corrupt those whose minds are open to such immoral influences and into whose hands a publication of this sort might fall."[10] The Hicklin standard was soon adopted on the other side of the Atlantic and remained in effect in the United States until it was superseded by *Roth v. United States* in 1957, at which point the Supreme Court modified it to include only that material whose "dominant theme taken as a whole appeals to the prurient interest"[11]—a step forward from the Hicklin test, which had allowed controversial passages to be judged out of context so that a novel like James Joyce's *Ulysses*, for example, could be deemed legally pornographic.

The Hollywood film industry, meanwhile, was subjected to an even steeper set of legal regulations than the literature of its time. In *Mutual Film Corporation v. Industrial Commission of Ohio* (1915), the Supreme Court ruled that the First Amendment could not be used to defend the content of motion pictures. Because the movie industry was "a business, pure and simple" and could so easily "be used for evil," the Court declared, it did not consider the censorship of the cinema to be "beyond the power of government."[12] As a result, state and local censor boards were legally permitted to trim, truncate, and ban classical Hollywood films to their heart's content. This decision would not be overturned until *Joseph Burstyn, Inc. v. Wilson* (1952), commonly known as the "Miracle Decision" because it dealt with the banning of Roberto Rossellini's "sacrilegious" short film *The Miracle* (1948).[13] In this decision, film was finally determined to be a "significant medium for the communication of ideas" that deserved to be granted the Constitutional right of free speech.[14] Over the course of the following decade, the proscriptive powers of state and local censors were gradually dissolved by a series of Supreme Court verdicts until, in the mid-1960s, the motion picture industry was effectively freed from the shackles of legal censorship altogether.

As important as these juridical developments were to the construction of the artistically forbidden, the books and films that I will be discussing in this study were in little danger of being seized or banned on legal grounds. There is, however, another form of censorship that has the ability to affect even the most mainstream and respectable of texts—the de facto censorship of the marketplace. The more that industrialization and capitalism flourished in nineteenth-century England, the more a book's perceived literary merit came to be dependent upon its anticipated bottom line. Moreover, as literacy began to extend to the working classes who could not afford to purchase their novels, library owners like Charles Mudie were given an even more specific type of censorious power: if the "notoriously straight-laced, hymn-writing Mudie"[15] did not approve of a given novel's moral tone, he could withhold it from general circulation and more or less ensure its financial failure (as he did with George Meredith's *The Ordeal of Richard Feverel* [1859], for example). The most outspoken attack on this branch of censorship can be found in George Moore's 1885 polemical pamphlet, *Literature at Nurse, or Circulating Morals*. In it, Moore heatedly condemns the restrictive policies of Mudie's literary "monopoly," and insists that "the old literary tradition coming down to us through a long line of glorious ancestors, is being gradually obliterated to suit the commercial views of a narrow-minded tradesman. Instead of being allowed to fight, with and amid, the thoughts and aspirations of men, literature is now rocked to an ignoble rest in the motherly arms of the librarian."[16]

In early Hollywood, the most influential set of "motherly arms" belonged to a small cohort of Catholic men, who gathered together in the fall of 1929 to compose a formal document that would lay out definitive moral rules for Hollywood filmmakers to follow. Responding to the complaints of religious and secular protest groups that had increasingly been lodged against the motion picture industry, Father Daniel Lord, Father FitzGeorge Dineen, and the Catholic newspaper publisher Martin Quigley wrote up a list of three "General Principles," twelve "Particular Applications"—with forty-three even more "particular" subcategories woven among them—followed by pages upon pages of "Reasons Supporting the Preamble of the Code," "Reasons Underlying the General Principles," and "Reasons Underlying the Particular Applications." It is a fascinating document to read through, rife with the most grandiose of moralistic claims ("If motion pictures consistently hold up for admiration high types of characters and present stories that will affect lives for the better, they can become the most powerful natural force for the improvement of mankind") and the most precise of prudish proscriptions ("Dances with movement of the breasts, excessive body movements while the feet are stationary, violate decency and are wrong").[17] In its length and in its careful attention to sordid detail, the Production Code is an exemplary model of the "discursive explosion" outlined by Foucault.

But even though, as Leonard Leff and Jerold Simmons have pointed out, the content of the Code "concerned morals, the *adoption* of [the] Code . . . concern[ed] money."[18] For it was no coincidence that the Code was formally adopted by the Motion Picture Producers and Distributors of America (MPPDA) less than six months after the stock market crash of 1929. Hollywood studios had been borrowing large sums of money from New York investment bankers ever since 1919, primarily for the purpose of expanding their exhibition empires. When the bankers lost almost everything a decade later, they suddenly became highly motivated to protect their Hollywood investments at all costs. One way that they attempted to do this was by putting pressure on the studios to create products that would be as broadly appealing (and fiscally lucrative) as possible. Since the self-proclaimed goal of the Production Code was to make movies harmless and appropriate for everyone—"for the masses, for the cultivated and the rude, the mature and the immature, the self-respecting and the criminal"[19]—its implementation was Hollywood's way of assuring New York and the rest of the country that they were going to make a change for the better, both morally and financially. At the time, the moguls believed that publicizing their compliance with this new system of self-imposed censorship would satisfy the demands of their opponents without requiring them to make any significant changes to the way they ran their businesses. By 1934, however, moral protesters were on the offense again, insisting that the Code was not being sufficiently enforced and that Hollywood films were as indecent as ever. In an attempt to evade proposed boycotts, MPPDA president Will Hays changed the name of his censorship division to the Production Code Administration and brought on a new, more pugnacious leader to tighten the division's reins: Joseph Breen. Under Breen's direction, the Code became a more conservative and effectual censorship tool, and what is now regarded to be the most stringent epoch of cinematic purity began in earnest.

With so many legal and extralegal forces working against them, one would imagine Victorian novels and classical Hollywood films to have been creatively stymied to the point of suffocation. And, in truth, there were some characters and ideas that the two genres were forced to censor virtually out of existence. As compellingly as postcolonial and queer studies scholars have explored the undercurrents of multiculturalism and homosociality that trickled through such novels and films, for example, it cannot be denied that the world presented within them was, for the most part, a blindingly white, compulsorily heterosexual place. But there were other ways in which the moral censor's attempts to regulate the genres failed—or, at least, resulted in some highly unexpected permutations. Following the basic model of Freud's "return of the repressed," these permutations bobbed up from below the surface at regular and irregular intervals, in various guises and with various effects. It is the goal of this book to trace the curves and contours of censorship's unintended consequences, both as they apply to internal textual elements (plot, character, language, imagery, tone) and to the external production and reception of the text.

My chapters are arranged thematically, each using one British novelist and one Hollywood director to investigate the theme at hand. By configuring my analyses in this way, I realize that I am setting up something of a false symmetry between the authorship of the novelist and the authorship of the film director. To be sure, filmmaking is a far more collaborative process than the relatively private act of writing a novel, and I do not mean to elide or ignore the artistic contributions made by film producers, writers, cinematographers, editors, composers, costumers, actors, et al. But the directors of the films that I have chosen to discuss were the individuals who dealt most directly with the mandates issued by the Hays Office, and they were the ones responsible for combining all the various cinematic threads together in an effort to satisfy the moral censor's demands and fulfill the film's artistic promise at one and the same time. I also purposely selected directors who tend to be identified with one particular film style and whose names carry with them certain specific cinematic connotations. "Sturges," "Cukor," "Capra," and "Kazan" are shorthand for more elaborate ideas about films and filmmaking, just as "Thackeray," "Austen," "Dickens," and "Brontë" are shorthand for more elaborate ideas about novels and novel writing.

Another factor that I took into consideration when determining which artists to single out in my chapter analyses was the extent to which their works narrativize, either directly or indirectly, the issue of moral censorship. Though the four novels and four films that will serve as the primary textual subjects of this study are by no means the only (or even the most obvious) examples of Victorian and classical Hollywood narratives concerning themselves with the rules and regulations of social acceptability, each of them does so in a way that is of particular interest to me. My chapter pairings are based largely on the connections that I see between specific novels and films, and between the personal attitudes of the artists who created them. What is lost in using this organizational approach, of course, is a sense of chronology; the story of censorship that I am telling has no distinct beginning, middle, or end. As appealing as a progressive structural framework might be, I believe that forcing such a framework onto the history of cultural censorship would be reductive and misleading. The censorship practices and evasion techniques that I will be analyzing do not belong exclusively to the Victorian or Production Code eras, and they are marked more by fluidity than by abrupt or systematic change. Yet it is still the case that Victorian novelists and classical Hollywood filmmakers have come to occupy similar positions within our literary and cinematic imaginations, especially in terms of their perceived willingness to abide by what John Stuart Mill termed the "tyranny of the prevailing opinion."[20] In the chapters that follow, I do not entirely refute this view of the popular artists under consideration. But I do question the assumption that the artists' acts of direct and indirect obeisance were solely (or even predominantly) harmful to their ideological and aesthetic designs.

My story with no beginning begins with scandal. Not a particular historical or fictional scandal, but the paradoxical logic of scandal according to which discourse is increased by feelings like shock and moral indignation rather than silenced by them. To understand the ramifications of this logic in Victorian literature and classical Hollywood film, I look at the works of William Makepeace Thackeray and Preston Sturges, two artists who share a penchant for thematizing the subject of scandal (and, by extension, the subject of censorship) throughout the course of their storytelling. Indeed, the plots of Thackeray's novels and Sturges's films are routinely, almost compulsively concerned with the public response to the private taboo. Focusing on two of the artists' most scandal-ridden texts, Thackeray's *Vanity Fair* (1848) and Sturges's *The Lady Eve* (1941), I discuss the ways in which the authors harness the perverse powers of the logic of scandal to their own artistic advantage. By repeatedly pointing out to their audiences all the things that they, in the name of propriety, should not and will not say, Thackeray and Sturges are simultaneously able to condemn, ridicule, and appease the more squeamish and conservative members of those audiences. One narrative trick that this chapter examines in particular is that of manipulating the connections between a text's visual and verbal elements in order to circumvent the rules of moral censorship. Thackeray and Sturges are the ideal artists to demonstrate this trick, Thackeray being the rare novelist to draw all his own illustrations and Sturges being the first director of the Hollywood sound era to write all his own screenplays. Throughout their respective works, words and images are played off of one another in a well-orchestrated juggling act that allows the artists to show us that which they "cannot" tell us, and to tell us that which they "cannot" show.

My second chapter considers the relationship between censorship, sophistication, and gender. Film censors have traditionally defined sophisticated content to be that which can only be understood by the adult, urban, and male members of the audience, and have encouraged writers and filmmakers to speak in a carefully bifurcated language "from which," as one Code administrator put it, "conclusions might be drawn by the sophisticated mind, but which would mean nothing to the unsophisticated and inexperienced."[21] In this chapter, I draw connections between this gendered form of film censorship and the desire to protect the "young and virtuous female reader" that permeated discussions of the nineteenth-century British novel. Following Joseph Litvak's lead in declaring Jane Austen to be "the first 'Victorian' novelist,"[22] my discussion of sophistication is framed around the archetypically sophisticated romantic comedies of Austen's *Emma* (1815) and George Cukor's *The Philadelphia Story* (1940)—two stories in which the censor's presumptions about the inexperienced, vulnerable female mind are pointedly undercut by the feminized inflection of the texts' most allusive, suggestive discourse. Each of these works is, in its own way, a *bildungsroman* of sophistication— Emma Woodhouse must learn, over the course of her narrative, how to target her communications in a more sophisticated manner, while Tracy Lord must learn how *not* to be an unsophisticated, judgmental prude. Ultimately, in these works, sophistication becomes more than a strategy to make controversial content more palatable; it becomes a means of freeing the female protagonist (and, by extension, the female reader/viewer) from the social expectation of moral perfection.

As seminal as Eisenstein's comparative analysis of Charles Dickens and D. W. Griffith may be, in my third chapter I locate more parallels between Charles Dickens and Frank Capra. In addition to the many formal and stylistic similarities that I see in and among their best-known works, I also see a striking resemblance between their narrative treatments of controversial material. More, perhaps, than any of the other figures I am examining, Dickens and Capra valued popular success and the idea of artistic respectability. But they also shared lofty ideas about the importance of social truth in art, and worked hard to create texts that would carefully walk the line between pleasing innocuousness and gritty realism. To that end, both artists created stories that were sharply critical of social and political ills but that still managed to exude an impression of soft-hearted idealism, even sentimentalism. As conflicting as the impulse to critique and the impulse to idealize may seem to be, I read the latter impulse as a calculated strategy for achieving the former—in other words, I believe that Dickens and Capra intentionally infused their texts with an exaggerated aura of innocence and purity in order to make their most challenging notions acceptable and marketable to as large an audience as possible. This is especially true of Dickens and Capra's iconically wholesome holiday classics, *A Christmas Carol* (1843) and *It's a Wonderful Life* (1946), each of which offers the audience a warm, inviting, Christmassy façade that artfully overshadows the darker, more pessimistic implications at its core.

For my fourth chapter, I delve into the psychological and libidinal pleasures of the forbidden fruit by examining the highly charged romantic encounters in Charlotte Brontë's and Elia Kazan's texts to see how barriers of resistance work to perpetuate and propel interest and desire. The final works that I examine in my project are, therefore, two intensely psychological stories of women whose lives appear to be damaged and even destroyed by the forces of sexual repression: Brontë's *Villette* (1853) and Kazan's film adaptation of *A Streetcar Named Desire* (1951). The latter stands apart from the other texts I am analyzing in that it does have a reputation for being a "censored" work of art, primarily due to the four minutes of footage the Catholic Legion of Decency excised from the final cut of the film without Kazan's compliance or consent. But I am interested less in those four missing minutes than in the 122 minutes that did manage to make their way into movie theaters in 1951, and in Kazan's unexpectedly productive dealings with the Hays Office as he worked to bring Tennessee Williams's unexpected portrayal of sexual repression to the silver screen. For Blanche DuBois and her "old-maid-school-teacher-ish" compatriot Lucy Snowe are not only shown to be victimized by the repressive forces that surround them; they are also shown, repeatedly and emphatically, to construct and reinforce sexual barriers themselves in an effort to heighten their own sensations of desire. Similarly, I argue, Brontë's and Kazan's interactions with their respective moral censors were marked less by victimization and oppression than by stimulation and inspiration. Both artists were, in the end, paradoxically motivated by the moral complaints lodged against them to communicate their ideas in subtler, richer, and more powerful ways.

In an often-cited story from Charlotte Brontë's childhood, we are given a key to understanding the paradoxical nature of the restraint imposed upon Victorian writers and their classical Hollywood counterparts. Describing his unconventional child-rearing techniques to biographer Elizabeth Gaskell, Patrick Brontë recounts:

> When my children were very young, when, as far as I can remember, the oldest was about ten years of age, and the youngest about four, thinking that they knew more than I had yet discovered, in order to make them speak with less timidity, I deemed that if they were put under a sort of cover I might gain my end; and happening to have a mask in the house, I told them all to stand and speak boldly from under cover of the mask.[23]

Though the goal of such moral censors as Charles Mudie and Joseph Breen was certainly *not* "to make [artists] speak with less timidity," the metaphoric mask that their censorship efforts placed upon Victorian and classical Hollywood artists inadvertently helped to achieve that goal nonetheless. The novels and films that I will examine in this project still resonate today because they speak so boldly and eloquently from "under the mask," because they make such cunning use of the cultural restrictions imposed upon them, because they require their readers and viewers to think and question as they read and view. And that, in effect, is the gift of censorship: by forcing certain narrative impulses underground, censorship creates an open space, between text and subtext, where the agile interpreter within each one of us can come out to play.

1

The Sounds of Silence
W. M. Thackeray and Preston Sturges

> Here I am smothering dear old Mrs. Grundy's
> objections, before she has opened her mouth.
> —*W. M. Thackeray*

> It was actually the enormous risks I took with
> my pictures, skating right up to the edge of non-
> acceptance, that paid off so handsomely.
> —*Preston Sturges*

IN THE COURSE OF REJECTING the modern world's repressive hypothesis, Michel Foucault nominates the anonymous author of the Victorian pornographic confessional *My Secret Life* to replace Queen Victoria as the "central figure" of nineteenth-century Western sexuality. The reason for this striking substitution, Foucault explains, is that "[r]ather than seeing in this singular man a courageous fugitive from a 'Victorianism' that would have compelled him to silence, I am inclined to think that, in an epoch dominated by (highly prolix) directives enjoining discretion and modesty, he was the most direct and in a way the most naïve representative of a plurisecular injunction to talk about sex."[1] Yet as deliciously perverse as it may be to strip a sovereign queen of her iconic status in favor of a nameless pornographer, I believe we can learn more about the ways in which the Victorian era's "directives enjoining discretion" both collided and intersected with its "injunction to talk about sex" if we focus our attention on less naïve, less directly marginalized material. To that end, the following chapter will nominate a very different nineteenth-century writer to stand in as his culture's discursive representative: William Makepeace Thackeray.

One reason that Thackeray's novels serve as a particularly good point of departure for my discussion of Victorian censorship is that so many of them point out and bemoan the kinds of social and marketplace limitations that were implicitly placed upon writers in his day. Thackeray was, of course, very much invested in the market success of his fictional works; having lost the majority of his patrimony to gambling debts that he accrued during college and having already failed in several other vocational endeavors, he entered the novel-writing profession more for financial than aesthetic reasons. But he was also able to view the hypocrisies of the English way of life with the skepticism of an outsider's perspective, having spent his early childhood in India, and he specifically chose to make those hypocrisies one of the central thematic concerns of his fiction. Thackeray was, in fact, responsible for coining one of the key terms used to describe the "tyranny of the prevailing opinion"[2] that was so powerful within the Victorian era: Grundyism. Mrs. Grundy was originally a character in Thomas Morton's 1798 play, *Speed the Plough,* who never appears on stage but whose moral judgment is of extreme importance to her neighbors; "What will Mrs. Grundy think?" is their perennial refrain. But it was thanks to Thackeray's repeated use of her name in his personal and fictional writing (see, for example, this chapter's epigraph) that "Mrs. Grundy" came to signify "an unseen censoring element" on a broader level. By constructing a disembodied, hypothetical figure to symbolize his culture's priggishness and conservatism, Thackeray was able to mock and critique such impulses without attacking any of his moral censors personally. His writing managed, in other words, to be ostentatiously vocal about its inability to vocalize the forbidden truth.

Perhaps the best example of this noisy silence on Thackeray's part can be found in the middle of his best-known work, regarding his best-known character. The sixty-fourth chapter of *Vanity Fair* (1848) opens with the narrator's bluff announcement that he is about to censor himself: "We must pass over a part of Mrs. Rebecca Crawley's biography with that lightness and delicacy which the world demands—the moral world, that has, perhaps, no particular objection to vice, but an insuperable repugnance to hearing vice called by its proper name."[3] What follows this promise of delicate avoidance, however, turns out to be an overt and uncompromising attack on the hypocrisy of Victorian "modesty," followed by an articulation of the strategy that Thackeray has chosen to employ in response to such hypocrisy:

> [I]t has been the wish of the present writer, all through this story, deferentially to submit to the fashion at present prevailing, and only to hint at the existence of wickedness in a light, easy, and agreeable manner, so that nobody's fine feelings may be offended. I defy any one to say that our Becky, who has certainly some vices, has not been presented to the public in a perfectly genteel and inoffensive manner. In describing this syren, singing and smiling, coaxing and cajoling, the author, with modest pride, asks his readers all round, has he once forgotten the laws of politeness, and showed the monster's hideous tail above water? No! Those who like may peep down under waves that are pretty transparent, and see it writhing and twirling, diabolically hideous and slimy, flapping amongst bones, or curling round corpses; but above the water line, I ask, has not everything been proper, agreeable, and decorous, and has any the most squeamish immoralist in Vanity Fair a right to cry fie? (637–38)

Thackeray's description of the politely bifurcated style of storytelling demanded of him by the Moral World in which he lives bears a striking resemblance to the cinematic style that would be encouraged by Code administrators almost a century later—a style that, as one such administrator explicitly put it, would be able to "please the sophisticated, without causing the unsophisticated to blush, which allows everybody in the audience to draw the inference he wishes."[4] Victorian moralists and Code censors were not, in other words, enjoining the artists working under their purview to be silent; they were enjoining them to be *coy*.

The filmmaker I have chosen to pair with Thackeray in order to explore this coyness is Preston Sturges, another highly popular artist whose works are not generally thought to be shocking, obscene, or particularly censorable. Sturges began his artistic career writing Broadway plays and Hollywood screenplays, some of which were successful and some of which were not. But it was his 1940 foray into directing—and, more specifically, into directing what he himself had written—that turned Sturges (at age forty-two) into the new Hollywood "boy wonder."[5] The string of critical and financial hits that were to follow within a time span of only a few short years, including *The Great McGinty* (1940), *Christmas in July* (1940), *The Lady Eve* (1941), *Sullivan's Travels* (1941), *The Palm Beach Story* (1942),

The Miracle of Morgan's Creek (1944), and *Hail the Conquering Hero* (1944), was unprecedented. By the end of this series, Sturges was the most touted director in the country, and he had the paycheck to prove it. But his success was also unprecedentedly short-lived, for it was soon after the filming of *Hero* that Sturges got into a contract dispute with his home studio at Paramount and decided to set off to become his own boss. To that end, he joined forces with the equally eccentric and entrepreneurial Howard Hughes to create the California Pictures Corporation, which Hughes was to finance and Sturges was to run. The venture was, however, an unmitigated failure, and the two parted ways after only two years without releasing a single film. Sturges's next move was to Twentieth Century Fox, where he was given an enormous salary and creative carte blanche. But his good fortune seemed to have run out, as the first two films he made there were both box-office disasters and Fox decided to let him go. And that was pretty much it for Sturges. He spent the rest of his life living in Paris, where he wrote a play here, a screenplay there, but never made enough money to pay for his expensive habits or the alimony he owed to the four ex-wives that he had accumulated over the years.

Sturges may not share Thackeray's habit of conspicuously raising the issue of moral censorship throughout the course of his storytelling, but he does share a similar authorial tone of sly irreverence that is seen by many contemporary critics as a form of rebellion against his culture's restrictive, conservative values. The two artists were not always considered to be such rebels, however. In Sturges's case, the earliest wave of serious criticism of his work found it to be too "hollow" and "frothy" to be an effective mouthpiece for social change. James Agee reproached Sturges for "his exaggerated respect for plain success," which led him to "produc[e] some of the most intoxicating bits of nihilism the screen has known, but always at the expense of a larger excellence"; Manny Farber and W. S. Poster observed that his "Barnum-and-Bailey showmanship and dislike of fixed purposes often make the typical Sturges movie seem like a uniquely irritating pastiche"; and Siegfried Kracauer accused him of possessing "a conformist attitude" and of "us[ing] the tools of social criticism, only to destroy its constructive power."[6] But this dissatisfied view of Sturges—as a talented showman who failed to live up to his own artistic and political potential—has been slowly eroded over the years by a string of more appreciative French film theorists, including André Bazin, who feels that Sturges "restores to American film a sense of social satire that I find equaled only . . . in Chaplin's films," and François Truffaut, who finds in Sturges's work a pleasingly "subversive way of thinking."[7] Sturges now retains the peculiar status of a sort of cult mainstream figure: in spite of the fact that so many of his films are considered, as Turner Classic Movies would put it, "the essentials," his name is much less recognizable to the contemporary public than are the names of other classical Hollywood auteurs such as Alfred Hitchcock, Orson Welles, or Billy Wilder. Those who do discuss him today, however, almost always agree with the French theorists' complimentary appraisal of his works; he is considered "radical" and "visionary," when considered at all.

Thackeray's image, too, has undergone a series of transformations over the past century and a half. By his contemporaries, he was widely regarded to be a shrewd, often scathing social satirist; Charlotte Brontë even went so far as to see him "as the first social regenerator of the day, as the very master of that working corps who would restore to rectitude the warped system of things."[8] After his death, however, more and more critics began to complain of the lack of continuity and unity in Thackeray's novels. Like Sturges, Thackeray's "showmanship" and "dislike of fixed purposes" made many critics accuse his works of feeling like mere "pastiche," or worse—N. N. Feltes, for one, has condemningly labeled *Henry Esmond* (1852) "a commodity-book, of which bourgeois moralism is a distinctively intrusive ideological determination."[9] The problem, according to biographer Catherine Peters, was that Thackeray posthumously came to be "revered as the typical exponent of Victorian middle-class values," so that when those values came to be seen as stuffy and outdated, "Thackeray's reputation suffered a decline from which it has never really recovered."[10] Although Thackeray's reputation may not be now what it once was, Foucault's reassessment of Victorian values has inspired recent critics to reassess Thackeray's political and moral emphasis; indeed, the vast majority of post-Foucauldian analysis of Thackeray's work tends to focus its energy on demonstrating how very much that work was able to get away with. Nina Auerbach has, for instance, professed that she "can think of no mid-Victorian novel more incisively outspoken" on the subject of "the dispossession of actual women" than Thackeray's *Henry*

Esmond; Eve Kosofsky Sedgwick has seen in the same text a "radical and *a*historical critique of patriarchy"; and Peter Shillingsburg has found Thackeray's "psychological realism" to be "profoundly subversive to the establishment."[11] According to all of this critical imagery, Thackeray is positioned on one side of the ideological battle line, with the conservative moral censor positioned antagonistically on the other.

In looking at the way Thackeray and Sturges spoke about the subject of censorship in their personal writing, however, we find something a bit more complex than mere animosity. Consider, for example, Sturges's remarks about his most controversial and, perhaps not coincidentally, most financially successful film, *The Miracle of Morgan's Creek*. Although Sturges was forced by the PCA to make some "moral changes" to his story about accidental pregnancy, contemplated suicide, and attempted bigamy in order to get it released, the slightly censored version that made its way into theaters over a year after production wrapped still caused right-wing Catholics to call for a boycott and multiple reviewers to comment on the "miracle" of its having gotten past the Hays Office at all—see Bosley Crowther's comments in the *New York Times* ("The watchmen for the usually prim Hays office certainly permitted themselves a Jovian nod when confronted with the irrepressible impudence of Preston Sturges's *The Miracle of Morgan's Creek*"), or, more graphically, James Agee's in the *Nation* ("the Hays office has either been hypnotized into a liberality for which it should be thanked, or has been raped in its sleep").[12] Reflecting on the religious and parental protests against his film in his posthumously published "semi-autobiography," Sturges laments the fact that "[e]fforts to make all motion picture plays suitable to all ages from the cradle to the grave have so emasculated, Comstocked and bowdlerized this wonderful form of theatre that many adults have been driven away from it entirely."[13] Yet he also maintains that anyone who was offended by *Morgan's Creek* must have been reading it incorrectly, since his "intention" in telling the story was simply "to show what happens to young girls who disregard their parents' advice and who confuse patriotism with promiscuity. As I do not work in a church, I tried to adorn my sermon with laughter so that people would go to see the picture instead of staying away from it."[14] Sturges had, in fact, attempted to put a clergyman character in the movie to "preach" that point for him. For a scene that was, ironically, "removed at the request of the studio because it was felt that it could be interpreted as showing a clergyman in a humorous light," Sturges had written a lengthy sermon that was to conclude with the rector imploring his wartime congregation: "Beware of the spell cast by jingling spurs . . . of the hasty act repented at leisure . . . of confusing patriotism with promiscuity . . . of interpreting loyalty as laxity. Beware, young women!"[15] And "that," insists Sturges, "was my moral. I am sorry that it was left out."[16]

Along similar lines, reading through Thackeray's letters gives one the mixed impression that he was both a staunch opponent of censorship's judgmental self-righteousness ("And it seems to me hence almost blasphemous: that any blind prejudiced sinful mortal being should dare to be unhappy about the belief of another; should dare to say Lo I am right and my brothers must go to damnation—I Know God and my brother doesn't"[17]) and a pious moralizer in his own right ("And indeed, a solemn prayer to God Almighty was in my thoughts that we [novelists] may never forget truth & Justice and kindness as the great ends of our profession . . . [which] seems to me to be as serious as the Parson's own"[18]). This apparent ideological ambivalence is also prevalent between the covers of Thackeray's fictional works. In the preface to *Pendennis* (1850), for example, Thackeray lodges one of Victorian literature's most biting complaints against censorship when he proclaims that "[s]ince the author of *Tom Jones* was buried, no writer of fiction among us has been permitted to depict to his utmost power a MAN."[19] In particular, Thackeray addresses the "many ladies" who have been boycotting his novel "because, in the course of the story, I described a young man . . . affected by temptation." What these ladies have failed to appreciate, he explains, is that his perfectly innocent "object" in depicting such a character is "to say that he had the passions to feel, and the manliness and generosity to overcome them."[20] Or, when discussing his exceptionally salacious take on the Newgate school of crime fiction, *Catherine: A Story* (1840), Thackeray avers that his primary goal in writing such an off-color work has been "to make readers so horribly horrified as to cause them to give up or rather throw up the book and all of it's [*sic*] kind."[21] The problem with Newgate novels, he moralistically contends, is that they portrayed their criminal heroes in a dangerously appealing way. To the genre's best-known practitioners (Dickens, Bulwer-Lytton, etc.), *Catherine*'s narrator offers some specific moral advice: "[L]et your rogues in novels act like rogues, and your honest men like honest men; don't let us have any juggling or thimblerigging with virtue and vice, so that, at the end of three volumes, the bewildered reader shall not know which is which."[22] In these and other reflexive remarks, Thackeray and Sturges are claiming that the illicit content of their works serves as a necessary set-up for the moral lessons they are trying to impart. The reason, they insist, that they describe so many depraved and dissolute acts is to caution their readers and viewers against engaging in such activity themselves.

What Thackeray and Sturges are exploiting in such claims is what I will refer to throughout this chapter as the logic of scandal, which is a sort of commonsense cousin to the "incitement to discourse" theorized by Foucault. It is the logic wherein speech is authorized and amplified by feelings like shock and moral indignation rather than stymied by them; scandal, that is, like censorship, fosters that which it purports to suppress. To explore the causes and effects of this discursive paradox, I will turn my attention to two works by Thackeray and Sturges that use the logic of scandal to propel their narratives forward but also to comment indirectly on the subject of censorship: Thackeray's *Vanity Fair* and Sturges's *The Lady Eve*. The most obviously subversive element that *The Lady Eve* has in common with *Vanity Fair* is the discomfiting presence of its morally ambiguous antiheroine, Jean Harrington (Barbara Stanwyck). Like Becky Sharp before her, Jean is an "adventuress on the high seas" whose narrative job it is to disrupt the order and equanimity of the patriarchal Moral World. In Sturges's telling, this world is personified by the priggish millionaire with whom Jean falls in love, Charles "Hopsie" Pike (Henry Fonda). Charles's main problem is that he cannot see past the categories of "good" and "evil" that the Moral World has prescribed for him; or, as Jean explains to him in what becomes something of the film's mantra, "You see, Hopsie, you don't know very much about girls; the best ones aren't as good as you probably think they are, and the bad ones aren't as bad—not nearly as bad."

This mantra is, of course, directly antithetical to that of the Production Code, which insists that "evil" may only be presented in a Hollywood film if, "throughout, the audience feels sure that evil is wrong and good is right."[23] Joseph Breen, the de facto head of the PCA from 1934 to 1954, worked hard to rid *The Lady Eve* of its blurry morality, and believed that the best way to do so was by making moral improvements to the character of Jean. Because one of the worst crimes that a woman could commit, in the eyes of the Hays Office, was the "crime" of promiscuity, Breen's most unbending demand was that Sturges "entirely eliminate" a scene from the film that contained "the definite suggestion of a sex affair between your two leads," as he described it.[24] Although, as we shall later see, Sturges did not heed all (or even most) of Breen's censorship recommendations, he did fully excise the scene in question from his film, though the ramifications of that excision may not have been quite what the PCA intended them to be. The scene was supposed to occur on the second night of Charles and Jean's shipboard romance, after Charles has made his romantic "I've always loved you" speech and Jean has prevented her father from cheating Charles out of too much money at cards. Following this card game, Charles was supposed to be called away from the table by the ship's purser, who would then show him an incriminating photo of Jean and her father that labeled them as professional con artists. And it was at this point that Charles was supposed to engage in the "definite sex affair" with Jean—after he knew of her disreputable past and knew that marriage would not be in their future. In this version of the script, Charles *is* guilty of the conniving cruelty that Jean wrongly attributes to him in the final version: "If you were just trying to make me feel cheap and hurt me," she tells him, "you succeeded handsomely." Yet as censorable as such extramarital activity may have appeared to Breen in his reading of the script, the removal of that activity actually stripped the film of its one moment of assertive male power—the one moment where the hero knows more than the heroine and willfully controls the sexual interplay. By forcing Sturges to take out this moment, the PCA inadvertently helped to reinforce the film's feminist tendencies. In the final cut, Jean maintains her sexual control throughout the story and seeks revenge not because she is a poor, damaged creature who has been taken advantage of by a manipulative man, but because she wants to knock the man (her moral censor) off of his high-minded, sanctimonious pedestal.

Becky Sharp wages a similar battle against her culture's self-righteous censoriousness in *Vanity Fair*, though gender plays a very different role in her struggle. Because Thackeray uses the image of the prudish, judgmental Mrs. Grundy figure to personify the Moral World as he sees it, he pits

Becky against an army of female characters who are priggishly scandalized by her refusal to be quiet and submissive and "know her place." The list of Mrs. Grundies that Becky encounters throughout the course of the story is a lengthy one indeed, and includes the likes of Miss Pinkerton, Mrs. Bute Crawley, Miss Firkin, Miss Briggs, Miss Crawley, Lady Gaunt, Lady Bareacres, Lady Southdown, Lady Steyne, and even Amelia Sedley, whose first few lines of dialogue in the text are all markedly Grundy-ish in tone. When Becky rebelliously throws her copy of Johnson's "Dixonary" out the carriage window as they drive off from Miss Pinkerton's Academy, Amelia chides, "How could you do so, Rebecca?"; when Becky fantasizes about seeing Miss Pinkerton floating, dead, in the Thames, Amelia cries, "Hush!"; and when, "greatest blasphemy" of all, Becky reflects that it was her French-speaking skills that caused Miss Pinkerton to release her from her duties and flippantly exclaims, "Vive la France, Vive l'Empereur, *Vive Bonaparte!*", Amelia responds with horror, "O Rebecca, Rebecca, for shame!" (10). Although Amelia and Becky spend most of the rest of the story far away from one another leading their own separate lives, the moral juxtaposition of their characters that is introduced in this opening scene continues to serve as a primary narrative concern. Many readers of *Vanity Fair* have gleaned from this juxtaposition a similar lesson to that taught by *The Lady Eve*, about "good girls" not being as good as people think they are and "bad girls" not being as bad. For as much as Becky may officially function as the novel's irredeemably corrupt villainess, there is an unmistakable textual undercurrent that seems to give preference to her characteristics of intelligence, humor, and cunning over Amelia's attributes of obsessive-compulsiveness, masochism, and hypocrisy.

In fact, as several critics have previously noted, the characters of Becky Sharp and Jean Harrington are given *such* preference within their respective narratives that they are effectively granted a sort of surrogate authorial status. Though the two heroines aspire to be neither novelists like Thackeray's Arthur Pendennis nor filmmakers like Sturges's John Sullivan, they are both unmistakably "artists" of another variety: con artists, performers, storytellers par excellence. This artistic identification does not, in and of itself, necessarily mark Becky and Jean as authorial stand-ins for Thackeray and Sturges, but early moments in their respective texts do draw specific parallels between Becky and Jean's cagey artistry and

Thackeray and Sturges's narrative art. In *The Lady Eve,* this parallelizing is most visible in the shipboard scene that shows Jean peering through her rectangular, movie-screen-shaped compact mirror at the failed attempts of her fellow female passengers to capture Charles's sexual attention. Stanley Cavell pays particular attention to this scene in his *Lady Eve* chapter of *Pursuits of Happiness,* noting all the directorial powers that Jean is granted within it—from framing and blocking the other characters' actions to scripting and narrating the other characters' lines—and concluding that Jean must be meant to "represent" Sturges: "That the woman is some kind of stand-in for the role of director fits our understanding that the man, the sucker, is a stand-in for the role of audience."[25] It is significant to note that, both by positioning Jean's vision as the lens through which we are watching the action unfold and positioning Charles as the sexualized object of all the female passengers' man-hungry glances, Sturges is inverting classical Hollywood's much-discussed tendency to present its female characters as the victimized objects of the male gaze.[26]

In *Vanity Fair,* there is a comparable early moment in which Becky is permitted to usurp Thackeray's narrative (and illustrative) power, when she writes a pair of lengthy letters to her "dear friend" Amelia satirically narrating all of her initial experiences at Queen's Crawley and includes a sketch caricaturing two of her female rivals for Rawdon Crawley's attention. The fact that Becky's sketch bears no visible stylistic difference from the rest of the illustrations in the novel is rarely seen as a case of poor craftsmanship on Thackeray's part; it is, instead, viewed as a way in which "Becky's" mockery is subtly connected with Thackeray's own mockery—as is Becky's distinctly Thackerayan epistolary tone. Thackeray is, however, careful to contradict this implied connection on an official level: "Otherwise," he defends, "you might fancy it was I who was sneering at the practice of devotion, which Miss Sharp finds so ridiculous; that it was I who laughed good-humouredly at the reeling old Silenus of a baronet—whereas the laughter comes from one who has no reverence except for prosperity and no eye for anything beyond success" (84). But the specific language of this passage, with its references to Becky's keen sense of "ridicule" and her "good-humoured" laughter, does more to reinforce the Becky-Thackeray connection than to dismantle it. It is, rather blatantly, a protesting-too-much sort of moment—in so adamantly denying that Becky's satirical view of the world has anything to do with his own, the narrator effectively calls our attention to the possibility that her view is little more than a thinly veiled substitute for his own view, dangerously irreverent as it may be. Because, then, the morally rebellious heroines of *Vanity Fair* and *The Lady Eve* are so often and so obviously aligned with their respective authors, their diegetic battles against moral prudery and censoriousness would seem to be a metaphor for Thackeray and Sturges's artistic struggles with those same forces.

Even if we accept this premise to be true, however, a closer look at the diegetic battles in question reveals a far more complex relationship between the texts' "rebels" and "prudes" than a purely adversarial one. This is easier to see in *The Lady Eve*, since its alleged moral adversaries wind up falling passionately in love with each other. Significantly, Jean's romantic attraction to Charles seems to be directly related to his prim, proper, schoolboy demeanor; the more he blushes and stammers, the more sexually enticed she becomes. Although this could be said to stem from her desire to be the one in control of the relationship—think, for example, of the "little short guy" that she claims to envision as her romantic ideal, just so he will be forced to "look up" to her—it could also be said to stem from the perverse pleasure she finds in trying to outsmart and outplay the man her father describes as their "righteous," "narrow-minded" moral foe. When this perverse pleasure kicks into overdrive, of course, is after Charles romantically rejects her (on, it must be noted, a very "moral" basis—as soon as he finds out that she is a professional gambler, he no longer considers her to be morally qualified to be his wife). From this point on, the motivation for Jean's attraction to Charles is best summed up in her cutting remark, "I need him like the axe needs the turkey." This remark proves, however, to be even truer than Jean meant it to be: after she drops her metaphorical "axe" by verbally cuckolding Charles on their honeymoon train ride, Jean appears to feel an immediate sense of deflation and loss. Instead of reveling in her triumphant revenge and enjoying the sight of Charles slipping in the mud while deboarding the train, Jean watches his departure solemnly, almost sadly, as if she finds herself missing her moral opponent—her turkey—before he has even stepped out of sight.

But the sense of deflation in the face of victory that is hinted at through Jean's unhappy expression is explicitly described to us in *Vanity*

Fair. For Becky's great moment of triumph comes not when she achieves romantic, marital, or even financial success but rather when she conquers Society—when all of her moral opponents (her Mrs. Grundies) are finally forced to accept her into the most respectable, elite, upper-class social circles that England has to offer. Like Jean, however, Becky feels much less actual pleasure in this moment than she had anticipated:

> Becky has often spoken in subsequent years of this season of her life, when she moved among the very greatest circles of London fashion. Her success excited, elated, and then bored her . . . . Becky's former acquaintances hated and envied her: the poor woman herself was yawning in spirit. "I wish I were out of it," she said to herself. "I would rather be a parson's wife, and teach a Sunday School than this; or a sergeant's lady and ride in the regimental waggon; or, O how much gayer it would be to wear spangles and trowsers, and dance before a booth at a fair." (503–4)[27]

Ironically, the very end of the novel shows Becky performing at a very different kind of booth at a very different kind of fair—it is, we are told, a stall at a "Fancy Fair" whose proceeds are elicited "for the benefit of . . . hapless beings" (689). But her presence at this charity event is, we are also told, part of her strategy for winning yet another bout with her moral detractors—detractors who, in the face of her separation from Rawdon Crawley due to allegations of adultery and her suspicious inheritance of Jos Sedley's life insurance money, have more moral ammunition against her than ever: "She has her enemies. Who has not? Her life is her answer to them. She busies herself in works of piety. She goes to church, and never without a footman. Her name is in all the Charity Lists" (689). The fact that Becky chooses to return to a life of clawing her way up the moral respectability ladder after she has already discovered how dull it is to hang from the ladder's highest rungs demonstrates the degree to which Becky finds pleasure in the game of moral combat itself, rather than in the rewards to be reaped by winning the game.

In a way, then, Becky and Jean's perverse attraction to the more censorious figures in their respective stories—Charles in *The Lady Eve*, the string of judgmental Mrs. Grundies that Becky is constantly trying to win over in *Vanity Fair*—can be understood in terms of the pleasure of contention, of taking on a difficult challenge (pleasures that I will discuss in greater detail in chapter 4). But how are we to understand the censorious figures' magnetic attraction to Becky and Jean? In Charles's case, of course, sex is involved; from the moment he meets Jean, he is, as he puts it, "cockeyed" with lust. Yet this immediate attraction cannot be explained by her redolent perfume and his recent trip up the Amazon—where, as he murmurs, "they don't use perfume"—alone. For until Jean violently forces herself into Charles's acquaintance, he is portrayed as a man utterly *devoid* of lust, even in the face of the most overt seductive moves that his female shipmates can muster (most of whom, one would imagine, are doused in as much perfume as Jean is wearing, if not more). Instead, we must assume that there is something in Jean's personality that Charles finds to be particularly alluring, perhaps because it is so hard to define. Indeed, the morning after they meet, he admits to Jean that part of her appeal lies in her unpredictability and moral ambiguity: "I could imagine a life with you being a series of ups and downs, lights and shadows, sometimes irritation, but very much happiness." Although Becky's moral detractors might think that they are deriving less "happiness," more "irritation" from their encounters with her, the truth is that they are as fascinated—and, even, as pleased—by her inventively slick social maneuvers as Charles is by Jean's sexy perfume and unpredictable nature. This is why Becky, for all her dubious morals and dealings, is so much more socially visible, so much more "talked about," than *Vanity Fair*'s sweeter, purer, duller heroine, Amelia Sedley.

And it is this attribute of Becky and Jean that interests me most: their "to-be-talked-about-ness," to paraphrase Laura Mulvey's terminology.[28] In both *Vanity Fair* and *The Lady Eve*, the perverse admirability of the anti-heroines is reflected in the amount of discourse that they inspire. The more provoking their behavior, the more talked about they become. Though this to-be-talked-about-ness is partially related to their physical attractiveness (the very attractiveness that Mulvey considers to be so objectifying in classical Hollywood film), it is also very much related to the logic of scandal. Before examining the ways in which the logic of scandal plays out in Becky and Jean's narratives, however, I want briefly to consider another film of Sturges's whose plot is quite explicitly concerned with the discursive ramifications of scandal: *The Miracle of Morgan's Creek*. In it, the heroine Trudy Kockenlocker achieves such a high level of "to-be-talked-about-ness" that she finds herself being vigorously discussed by newspapermen, governors, even fascist dictators like Benito Mussolini (who reportedly "resigns" when he hears her story) and Adolf Hitler (who pugnaciously "demands a recount"). This extreme proliferation of discourse all stems from one morally ambiguous sexual act—Trudy's drunken elopement and one-night stand with a soldier whose name she can't quite remember, resulting in her highly scandalous pregnancy. Ironically, "proliferation" is precisely what saves Trudy and her feckless replacement boyfriend, Norval Jones, from the permanent social damage that such a scandal would ordinarily inflict upon them: because her sexual act yields so *much* fruit—sextuplets, to be exact—her town and state and country all desperately want to be able to claim her medical miracle as their own. And so, in a conclusion that demonstrates the power of patriarchal discourse while at the same time exposing its slippery falseness, Sturges has Morgan's Creek's state governor (and the governor's conniving mob boss) unilaterally declare Norval to be the sextuplets' real father, Norval and Trudy to have been married all along, and the "scandal" in question to be null and void.

But as discursively resonant as *The Miracle of Morgan's Creek* may be, *The Lady Eve* is more pointed in its derision of the logic of scandal, thanks to its story-within-a-story narrative structure. For in addition to the role that scandal plays in the romantic conflict between the film's primary characters (conflict that begins when the ship's purser hands Charles a picture that silently convicts Jean of belonging to the scandalous profession of con artist), the film also includes an important tale of scandal told *by* Jean, with the assistance of Sir Alfred McGlennan Keith (Eric Blore), who specifically gives it the "gaslight melodrama" title of "Cecilia, or the Coachman's Daughter." According to Jean and Sir Alfred's story, "Jean" and "Eve" are identical twins separated at birth, the product of an English noblewoman's illicit affair with a lowly coachman, "Handsome Harry," who takes one daughter with him to live the seedy life of a professional con artist (this, of course, being our Jean), but leaves one daughter behind to grow up thinking she is the perfectly legitimate heir to the Sidwich title and fortune (this being the Lady Eve). As outlandishly far-fetched as this saga may be, Charles "swallows" it—"like a wolf," we are told—because it allows him to "spiritually carve [Jean] in half, taking the good without the bad, the lady without the woman, the ideal without the reality, the richer without the poorer," as Stanley Cavell aptly describes it in his metaphysical reading of the film.[29] But Jean also succeeds with her palpably ridiculous ruse precisely because the ruse plays on what Charles considers to be his canny intellectual skepticism. As he condescendingly explains to his less intellectual but far more perceptive bodyguard Muggsy (William Demarest), "If she didn't look so exactly like the other girl I might be suspicious, but you don't understand psychology. If you wanted to pretend you were somebody else you'd glue a muff on your chin and the dog wouldn't even bark at you."

Interestingly, the sensational tale that Jean and Sir Alfred concoct for Charles is a somewhat altered version of the short story "The Two Bad Hats" upon which *The Lady Eve* was originally, if loosely, based. The story was first written by Irish playwright Monckton Hoffe but was significantly revised by screenwriter Jeanne Bartlett before Sturges began working on it. In it, a wealthy English socialite *does* run off with a lowly horse dealer and give birth to twin daughters, named Salome and Sheba, the first of whom is as "bad" as her disgraceful mother, the second of whom dies young but is resurrected (via impersonation) whenever the "bad" sister thinks it would be convenient to look "good." And this is where "The Coachman's Daughter" begins to bleed into *The Lady Eve*; like Jean, Salome falls in love with a proper, puritanical, wealthy young man (in "The Two Bad Hats," his name is Geoffrey Pallas rather than Charles Pike) and sets out to prove the error of his moralistic ways. She does this by alternately dating Pallas under the guise of each sister—the angelic Sheba and the devilish Salome—and showing him that the sister who he thinks is morally wrong for him is really the love of his life. As Bartlett explains in her version of the story, "To love her as Sheba is only loving himself, but to love her as Salome is honest love, because it's against his every conviction."[30] Much as Sturges may have strayed from Hoffe's and Bartlett's initial treatments in his reconstruction of the tale, he did choose to keep this perverse moral of the story implicitly intact.

I am, though, less concerned with the plot points from "The Two Bad Hats" that made their way into Sturges's screenplay than I am with the plot points that made their way into Jean and Sir Alfred's gaslight melodrama *within* Sturges's screenplay. For the key difference between *Eve* and "Cecilia" is that the latter is so blatantly marked for the film's viewers as a fiction of scandal, thereby allowing them to observe the discursive results of that fiction from a more knowing, complicit standpoint. Hence, in spite of Sir Alfred's ostensible attempts to prevent Charles from repeating the details of his "Coachman's Daughter" scandal to anyone else (i.e., "You must never mention a word of this to a soul," and "Silence! To the grave! And even beyond!"), the audience understands the extent to which Sir Alfred is invested in the dissemination of that story, since it will help to protect the sham identity that it has taken him so many "years to build up." Similarly, when Jean, as the honeymooning Lady Eve, unleashes the litany of details about her allegedly "scandalous" past to Charles, both she and the audience are aware that Charles's belief in those details will lead to another form of scandal that will publicly humiliate and shame him: the scandal of filing for divorce within the first week of his marriage. And so, in yet another scene that involves a group of high-powered men standing nervously around a telephone debating how to respond to the allegations of a woman's sexual misconduct—think *The Miracle of Morgan's Creek*—we see Charles's family lawyers trying desperately to keep Jean quiet. They don't want her to talk to Charles's father ("We can't allow that, that's entirely irregular!"), they don't want her to talk to Charles ("It's a trick!"), and, above all, they don't want her to tell her story to the world at large (as Jean's father explains, they are offering her hush-money: "They'll give you half when you leave for Reno and the balance at the end of six weeks"). Of course, in their efforts to silence the scandal, all we see the lawyers do is talk, talk, talk—and the more they talk, the more Charles is forced to feel the sting of his humiliation over and over again. What both Jean and Sir Alfred seem to realize is that the invocation of an unspeakable scandal is one of the quickest ways to induce prolific discourse. By having his characters intentionally manipulate the logic of scandal for their own self-serving and vengeful purposes, Sturges places particular narrative emphasis on the ironies and hypocrisies of that logic.

It is difficult, meanwhile, to think of a fictional character who better illustrates the logic of scandal than Becky Sharp, on both diegetic and non-diegetic levels. Diegetically, a substantial portion of the novel is devoted to discussing the other characters' discussion of Becky—as Thackeray puts it in his description of her triumphant performance in the charades at Gaunt House (a performance that is so talked about that it even makes it into the

Sunday papers): "All voices were for her" (515). Not surprisingly, within almost every conversation about Becky there is at least one comment that relates to her morally questionable upbringing or behavior; "Her mother was an opera girl, and she has been on the stage or worse herself" is a fairly representative remark (168). Of course, all of the petty grievances about Becky's bohemian background and flirtatious demeanor pale in comparison to the central moral complaint that is lodged against her in the course of the story, the complaint of marital infidelity. (This charge, incidentally, may or may not be true, though the truth of it does not really matter from a plot perspective; for, as Rawdon Crawley aptly puts it, "If she's not guilty . . . she's as bad as guilty" [555].) But even after Becky has seemingly passed the societal point of no return, we can see that she continues to play an active role in her community's discourse. When Rawdon walks out on Becky and their small home on Curzon Street, for example, we are told that "the late fair tenant of that poor little mansion was in the meanwhile—where? Who cared? Who asked after a day or two?" (556) In spite of this insinuation that Becky has stopped being "talked about," however, we are subsequently told, a mere two sentences later, that "[s]ome people said she had gone to Naples in pursuit of Lord Steyne; whilst others averred that his Lordship quitted that city, and fled to Palermo on hearing of Becky's arrival; some said she was living in Bierstadt, and had become a *dame d'honneur* to the Queen of Bulgaria; some that she was at Boulogne; and others, at a boarding-house at Cheltenham" (556). Thackeray's decision to provide us with a myriad of gossipy narrative options rather than have his omniscient narrator simply tell us where Becky has "really" gone is, I would argue, more than just another example of his authorial caginess; it is also a subtle indicator that the amount of Becky-related social discourse has not been too diminished by her new degree of disrepute.

On a narrative level, too, the text of *Vanity Fair* talks as much as ever about Becky Sharp after her fall from grace, in spite of Thackeray's repeated assertions that he is morally obligated to avoid such talk. For example, he tells us that "[i]f we were to give a full account of her proceedings during a couple of years that followed after the Curzon Street catastrophe, there might be some reason for people to say this book was improper," and that "the less that is said about her doings [during those years] is in fact the better" (638). These claims of self-imposed narrative reticence are, however, immediately contradicted by the fourteen-page-long, fairly detailed chapter describing Becky's post–Curzon Street life that follows them, in which we are explicitly told "of the gambling, and of the drinking, and of the going down on her knees to the Reverend Mr. Muff, Ministre Anglican, and borrowing money of him, and of her coaxing and flirting with Milor Noodle, son of Sir Noodle, pupil of the Rev. Mr. Muff, whom she used to take into her private room, and of whom she won large sums at *écarté*" and so on and so forth (644–45). Thackeray's narrative strategy seems, here, to be a variation on the logic of scandal. He tells us that he simply cannot discuss certain elements of Becky's life because they are too shocking, too dissolute, too immoral; then, after showing himself to be on the "side" of the morally indignant, he goes right ahead and discusses them anyway. As long as he keeps using words like "wicked" and "heartless" and "monstrous" to describe Becky—and keeps depicting her in his illustrations as a siren, a witch, a Circe, and even, "greatest blasphemy" of all, a female Napoleon Bonaparte (see fig. 1)—Thackeray is, it seems, free to talk about her crimes and misdemeanors to his heart's content.

FIGURE 1 *Villainous portraits of Becky Sharp. Illustrations from* Vanity Fair.

But the talk about Becky does not stop there. As Margaret Oliphant would snidely remark a few years after the novel's initial publication, "there is nothing to be said on the subject of *Vanity Fair*, which has not been said already."[31] Although the logic of scandal must surely have played a major role in the proliferation of public discourse regarding the novel—inasmuch as the more censorious members of Victorian society were licensed by such logic to talk vociferously about all of the flaws in Becky's character, in the name of moral condemnation—there is one review from the time period that hints at a more complex relationship between Becky's character and England's discursive practices. In this review, written by Lady Eastlake in 1848, we are told:

> A remarkable novel is a great event for English society. It is a kind of common friend, about whom people can speak the truth without fear of being compromised, and confess their emotions without being ashamed. We are a particularly shy and reserved people, and set about nothing so awkwardly as the simple art of getting really acquainted with each other. . . . But there are ways and means for lifting the veil which equally favour our national idiosyncrasy; and a new and remarkable novel is one of them—especially the nearer it comes to real life. We invite our neighbour to a walk with the deliberate and malicious object of getting thoroughly acquainted with him. We ask no impertinent questions—we proffer no indiscreet confidences—we do not even sound him, ever so delicately, as to his opinion of a common friend, for he would be sure not to say, lest we should go and tell; but we simply discuss Becky Sharp, or Jane Eyre, and our object is answered at once.[32]

Becky Sharp is, according to this description, more than an immoral character who narrowly escaped being censored out of existence by the repressive sensibilities of Victorian culture; she is one of the central figures around whom private Victorian discourse was generated.

Becky's ability to generate discourse cannot, of course, be attributed to the scandalousness of her behavior alone. Readers talk about her because she "so thoroughly satisfies our highest *beau idéal* of feminine wickedness"; but they also talk about her because she is so "excellently rendered," because the novel in which she "fills so important a place" is "one of the most original works of real genius that has of late been given to the world."[33] The final question I would like to consider in this chapter is, therefore, the extent to which Thackeray's—and Sturges's—artistic excellence may also be indebted to the dictates of censorship. For the very ambiguity that I have been seeing throughout my analysis as both the target and the result of censorship is, in fact, one of the primary ingredients that readers and viewers have come to expect of their "great" art. Censorship, in other words, creates the need for subtext, the need for diverse and ever-shifting modes of communication, the need for silences that speak louder than words. It is easier to recognize this kind of evasively nonverbal discourse in the medium of film than in the medium of literature, although, as we shall see, there are ways in which the novel is able to converse in this alternate register as well.

Because Sturges has, over the years, garnered so much attention for his dialogic agility (Andrew Sarris considers him to be "by far the wittiest scriptwriter the English-speaking cinema has known," Joe McElhaney declares his films to be "not only verbal but also *dominated* by words, by the act of speaking as a powerful bearer of meaning in and of itself," etc.[34]), his inspired use of nonverbal, indirect modes of representation is often underrated or outright ignored. This was not always the case, however. Many of the reviews written at the time of *The Lady Eve*'s initial release pinpointed Sturges's visual inventiveness as one of his great strengths as a director. Bosley Crowther, for example, effused that "the manner in which action is telescoped and commented upon by fast and hilarious glimpses is cinema at its very best," while the film critic from *Weekly Variety* commended Sturges for "inject[ing] several new touches in the unreeling: comedy animated cartoon background for main title decidedly novel; and the silent pantomimed montage passage bridging proposal to wedding is also new technique."[35] The reason that Sturges allows the visual to take over during this bridging montage is, in my opinion, twofold: on the one hand, he understood that the "sanctity of marriage"–defending Hays Office would not look too kindly upon a prolonged wedding ceremony that the audience knows to be something of a sham. On the other hand, by skimming over the wedding—and spending as much time showing the servants preparing for the big, extravagant party as the bride walking down the aisle—Sturges subtly undermines the importance of the ritualistic moment itself. The fact that the montage ends with Jean looking up at Charles and then back toward the camera with a glint in her eye that he reads as love (but that we know to be vengefulness) brings us to another of Sturges's key visual ploys. Throughout the film, from the initial seduction scene to the various card-table scenes to the horse-nuzzling proposal scene to the train revenge scene, Sturges repeatedly positions the camera in such a way that the audience is made privy to Jean's expressive, sardonic looks while Charles misses them entirely (see fig. 2).

But in the world of film, visual images do not constitute the only form of nonverbal communication. Sturges is also able to rely on certain auditory cues to help him make his point, such as the steaming, erupting boat whistles that carry on a suggestive conversation as Charles transfers from the womanless safety of his little launch to the man-hungry commotion of the S.S. *Southern Queen*, or the similarly suggestive train whistles that are interspliced with the names of Eve's alleged former lovers as she reveals them to her horrified new groom. Beyond these obvious audio effects, Sturges also takes advantage of a subtler kind of sound—the sound of his actors' voices, which is often able to relay much more

FIGURE 2 *Playing to the audience. Barbara Stanwyck and Henry Fonda in* The Lady Eve.

than what is found "on the printed page." For example, the scene of Barbara Stanwyck draping herself around Henry Fonda while running her fingers through his hair is, thanks to its visual staging as well as the erotically charged vocalizations of the actors, arguably one of the sexiest scenes of classical Hollywood cinema. Stanwyck's voice, a guttural blend of sandpaper and honey, and Fonda's voice, an agitated mix of schoolboy gulps and tremors, tug and pull at one another until they reach what is quite clearly the verbal equivalent of a sexual climax (see fig. 3). And yet, nothing in the screenplay's written dialogue appears to be particularly vulgar or risqué, as is evidenced by the fact that Joseph Breen gave the scene an uncontested green light when he read it in October 1940. After *The Lady Eve* was released, however, many state censor boards ordered the scene to be excised on the basis of its offensively "lewd" nature. Much like the Victorian moral watchdogs who bristled at the too-knowing intonations of music-hall performers (i.e., "It was not what she said, but the way in which she said it"[36]), these local censors objected to the very

FIGURE 3   *Erotic intonations. Henry Fonda and Barbara Stanwyck in* The Lady Eve.

sound of sexuality. What this means, of course, is that Sturges essentially outsmarted Breen, since Breen considered his job to be the weeding out of any material that state or religious groups might possibly deem objectionable. Or, looked at another way, this scene could also be viewed as a prime example of the subtlety of filmic phrasing that came as a result of the Production Code's ever-looming threat of verbal censorship.

For although the Code did make some attempt to prohibit certain nonverbal forms of representation—"Dances suggesting or representing sexual actions or indecent passions are forbidden;" "Scenes of *actual child birth*, in fact or in silhouette, are never to be presented"[37]—its primary emphasis was unquestionably on the spoken word. This can most easily be seen in the timing of the implementation of the Code, since, as is mentioned in the Code's preamble, it was specifically "[d]uring the rapid transition from silent to talking pictures" that Hollywood producers "realized the necessity and the opportunity of subscribing to a Code to govern the production of talking pictures."[38] Words had, in fact, been a source of censorship anxiety even before the emergence of sound technology; as Kevin Brownlow recounts in *Behind the Mask of Innocence*, many silent film viewers became fluent in the language of lip-reading, so that when, for example, director Raoul Walsh allowed his actors to "swear authentically at each other" in *What Price Glory?* (1926), Hays Office censors responded by including on their 1927 list of "Don'ts and Be Carefuls" a proscription against "pointed profanity—by either title or lip."[39] In the years following the Code's implementation, this verbal emphasis was also seen in the structure of the PCA's revision process: the vast majority of the Code's censorious "recommendations" were made when administrators read the screenplays of films in the preproduction phase of development, as opposed to when films were viewed after they had already been shot. As a result, classical Hollywood's dialogue was inherently subjected to a more rigorous censorship regimen than were the nonverbal elements of its films.

If we look at what Breen wanted to expurgate from the original draft of *The Lady Eve* that Sturges submitted to the Hays Office, for example, we can see that most of his recommendations relate to what the movie should not *say*, rather than what it should not *show*. Among the recommended verbal cuts are offensive words such as "puke," "nuts," and "damn," and suggestive lines such as "Don't you think we ought to go to bed?" Statistically, Sturges followed about half of Breen's recommendations—and utterly disregarded the other half. (One example of a recommended cut that Sturges chose simply to ignore was, incidentally, Sir Alfred's entire "Coachman's Daughter" scandal story, which Breen pronounced to be "not acceptable, by reason of its suggestiveness."[40]) It seems quite possible, in fact, that Sturges was employing a tactic similar to the one famously described by Mae West: "When I knew that the censors were after my films and they had to come and okay everything," West boasted, "I wrote scenes for them to cut! These scenes were so rough that I'd never have used them. But they worked as a decoy. They cut them and left the stuff I wanted."[41] Even though Sturges never explicitly made this claim about his own screenwriting, the central plot twist of *The Lady Eve* does seem to echo West's censorship evasion strategy, in that it involves Jean successfully assuaging Charles's qualms about her disreputability by dangling the decoy of the Lady Eve's rougher, more obviously objectionable past before him.

One element of Sturges's script that Breen did not object to was the series of slapstick sight-gags that were to take place over the course of the film. Breen was, of course, quite accustomed to the tradition of slapstick cinema, which had been popular since the advent of silent film and which was still very much alive in the "screwball" romantic comedy genre to which *The Lady Eve* appeared so neatly to belong. Brian Henderson has argued that Sturges's decision to follow the conventions of screwball comedy in *The Lady Eve* and *The Palm Beach Story* stemmed from a specific defense strategy on his part: "That these are the most genre-typed films that he made provides, besides their lightness itself, a built-in defense structure. No director is responsible for the subject or even the plot of a genre film—they are taken as given."[42] Yet the physical comedy in Sturges's version of screwball works quite differently than the physical comedy in most of the other exemplary models of the form. As Diane Carson outlines in her essay on sexism in screwball comedies, there are screwballs in which "the central male character spanks the woman (*It Happened One Night*), knocks her out with a punch (*Nothing Sacred*), kicks her (*The Awful Truth*), jabs her with a pin (*Twentieth Century*), throws her under a shower (*My Man Godfrey*), or pushes her over with a solid hand to the face (*The Philadelphia Story*)."[43] *The Lady Eve*, by contrast, starts off by reversing the direction of the physical violence when Jean intentionally trips Charles so that he falls flat on his face, and then continues to show Charles falling and humiliating himself throughout the film—not because Jean keeps tripping him, but because he simply cannot stop *looking* at her (which is, again, an important reworking of the disempowering male gaze that feminist film theorists have so often criticized within classical Hollywood cinema). The emasculation of Charles that is carried out through this progression of ever messier and more painful pratfalls is, I would argue, the same emasculation that resulted from Breen's demand that Charles's "objectionable" act of sleeping with Jean out of wedlock be cut. By knowing what would probably be able to make it past Code administrators (the visual) and what probably would not (sexual dialogue), Sturges was able to manipulate the mandates of censorship for his own artistic purposes: in this case, to upend gender stereotypes by granting his heroine an unconventional level of unchallenged autonomy.

Although Thackeray, as a novelist, does not have at his disposal the same set of nonverbal tools that are available to filmmakers like Sturges, part of why his satire is still vivid to us today is because it is so visual in nature. A good deal of this visuality stems from Thackeray's ability to "paint a picture" with his words—if we return to the passage describing Becky's "hideous tail" below the water line, for example, we notice that it carefully differentiates between what Thackeray's writing will allow his readers to *hear* about Becky's bad behavior (thanks, he tells us, to the Moral World's "insuperable repugnance to hearing vice called by its proper name" [637]) and what it will allow them to *see* ("Those who like may . . . see it writhing and twirling, diabolically hideous and slimy, flapping amongst bones, or curling round corpses" [638]). In addition to the skill of writing visually, however, there is one other narrative trick up Thackeray's sleeve that his fellow Victorian novelists did not possess: the trick of providing illustrations for all his own novels. From the engraved vignette title page showing a court jester gazing despondently at himself in a cracked mirror while a smirking Becky doll lies next to him on the ground, to the closing woodcut showing a jester's stick lying on the ground in a sort of miniature embrace with the "famous little Becky puppet" (xvi), *Vanity Fair*'s illustrations are ripe for interpretation indeed. The favorite illustration for this kind of interpretation seems to be that of "Becky's second appearance in the character of Clytemnestra," as Thackeray incriminatingly captions it, which depicts a terrified Jos Sedley pleading with Dobbin to rescue him from Becky's evil clutches as she lurks ominously in the shadows of the curtains nearby (fig. 4). Most feminist critics who discuss *Vanity Fair* find something to say about this particular illustration—about the darkly subversive power it grants Becky, about its foreshadowing of a more violent

FIGURE 4 *Murderous implications. Illustration from* Vanity Fair.

form of female rebellion, about its ability to "go where the text fears to tread."[44] For the most part, then, these critics are buying into the murderous implication of the sketch; in much the same way that Charles, in *The Lady Eve*, allows the purser's photograph to act as judge and jury in his estimation of Jean's character, these critics are letting one silent yet evocative illustration convict Becky of a crime that the novel specifically refuses to tell us whether she has committed or not.

It is interesting to compare this critical stance to the one taken by Lady Eastlake, who is often criticized by feminist scholars for her Grundy-ish treatment of moral and gender issues. In the final section of her review of *Vanity Fair* she does, after all, "advise" her readers "to cut out that picture of our heroine's 'Second Appearance as Clytemnestra,' which casts so uncomfortable a glare over the latter part of the volume," and to cling to the belief that Jos died from perfectly natural, biological causes—for, as she points out, the man had "been much in India . . . and his digestion was not to be compared with Becky's."[45] Before she arrives at this reactionary call for a sort of do-it-yourself censorship, however, it is important to note that she actually thanks Thackeray for the indirectness and ambiguity of the illustration in question: "We, therefore, cannot sufficiently applaud the extreme discretion with which Mr. Thackeray has hinted at the possibly assistant circumstances of Jos Sedley's dissolution. A less delicacy of handling would have marred the harmony of the whole design."[46] Lady Eastlake is, for want of a more flexible word, right; a more overt and unequivocal depiction of Jos's murder *would* have robbed *Vanity Fair* of the moral ambiguity that has been, and continues to be, one of its greatest attractions. Whether Thackeray avoided telling a story that definitively ends with a woman getting away with murder because he knew that such a story's lack of "compensating moral values" would have made it deeply objectionable to a host of Grundies the world over or because he artistically preferred such an ending cannot, of course, ever be known. The truth probably lies somewhere in the middle, with Thackeray being careful not to cross any lines that would make his book less popular or profitable, but also very much reveling in the shifty ambiguity that was, in effect, required of him. This can particularly be seen in an interview for *Appleton's Journal* that took place several years after *Vanity Fair* was published, in which Thackeray was asked point-blank whether or not Becky killed Jos. In response, Thackeray "smoked meditatively as if he was endeavouring to arrive at the solution of some problem, and then with a slow smile dawning on his face, replied, 'I do not know.'"[47]

Thackeray's smile during this interview is, I would argue, the same cagey smile that keeps figuratively appearing throughout his novels—the smile that we feel when he is dangling various narrative options before us but refusing to tell us which is right, the smile that we feel when he is exploiting the logic of scandal in order to tell us what he "shouldn't," the smile that we feel even when he is in the midst of one of his scathing anticensorship rants. In *Vanity Fair*, this smile takes a more concrete form by appearing on Becky's face in almost every sketch that Thackeray draws of her; in many sketches, in fact, a cunning grin is the only identifying feature to let us know we are looking at Becky at all. (See again, for example, the illustrations of Becky as sorceress at the opening of Chapter 63 and of Becky as Napoleon at the opening of Chapter 64 that are shown in fig. 1.) Interestingly, one place that the cagey smile does *not* appear is on the face of the court jester that Thackeray repeatedly draws to signify "himself" throughout the text. There is even one illustration, the tailpiece to Chapter 9, which is clearly a self-portrait of Thackeray, in full jester garb, holding a smiling fool's mask down in front of him to reveal the more contemplative expression that he has been hiding behind the mask (fig. 5). The author/illustrator's desire to assume the role of the serious

FIGURE 5 *Thackeray the Fool. Illustration from* Vanity Fair.

jester, who is able to speak more freely and audaciously about controversial subjects because of his status as a jolly, harmless "fool," can be interpreted as yet another sign that he was doing everything in his power to combat the restrictions of moral censorship. But it can also be interpreted in terms of its relationship to the proliferation of discourse.

For Thackeray's decision to fashion himself as a common Fool—along with his decision to give *Vanity Fair* the thought-provoking subtitle of "A Novel without a Hero"—anticipates not Foucault, this time, so much as Roland Barthes, who points out in *S/Z* that "the Fool, dressed in motley, a divided costume, was once the purveyor of the *double understanding*"; that this double understanding "far exceeds the limited case of the play on words or the equivocation and permeates, in various forms and densities, all classic writing"; and that "the reader is an accomplice, not of this or that character, but of the discourse itself insofar as it plays on the division of reception, the impurity of communication: the discourse, and not one or another of its characters, is the only *positive* hero of the story."[48] Although Barthes may, here, technically be speaking of the relationship between "the reader" and "classic writing," his description of discourse in all its "various forms" could be applied to the viewer and classic film as well. Thackeray and Sturges are, certainly, both double-dealing Fools in their own rights, and the multivalent discourse of their texts can quite easily be seen as the true "hero" of their narrative efforts. But, as I have hoped to show throughout this chapter, granting their discourse this heroic status does not turn censorship into the texts' patently degenerate villain. Just as the dichotomies of Amelia as heroine/Becky as villainess and Jean as "bad girl"/Eve as "good girl" prove to be overly simplistic and even just plain false, so too does the counterposing of discourse and censorship that has been accepted by so many readers, viewers, and critics for so long. It is only if we look beyond this false dichotomy that we can see how moral censorship, even in its subtlest state, transforms, complicates, and sometimes (greatest blasphemy of all) improves narrative art.

2

For Sophisticated Eyes Only
Jane Austen and George Cukor

> I do not write for such dull Elves as have not a great
> deal of Ingenuity themselves.
> —*Jane Austen*

> Sometimes I think there was more sex within the
> code than without it.
> —*George Cukor*

IN THE EYES OF MOST HOLLYWOOD HISTORIANS, the enforcement of Production Code standards in the years between the Code's implementation in 1930 and Joseph Breen's ascension to the Production Code Administration (PCA) throne in 1934 was so inconsistent and ineffectual that those years ought not even count as part of the Hays Code era; hence the misleading term "pre-Code Hollywood" was born. But if the Code did not gain its teeth until Breen took hold of the PCA's reins, it did receive some of its most influential and enduring features from the man who preceded Breen as Hollywood's self-censorship czar: the less dogmatic, less conservative, less well-known Colonel Jason Joy. Joy was brought on as the head of the Studio Relations Committee (SRC) (the MPPDA's original name for its censorship division) in 1927, at which point he helped to compose a list of "Don'ts and Be Carefuls" that would eventually come to be subsumed by the more comprehensive Code of 1930. The list contains less than half as many "Don'ts" as it does "Be Carefuls," and this ratio is representative of Joy's overall sense of his role as film censor: his job, as he saw it, was to make sure that a few specific subjects absolutely would "not appear" in Hollywood films ("Pointed pro-

fanity," "Any inference of sex perversion," "Ridicule of the clergy," etc.),
but also—and, to him, more importantly—that "special care [would] be
exercised" and "good taste [would] be emphasized" in the treatment of
a great many more (i.e., "International relations," "Sympathy for crimi-
nals," "Man and woman in bed together").[1] When Breen took over in
1934, he viewed his role quite differently: his goal was to turn as many
of Joy's tentative "Be Carefuls" into absolute "Don'ts" as possible—to
banish, in thought, word, and deed, any and all immoral material from
the world of film. In the face of such a rigid set of regulations, one might
expect "post-Code" Hollywood to have been left with nothing to produce but adaptations of Jane Austen novels. But thought, word, and deed
proved to be more difficult to police than Breen anticipated, particularly
in light of the censorship evasion strategy that Austen had so successfully
employed in her novels, and that Joy had so vocally encouraged throughout his SRC tenure: the strategy of sophistication.

The term "sophisticated" was frequently bandied about in early discussions of film content, in a variety of different ways. On one hand,
sophistication was something to be avoided and feared, a pseudonym
for the easy sexual liberty of the Broadway stage that threatened to undermine Hollywood's struggle to purify its own image. Yet at the same
time, producers and studio heads could not help but notice that "sophisticated" movies were gradually becoming more and more popular (and,
by extension, more and more lucrative). As Lea Jacobs chronicles in her
study of Hollywood in the 1920s, that decade witnessed "a decisive shift
in taste" away from films "that were dismissed as sentimental or simply
old-fashioned" and *toward* films "that came to be identified as 'sophisticated,' on the edge of what censors or more conservative viewers would
tolerate."[2] The task set before Joy, then, was to negotiate a space between
"objectionable" sophistication and "desirable" sophistication, so that
studios could continue to reap the profits of sophisticated filmmaking
without incurring the wrath of state censors or public morality groups.
The primary way that Joy did this, I would argue, was by regularly ask-
ing the producers, writers, and directors under his domain to speak in a
specific cinematic language, "from which," as he himself put it, "conclusions might be drawn by the sophisticated mind, but which would mean
nothing to the unsophisticated and inexperienced."[3] In other words, Joy

worked hard over the course of his SRC reign to set up a system of representation in which ambiguity and innuendo would be valorized rather than demonized—in which controversial content would be bifurcated rather than eliminated.

But if, under this formulation, content was supposed to be simultaneously geared toward two distinct types of viewer—"sophisticated" and "unsophisticated"—it is important for us to understand exactly what those classifications were taken to mean in Joy's day. On the most accepted level, the distinction was meant to refer to age; in the words of the Production Code, the conventional wisdom of the time was that "maturer minds may easily understand and accept without harm subject matter in plots which do younger people positive harm."[4] But the Code also makes reference to another widely accepted differentiation, this time based on region: "Small communities, remote from sophistication and from the hardening process which often takes place in the ethical and moral standards of groups in larger cities, are easily and readily reached by any sort of film."[5] Only slightly less direct, meanwhile, are the Code's allusions to a third, class-based distinction; when the Code complains that "it is difficult to produce films intended for only certain classes of people" due to the unfortunate fact that "[t]he exhibitors' theatres are built for the masses, for the cultivated and the rude, the mature and the immature, the self-respecting and the criminal," we can hear tacit echoes of the "sophisticated"/"unsophisticated" divide.[6]

One type of audience distinction that is conspicuously absent from the Code's field of vision is that of gender. But this does not mean that censorship discussions were never framed along gendered lines during the classical Hollywood era. What it does mean is that making official comments about the separate "sophistication" levels of men and women was, even in the 1920s and 30s, considered to be politically incorrect. (Political incorrectness did not hinder all censorship officials of the era, however; consider, for example, the blatantly misogynist remarks of the eccentrically named head of Chicago's local censorship board, Major Metellus Lucullus Cicero Funkhouser, who in 1917 unapologetically declared that his censoring policy was to eliminate scenes that "the male sex could stand" but that "might cause women to brood and lose their reason."[7]) The relationship between gender and Code censorship was in fact a complex one, both in terms of film content and film spectatorship. In the first place, even though there were certainly plenty of early Hollywood films that focused on masculine forms of vice—particularly in the male-dominated, vice-ridden gangster genre—it must be noted that the moral censors of the period spent a disproportionately large amount of their time and energy worrying about the abundance of *female* offenses that were being memorialized on film. This bias even comes across to some degree in the wording of the Code itself, as it singles out several female-specific areas of concern ("*The sale of women,* or a woman selling her virtue," "Scenes of *actual child birth,*" "dances with movement of the breasts"[8]), but no areas that are exclusively related to men. At the same time, however, it is important to remember that the largest group of foot soldiers in the battle against cinematic depravity belonged to the General Federation of Women's Clubs—a group that, at its peak, boasted some thirty million affiliated members.[9] As George Cukor complained in an interview about Code censorship that he gave late in his life: "There were all sorts of rules that were absolutely absurd. I know why they did it—they were scared to death of all the ladies' clubs, which have since disappeared but which were then very powerful."[10]

But if there were millions of women who actively worked to purify the movies, there were millions more who actively sought out the very kinds of movies they were socially expected to avoid. In a frequently cited *Variety* article from 1931 bluntly titled "Dirt Craze Due to Women," the perceived paradox of female prurience is described in no uncertain terms: "Women love dirt. Nothing shocks 'em. They want to know about bad women. The badder the better. . . . Women who make up the bulk of the picture audiences are also the majority readers of the tabloids, scandal sheets, flashy magazines, and erotic books. It is to cater to them all the hot stuff of the present day is turned out."[11] Even though, as Lea Jacobs appropriately points out, "[t]he reporter's statistics are dubious: there is no solid evidence that women made up either the bulk of motion picture audiences or the bulk of the readers of 'flashy magazines and erotic books,'"[12] the fact that such an article was written in 1931—and given front-page trade-paper status—demonstrates that the relationship between female moviegoers and controversial, "sophisticated" film content was not nearly as one-dimensional as the moral watchdogs of the era would have liked it to be. In this chapter, I will explore the intricacies of that relationship by focusing on the classical Hollywood genre that managed to be labeled as both predominately "feminine" and provocatively "sophisticated" at one and the same time: the romantic comedy.

This is not, of course, the only time that my project has or will set its sights on the cinematic tradition of romantic comedy; Preston Sturges's *The Lady Eve* (1941) is considered to be one of the genre's most biting examples, and Frank Capra's *It Happened One Night* (1934) is considered to be a founder of the form. But the romantic comedy director to whom I will be turning my attention in this chapter is one whose work (even when it strays outside of the romantic comedy genre, but particularly when it stays within it) is regularly, almost compulsively, referred to as both sophisticated and feminine: George Cukor. Indeed, it is difficult to find a piece of scholarly or biographical work written on Cukor that does not refer to his reputation as a "woman's director" in at least some way. This reputation stemmed primarily from his ability to elicit "undeniably superior performances" from the leading ladies of his films.[13] Cukor himself took offense at the term, not because he was ashamed of his close association with his female stars but because, as he dryly liked to put it, "There were men in those movies along with the ladies."[14] To be sure, three of those men—James Stewart, Ronald Coleman, and Rex Harrison—did go on to win Academy Awards for the roles that Cukor helped them to portray. Still, it is the incomparable list of female performances that he captured on film (Greta Garbo in *Camille* [1936], Vivien Leigh in *Gone with the Wind* [1939],[15] Ingrid Bergman in *Gaslight* [1944], Judy Holliday in *Born Yesterday* [1950], Judy Garland in *A Star Is Born* [1954], Audrey Hepburn in *My Fair Lady* [1964], Katharine Hepburn in their eight collaborations together, etc.) that continues to stand as Cukor's principal directorial claim to fame.

A less noted contributing factor to the reputedly "feminine" inflection of Cukor's films was the frequency with which he collaborated with female writers. To get a sense of just how frequent such collaborations were, we need only glance over a list of the "lady scribes" with whom Cukor worked over the course of his career, either by using their plays or novels as source material or by having them write his films' actual screenplays. In chronological order, the list includes Doris Anderson, Louise

Long, Edna Ferber, Gertrude Purcell, Zoe Akins, Adela Rogers St. Johns, Jane Murfin, Clemence Dane, Lucia Bronder, Frances Marion, Louisa May Alcott, Sarah Mason, Wanda Tuchock, Lenore Coffee, Gladys Unger, Margaret Mitchell, Clare Boothe Luce, Anita Loos, Rachel Crothers, Salka Viertel, Valerie Wyngate, I. A. R. Wylie, Marguerite Roberts, Ruth Gordon, Isobel Lennart, Dorothy Parker, Sonya Levien, Vera Caspary, Bella Spewack, and Jay Presson Allen. And the influence of women upon his scripts was not limited to the professional realm; he often sought the unofficial creative advice of his close female friends. According to his childhood friend Stella Bloch, for example, "When George got a script, he used to send it to me and ask me what I thought about it. He'd say, 'I have a script I'm supposed to direct and I'd like your opinion on it— whether any of the scenes are demeaning to women.'"[16] Since Cukor is the only director studied in this project who did not participate in any direct way with the writing of his scripts—"Now I, having started in the theatre, am for better or worse an interpretative director, and the text always determines the way I shoot a picture," he freely admitted[17]—it is important to keep these women's voices in mind when considering the general tone and impact of his oeuvre. Indeed, in the absence of *any* female directors of romantic comedy during the Production Code era, the contribution of female writers to the genre needs to be properly acknowledged, and studying the "feminine" works of George Cukor is one of the easiest ways to perform that act of acknowledgment.

Referring to Cukor as a "sophisticated" filmmaker, meanwhile, is only slightly less of a critical commonplace than referring to him as a woman's director. Gene Phillips, for example, has praised "Cukor's flair for imparting a brisk pace and a light touch to sophisticated comedy"; Douglas Edwards and David Goodstein have described Cukor as the "legendary director of . . . dozens of titles that set new standards of sophistication, wit and cinematic polish"; and actress Claire Bloom has explained that "[t]he difference between George and other directors was that he was an extremely sophisticated European gentleman, with irony, wit, and delicacy."[18] (Cukor would surely have derived the most pleasure from hearing this last remark; as the son of "just barely middle class" Hungarian-Jewish immigrant New Yorkers, he always went out of his way to come across as more "gentlemanly" and "European" than he really was.) Certainly part of the basis for this labeling stems from the five-year stint that Cukor spent directing successful plays on Broadway before being summoned to Hollywood in 1929; in his own words, "When I came to Hollywood from New York theater, everyone immediately typed me as a New York sophisticate."[19] But there is another aspect of Cukor's life that may have contributed to his "sophisticated" reputation in a more surreptitious manner: his relatively uncloseted homosexuality.

In *Strange Gourmets*, Joseph Litvak's compelling literary and cultural analysis of sophistication, he argues that "while sophistication cannot be reduced simply to homosexuality, . . . gay people—especially gay men—have traditionally functioned as objects of such distinguished epistemological and rhetorical aggressions as urbanity and knowingness," and that "in the Western *imaginaire*, gay people also function as subjects of sophistication."[20] To support this claim, Litvak helpfully reminds us of the etymological history of the term: "its older meaning, as well as its normative meaning, deriving from the rhetorical aberration known as sophistry, is 'corruption' or 'adulteration,' and its opposite would be something like *naturalness*, which, if etymologically related to *naïveté*, enjoys a considerably better press."[21] In the intensely homophobic world of Hollywood's studio system, then, the fact that Cukor was so relentlessly labeled as a "sophisticated" filmmaker might not have been quite as complimentary as our current use of the word would seem to imply. Although Litvak does not turn his critical gaze upon the medium of film in *Strange Gourmets*, the book's overriding argument that "the class politics of sophistication are inseparable from its sexual politics"[22] is as relevant to my discussion of classical Hollywood's most sophisticated, most openly gay director as it is to Litvak's discussion of certain nineteenth- and twentieth-century novelists and theorists.

It might be a bit surprising to learn that one of the primary novelists Litvak uses to illustrate his point about the "perverted," "homosexual" inflection of the term *sophistication* is Jane Austen. Yet as compulsorily heterosexual as her works are generally perceived to be, Litvak opens his argument with an extended discussion of Austen's "sophisticated" technique: "If the history of modern sophistication in some sense begins with the Victorian novel," he insists, "then Jane Austen is the first 'Victorian' novelist."[23] In this chapter, I agree with this proto-Victorian positioning of Austen on the basis of her narrative sophistication, but I will also demonstrate the extent to which Austen can be claimed as a Victorian novelist from a censorship perspective since, as so many historians of English morality are beginning to acknowledge, "the culture of Victorianism was set deeply within the English psyche before Victoria was crowned in 1837; in fact, most of the praise and the censure (the latter much more common) that critics have heaped on the Victorian years applies in much the same way to the preceding generation."[24] The true impetus for the adoption of "Victorian values" as we now tend to define them, such historians argue, had its roots in the complicated moral aftermath of the French Revolution.

In some ways, the bloody revolt being waged on the other side of the Channel released a spirit of radicalism, libertinism, and rebellion in English writing, as can be seen in such varied texts as Thomas Paine's *Rights of Man* (1791), Mary Wollstonecraft's *A Vindication of the Rights of Woman* (1792), and Matthew Lewis's *The Monk* (1796). But there was also a fierce and indignant backlash against such radicalism. In the early decades of the 1800s, this backlash resulted in what Anthony Mandal has described as "the depolemicization (if not the depoliticization) of fiction, leading to its reconstruction as a 'proper' vehicle for middle-class expression."[25] This was, for example, the era in which physician Thomas Bowdler performed one of England's most infamous acts of moral censorship when he edited out large portions of Shakespearean dialogue in the name of female protection: "It is my wish, and it has been my study," he explained in his preface to the second edition of *The Family Shakespeare* (1818), "to exclude from this publication whatever is unfit to be read aloud by a gentleman to a company of ladies."[26] But it was also, perhaps more significantly, the era in which the Evangelical moral reform movement, led by the dynamic politician William Wilberforce, achieved its highest levels of visibility and success.

It is my contention that Wilberforce's Society for the Suppression of Vice had a great deal in common with the Production Code Administration of the 1930s to the 1960s, starting with the tenacious, self-righteous spirits of their best-known leaders. Both Wilberforce and Breen considered it to be their personal, God-given mission to "save" their respective cultures' predominating popular art forms from the corrupting forces of obscenity, licentiousness, and profligacy. Wilberforce proclaimed that

"God almighty has set before me two great objects, the suppression of the slave trade and the reformation of manners," while Breen felt "a sacred duty to protect the spiritual well-being of the innocent souls who fluttered too close to the unholy attractions of the motion picture screen."[27] Like the PCA, the Evangelical reformers enjoyed an extralegal but distinctly powerful "say" in terms of what was considered to be morally acceptable and what was not. Like the PCA, the Evangelical reformers felt particularly threatened by the sophisticated "other" that lay to the East: English conservatives feared French cosmopolitanism in much the same way that Hollywood conservatives feared Broadway urbanity and wit.[28] Like the PCA, the Evangelical reformers were even more concerned about "the open female debauchery of the age" than they were about male forms of lewdness. And, like the PCA, they believed one major cause of that debauchery to be the excessive female interest in the latest popular art form; in Hannah More's *Strictures on the Modern System of Female Education* (1799), for example, she particularly complains that "the corruption occasioned by these [novels] has spread so wide, and descended so low, [that] among milliners, mantua-makers, and other trades where numbers work together, the labour of one girl is frequently sacrificed that she may be spared to read those mischievous books to others."[29]

It was during this reformatory, Bowdlerizing era that Jane Austen wrote and published all of her works. The question becomes, then, to what extent did this historical context determine or influence the way that Austen composed her stories? Or, for the purposes of this study: In the absence of any legally or administratively enforced "code" of censorship, to what extent did Austen effectively censor herself? The answers to these questions are difficult to come by, in part because of the elaborate censoring of Austen's firsthand accounts of her own thoughts and feelings that was performed by her sister Cassandra, whose goal it was to preserve Austen's image as a respectable, well-bred sister and aunt; indeed, according to Deirdre Le Faye's best estimate, "Jane Austen probably wrote about 3,000 letters during her lifetime, of which only 160 are known and published."[30] What we can tell from the private papers that Cassandra did not reduce to ashes is that Austen was deeply, even obsessively, interested in how her novels were being received. This is perhaps most evident in her carefully transcribed compilations of various friends' and family members' "Opinions" of some of her works—of *Emma* (1815), for example, she scrupulously records that "Captain Austen.—liked it extremely, observing that though there might be more Wit in P & P—& an higher Morality in M P—yet altogether, on account of it's peculiar air of Nature throughout, he preferred it to either. . . . Mr Sherer—did not think it equal to either M P—(which he liked the best of all) or P & P.—Displeased with my pictures of Clergymen. . . . Mr Cockerelle—liked it so little, Fanny would not send me his opinion"; and the list goes on and on.[31] The fact that Austen paid as much attention as she did to her readers' praises and censures would seem to imply that public opinion did in fact matter to her on at least some level. Yet we have almost no direct evidence that she catered any of her subsequent fictional efforts to the whims of her readers' tastes. (One small exception can be found in her removal of an off-color joke about a "natural daughter" from the second edition of *Sense and Sensibility* [1811], apparently in deference to objections that were raised after the publication of the first.) On the other hand, we are aware of several remarks that she made that seem directly to contradict the assumption that pleasing her audience was high on her artistic agenda, the most famous being her proclamation that, in *Emma*, she intended to create "a heroine whom no one but myself will much like."[32]

If we attempt to use Austen's attitude toward "Evangelicalism" as a way of understanding her feelings about moral censure, we again find ourselves confronted with markedly mixed signals, ranging from her flat assertion of 1809, "I do not like the Evangelicals," to her 1814 concession that "I am by no means convinced that we ought not all to be Evangelicals, & am at least persuaded that they who are so from Reason & Feeling, must be happiest & safest."[33] Critics have long debated the degree to which Austen can be classified as a social or religious conservative, and have often relied on one or the other of these statements to help support their different points of view. What does seem clear is that Austen found much to mock and criticize in the narrative tendencies of the major Evangelical novelists of her day; of Hannah More's *Coelebs in Search of a Wife* (1809), for example, she notes at one point that her "disinclination for it before was affected, but now it is real" and derides it for the pretentiousness of the diphthong in its title character's name ("the only merit [the book] could have, was in the name of Caleb, which has an honest, unpretending sound; but in Coelebs, there is pedantry & affectation.—Is it written only to Classical Scholars?"), while of Mary Brunton's *Self-Control* (1811) she declares that her "opinion is confirmed of its' [*sic*] being an excellently-meant, elegantly-written Work, without anything of Nature or Probability in it" and sarcastically plans to "redeem" her "credit" with one of her acquaintances who has disparaged her work "by writing a close Imitation of 'Self-control' as soon as I can;—I will improve upon it;—my Heroine shall not merely be wafted down an American river in a boat by herself, she shall cross the Atlantic in the same way, & never stop till she reaches Gravesent."[34]

In trying to explain why Austen was so opposed to the "Evangelical" style of writing, a close friend of Austen's named Ann Barrett hit upon some helpful points for us to consider:

> [She] had on all the subjects of enduring religious feeling the deepest and strongest convictions, but a contact with loud and noisy exponents of the then popular religious phase made her reticent almost to a fault. She had to suffer something in the way of reproach from those who believed she might have used her genius to greater effect; but . . . I think I see her now defending what she thought was the real province of a delineator of life and manners, and declaring her belief that example and not "direct preaching" was all that a novelist could afford properly to exhibit.[35]

Where Austen differs radically from the literary emissaries of the Evangelical reform movement, then, is in her aversion to being too noisy, too preachy, or too direct. In fact, if we subscribe to Ann Barrett's assessment of her motives, we are led to believe that Austen's disdain for the Evangelicals (who were, almost certainly, the "loud and noisy exponents of the then popular religious phase" to whom Barrett was referring) was what actively inspired her to banish religious and moralistic discourse from her novels. Instead, Austen preferred to be more "sophisticated" in her treatment of moral issues—to write with what Virginia Woolf would call an "infallible discretion."[36]

As a result of that discretion, trying to figure out where Austen stood on censorship from a close reading of her fiction is an equally perplexing business. Overall, Austen scholars seem to have gathered themselves into two distinct camps regarding the matter. There are those who believe that Austen sided squarely with the moral censors of her day and served as a steadfast literary proponent of the patriarchal status quo (see, for example,

Alistair Duckworth's *The Improvement of the Estate*, in which he views "the typical pattern of Jane Austen's plots, not as an expression of her submission to social pressures or as a fictional response to her own biographical predicament, but as an indication of her attitude to society and to the individual's place in society"), and those who believe that Austen brazenly faced up against the censorious powers-that-be and consciously infused her texts with controversial and subversive material (see Jillian Heydt-Stevenson's *Austen's Unbecoming Conjunctions*, in which she insists that "Austen's comedies of the flesh may sometimes shock, but they shock because she wanted them to, as she exposes a multitude of worlds, some of them unsavory indeed, within the well-known worlds of courtship and marriage").[37]

To this ongoing debate—which, it should be noted, almost never uses the word *censorship* to describe the cultural or literary injunctions at play—I hope to add a new dimension by considering the role that "sophistication" plays in Austen's literary technique. Her technique is sophisticated, certainly, in the sense of its being elegant, refined, intricate, cultivated, and all the other positive connotations of the term. But it is also sophisticated in the way that Jason Joy wanted the movies produced under his domain to be sophisticated, by simultaneously working on two different levels—one that is legible and appropriate for all audiences, one that is for certain eyes only. In Austen's well-known remark that serves as the epigraph to this chapter, she draws a Joy-ian distinction between those of her readers who are "dull Elves" (meaning: unsophisticated) and those who possess "a great deal of Ingenuity" (meaning: sophistication) themselves, and admits that her works are written specifically "for" the latter. According to the moral censor's preconceived notions of sophistication, the "dull Elves" to whom Austen is referring should necessarily consist of her young, rural, and female readers, while her intended "smart Elf" audience should, by contrast, consist of grown-ups, city-dwellers, and men. There is, of course, something fundamentally wrong with the gender dynamics of this picture. Not only are Austen's novels widely perceived to be un-male, they are also, as D. A. Miller has pointed out, widely perceived to be unmanly: "Like a handbag or fragrance, the works of Jane Austen [are] deemed a 'female thing'; and just as they [are] considered to bespeak the most distinctive depths of womanly being, so they [are] equally regarded as unreadable by those out of their natural element there."[38] Much, then, as George Cukor's reputation for sophistication is connected, in some unspoken way, with his persistent labeling as a "woman's director," Austen's sophisticated narrative technique—what Miller calls her "Style"—is what marks her as a "woman's writer" par excellence. Taken together, the works of Austen and Cukor tell us much about the covert relationship between sophistication and gender, particularly as they collide, conflate, and commingle in the "sophisticated"/"female" genre of romantic comedy.

. . .

We can see a common ground between Austen's novels and classical Hollywood romantic comedies in two seemingly contradictory ways. On one hand, as Thomas Doherty has expressly argued, the romantic comedies in question were required by the Code to employ an "Austenian" brand of verbal and sexual restraint: "The moral universe of classical Hollywood cinema—the world of reticence, constraint, discretion, untruths, and unspokens—comes from out of the past as another century where they do things differently. Packed tight with coded repression, it plays like the cinematic version of a Jane Austen novel."[39] At the same time, however, the romantic comedies certainly also mirror Austen's sense of linguistic playfulness and insouciant wit—the kind of wit to which Maria DiBattista is referring when she traces the lineage of the Hollywood romantic comedy back through its theatrical roots: "For inspiration and ease in the use of words," she argues, "the comic heroines of the talkies looked to the talkative women of stage comedy, from Shakespeare through the Restoration playwrights to Wilde, Shaw, and Coward."[40] While not all of Austen's heroines fall into this playfully "talkative" model of womanhood (least of all Elinor Dashwood and Fanny Price, for example), Austen is perhaps best known—and best loved—for her creation of two of literature's reigning female wits, Elizabeth Bennet and Emma Woodhouse. In this chapter, I have chosen to focus on *Emma* rather than *Pride and Prejudice* (1813) because of its more intricate treatment of the concepts of "sophistication" and "interpretation" that are so central to my discussion of censorship; *Emma* is, as Marilyn Butler has argued, "the greatest novel of the period because it puts to fullest use the period's interest in articulate, sophisticated characters, whose every movement of thought finds its verbal equivalent in a nuance of speech."[41] And I have chosen to pair *Emma* with the Hollywood romantic comedy that is, to my mind, the most explicitly about those same concepts: Cukor's *The Philadelphia Story* (1940). Sophistication not only shapes these texts from without, it shapes them from within. Each tells the story of a young woman who must learn, over the course of her narrative, how to harness the powers of discursive sophistication in order to circumvent her culture's rigid expectations of moral perfection, just as Austen and Cukor use strategies of sophisticated narration to circumvent their cultures' rigid rules of moral censorship.

As I will demonstrate, the entire plot of *The Philadelphia Story* can be read as an epistemological defense of sophistication—a defense that was as important to the arc of Cukor's career as it was to the arc of Katharine Hepburn's. The pivotal role that the text played in Hepburn's professional life is already part of Hollywood folklore. It is well known, for example, that the role of Tracy Lord was specifically written for Hepburn by playwright Philip Barry, that she starred in the Broadway version to great acclaim at a time when she was considered to be "box-office poison" in Hollywood, that she bought the rights to the play to ensure that she would be cast in the film version, and that the success of the film single-handedly (and permanently) returned her to Hollywood's A-list. Critics who focus on this biographical backdrop for the text tend to read it in strictly Hepburnian terms; Andrew Sarris, for example, has maintained that "[t]he play was about Katharine Hepburn herself, and what the American people thought about Katharine Hepburn in 1939, and what Katharine Hepburn realized that she had to do to keep her career going. *The Philadelphia Story* . . . is Katharine Hepburn getting her comeuppance at long last, and accepting it like the good sport she was."[42] But if Sarris is right that the text is fundamentally about what it means to be "Katharine Hepburn," it is important for us to remember how much Cukor was involved in the fabrication and dissemination of that meaning. As writer Dan Callahan has aptly noted:

> In Hepburn, Cukor found a woman who exemplified everything he believed in and everything he wanted to be. Thus, a butch but vulnerable actress became the seminal artistic creation of a sensitive but thrillingly earthy gay man.

There's a 1940s photograph of the two of them with matching open-mouthed smiles: they have become each other, for a moment or more, and together they created the idea of Katharine Hepburn, a grand and ennobling and essentially solitary idea. George Cukor *is* Katharine Hepburn, and vice versa. They helped, long before it was fashionable, to de-stabilise the sexes, and they provided an example to lyrical loners everywhere.[43]

Although Cukor and Hepburn's collaborative "artistic creation" was, ultimately, an indisputable and unparalleled success (Hepburn currently ranks as the American Film Institute's greatest female star of all time, holds the record for most Best Actress Oscar wins, etc.), that success was in serious jeopardy at the time of *The Philadelphia Story*'s conception. But why? What was so "poisonous" about the idea of Katharine Hepburn to audiences of the late thirties? The key, it seems, to understanding the box-office poison list of 1938 on which Hepburn was so famously and pejoratively placed is to bear in mind the identity of the list's author: Harry Brandt, the president of the Independent Theater Owners of America (ITOA). Brandt's goal in taking out a full-page ad in the trade press declaring the toxic status of stars like Hepburn, Greta Garbo, Marlene Dietrich, Joan Crawford, and Fred Astaire was to protest the studio practice of "block booking"—a practice wherein independent exhibitors were forced to pay for blocks of several different films in order to rent the one film that they actually wanted to play. Brandt's list was, therefore, meant to discourage the studios from casting the actors and actresses who were considered to be "unappealing" by the ITOA's primary clientele. Unappealing on what grounds? In film scholar Kathrina Glitre's opinion, the problem was that the "androgynous, exotic and *sophisticated* allure of these particular stars did not go down well in rural areas, where most of the independent exhibitors were located" (emphasis mine).[44] Hepburn's sophistication can, then, be seen as one of the major contributing factors that led to her temporary professional downfall. Significantly, however, Hepburn did not choose as her comeback vehicle a work that demonized the concept of sophistication, or that cast her in a more box-office-friendly, *un*sophisticated role. She chose, instead, to play the most sophisticated character in a sophisticated comedy by Broadway's most sophisticated playwright. And when it came time to bring all of this unapologetic sophistication to the big screen, she specifically chose to be directed by her good friend Cukor, who was also going through a low point of his career—and on similarly "sophisticated" grounds.

For the year that Hepburn was labeled as box-office poison was also the year that Cukor worked arduously on the preproduction of the most eagerly anticipated, most highly publicized movie of all time, *Gone with the Wind*, only to be humiliatingly replaced by director Victor Fleming two weeks into the shoot. There are conflicting opinions about what the real reason for Cukor's dismissal was, but Cukor himself certainly believed it had something to do with his very strained relationship with Clark Gable, who feared that Cukor was focusing too much on the leading ladies' performances at the expense of his own. In an oft-quoted interview, *Gone with the Wind*'s contributing screenwriter Ben Hecht described this version of the rationale behind Cukor's firing in particularly dismissive terms: "[Cukor] didn't know anything, except one thing. He didn't know anything about stories, he didn't know anything about directing, sets, technique. He had a flair for women acting. He knew how a woman should sit down, dress, smile. He was able to make women seem a little brighter and more sophisticated than they were, and that was about the only talent he had."[45] Like his compatriot Katharine Hepburn, however, Cukor did not respond to being negatively typed as a "sophisticated," "woman's" director by turning away from either female-centered material (his very next film would be the man-less *The Women* [1939]) or sophisticated Broadway fare (his next six films would be adaptations of former Broadway plays). Above all, Cukor's disheartening experience working on *Gone with the Wind*—which, he felt, its producer David O. Selznick was turning into "an overblown, almost purple melodrama, lacking a speck of truth"[46]—made him fervently want to return to the genre that he always considered to be his artistic safe haven, the genre of romantic comedy.

Although Austen never completely strayed from the comfort zone of that genre herself, the closest that she came to doing so was certainly in the novel that directly preceded her composition of *Emma*, *Mansfield Park* (1814). *Mansfield Park* is generally regarded to be Austen's most conservative, most "Evangelical" work; the one in which, "most clearly, the 'official' censor intervenes on behalf of society to suppress insurgent individualism."[47] And while that conservatism does appear, in some ways, to have "paid off" for Austen—the first edition of *Mansfield Park* generated a profit of £320, which was more than she made as a whole on the other three novels that were published during her lifetime[48]—Austen also suffered some serious disappointments when it came to the reception of *Mansfield Park*, most notably in the utter lack of attention that was paid to it by the literary reviewers of the time: not a single critical review was written upon its initial release. Austen did not comment upon this fact directly in any of her surviving letters, but she did demonstrate the extent to which her ego could be wounded by such an oversight in a letter that she wrote to her publisher John Murray in 1816 after he sent her Sir Walter Scott's review of her body of works, which, again, failed to make any mention of *Mansfield Park*: "I return you the Quarterly Review with many Thanks. The Authoress of *Emma* has no reason I think to complain of her treatment in it—except in the total omission of Mansfield Park.—I cannot but be sorry that so clever a Man as the Reviewer of *Emma*, should consider it as unworthy of being noticed."[49] The "reviews" of her friends and family that she so meticulously kept track of were, meanwhile, only a mixed bag at best. While a few of her friends professed to like *Mansfield Park* better than any of her works to date, the vast majority of them could not help but admit that they did not find in it quite the "Spirit," "brilliance," or "Wit" of *Pride and Prejudice*. Those who did grant it praise almost always focused upon "the pure morality with which it abounds" or, more specifically, upon "the Manner in which the Clergy are treated."[50] But even some of those glimmers of praise were qualified in the end; as one acquaintance candidly explained, "I think it excellent—& of it's good sense & moral Tendency there can be no doubt . . . but as you beg me to be perfectly honest, I must confess I prefer P&P."[51]

One gets the sense, from Austen's correspondence, that she preferred "P&P" herself—she even refers to it as "my own darling Child" in one of her most giddily excited letters to her sister Cassandra. Later in the same letter, too, she reveals her partiality toward the novel's heroine, Elizabeth Bennet: "I must confess that *I* think her as delightful a creature as ever appeared in print, & how I shall be able to tolerate those who do not like *her* at least, I do not know."[52] Why, then, did Austen create a heroine so very different from Elizabeth in her next novel, *Mansfield*

Park? (*Mansfield Park* is, after all, the one novel in which Austen actually uses the term "sophisticated" to describe her female protagonist, albeit in its negative form: when Henry Crawford is beginning to feel attracted to Fanny Price, he thinks to himself that "It would be something to be loved by such a girl, to excite the first ardours of her young, unsophisticated mind!"[53]) One hypothesis is that Austen enjoyed the artistic challenge of variation—to be sure, just after her comment about Elizabeth's "delightfulness," she notes that "Now I will try to write of something else;—it shall be a complete change of subject—Ordination."[54] In order to understand why Austen would consider such a change to be creatively beneficial, we may look to one of her most famous comments about her own literary work (in this case, *Pride and Prejudice*), which can be found in another letter that she wrote to Cassandra just short of a week later:

> The work is rather too light & bright & sparkling;—it wants shade;—it wants to be stretched out here & there with a long Chapter—of sense if it could be had, if not of solemn specious nonsense—about something unconnected with the story; an Essay on Writing, a critique on Walter Scott, or the history of Buonaparte—or anything that would form a contrast & bring the reader with increased delight to the playfulness & Epigrammatism of the general stile.[55]

It is possible, I would argue, to read Austen's entire foray into the pious, "Evangelical" world of *Mansfield Park* as an exercise in contrast, with the goal of making her return to the sophisticated, irreverent epigrammatism of *Emma* all the more "delightful" to her readers in the end. For although some critics have been able to read in *Emma* a continuation of the conservative impulse that Austen began to explore in *Mansfield Park*, many others dispute such a reading and vehemently argue for *Emma's* place at the table of radical and feminist ideas. One of the primary components of the novel that critics use to defend the latter stance is the presence of its eponymous, autonomous heroine. Like Tracy Lord in *The Philadelphia Story*, Emma Woodhouse is positioned at the center of her fictional world and granted an unflinching sense of social and economic empowerment from the start. Both Tracy and Emma are, to use Austen's opening words, "handsome, clever, and rich," and both are very much accustomed to having their own way.[56]

But do Emma and Tracy really possess as much power as their sovereign positions within their respective stories would seem to suggest? Some scholars believe not, pointing to the "put her in her place" narrative structure that is ostensibly followed by each text. A common reading of *Emma*, for example, finds that "[b]y the conclusion of her story, Emma is brought low, and marriage saves her,"[57] while a typical reading of *The Philadelphia Story* points out that, in the end, Tracy "becomes inebriated, is carried semiconscious from the pool, apologizes repeatedly, cries because of her alienating 'magnificence' . . . [and] happily parrots lines spoken for her by her ex- and soon-to-be husband, C. K. Dexter (Cary Grant)."[58] According to such readings, the heroines' unfettered power is treated as a "problem" that must be "fixed" by narrative's end, in a misogynist version of compensating moral values. Adding to this impression of sexist conventionality is the fact that, in each case, it is the male romantic partner who is assigned the censorious task of fixing the heroine. "Indeed," as Claudia Johnson has noted, "Mr. Knightley does look like the benevolent, all-seeing monitor crucial to the conservative fiction of Austen's day. Hovering like a chaperon around the edges of every major scene—the portrait party at Hartfield, the dinner at the Coles, the word game at the Abbey, the outing at Box Hill—he is always on the lookout for wrongdoing and nonsense."[59] Dexter also does a great deal of hovering around the outskirts of the narrative action in his story, though he chooses to adopt a decidedly less strict chaperoning style than that of Mr. Knightley; in the words of Stanley Cavell, his "is a power not to interfere in [events] but rather to let them happen."[60] Still, Dexter is as ready to lecture Tracy as Mr. Knightley is to lecture Emma, and from a similarly fraternal, if not quite paternal, standpoint—just as we are repeatedly reminded of Emma and Knightley's sibling-in-law status, so too are we reminded on several different occasions that Tracy and Dexter "grew up together."

But unlike Emma, who finds her only moral lecturer in Knightley—"Mr. Knightley, in fact, was one of the few people who could see faults in Emma Woodhouse, and the only one who ever told her of them" (5)—Tracy is subjected to the lectures of virtually every man around her. While this pedagogical format may appear to fulfill the gendered expectations of moral censorship, the ironic twist of *The Philadelphia Story* is that almost all of the men are lecturing the woman to be *less* prudish, *less* judgmental, *less* censorious. The bluntest such lecture comes from Tracy's father, who in the course of a few short minutes manages to call her an unattractive, unloving daughter, a heartless prig, a jealous woman, and a perennial spinster who "might just as well be made of bronze." Only slightly less severe, meanwhile, are the speeches made by the film's two competing romantic heroes, Dexter and Mike "Macaulay" Connor (James Stewart); the former condemns Tracy for being "generous to a fault . . . except to other people's faults" and warns her that she'll "never be a first class human being or a first class woman until you've learned to have some regard for human frailty," while the latter rebukes her for possessing all the self-righteous "arrogance of your class." According to the perverse moral logic of the film, Tracy must learn to shed her "exceptionally high standards," her "prejudice against weakness," and her confident discrimination between right and wrong in order to qualify as a "good" person by the story's end.

Importantly, however, this expectation of moral laxity is a two-way street; Tracy is allowed and, even, encouraged to indulge in "sophisticated" transgressions as much as the male characters ask her to overlook their own. Most obviously, Dexter's renewed romantic interest in Tracy is directly contingent upon her learning to let her "own foot slip a little." Hence the genuine delight that he appears to feel when he sees Tracy and Mike stumbling back from their drunken, late-night dip in the pool— no bitterness, no jealousy, no moral condemnation. Quite the opposite, in fact: Tracy effectively wins back Dexter's love and respect by getting drunk, getting naked, and getting physically intimate with another man. Mike's attraction to Tracy is less blatantly tied to his sense of her immorality, but it does begin when he sees her reading his book of short stories in the library, an act that he jokingly refers to as being a moral danger in and of itself: "Are you sure you're doing the right thing? You know what happens to girls like you when they read books like mine—they begin to think. That's *bad*." At the peak of their romantic encounter, too, Mike specifically describes his love for Tracy in terms of her fallibility rather than her perfection. "I don't seem to you made of bronze?" she asks. "No," he croons in response, "You're made out of flesh and blood. That's the blank, unholy surprise of it!" Tracy's appeal, then, for both Mike and Dexter, is her surprising capacity for fallibility and misconduct underneath her pristine shell of moral purity. And, in the end, Tracy comes to realize that she is no more attracted to moral perfection than either of the film's male protagonists is, for as much as she tries to convince herself that the man she desires is her fiancé George (John Howard)—with his "very high morals; very broad shoulders"—she ultimately rejects him on the grounds of his being "too good" for her, "a hundred times too good."

George is, in fact, the only character who looks at life from a more predictably "moral" standpoint, and is repeatedly ridiculed by the other characters for doing so. When, for example, he discovers Tracy in a heated tête-à-tête with her ex-husband and stiffly remarks, "I suppose I should object to this twosome," Dexter drolly brushes his objection aside by explaining that "*That* would be most objectionable." Or, when Tracy reads aloud the letter that George has written after finding her draped over Mike's arms on the eve of their wedding ("My dear Tracy, Your conduct last night was so shocking to my ideals of womanhood that my attitude toward you and the prospect of a happy and useful life together has been changed materially . . ."), Dexter, Mike, and Liz must all force themselves to stifle derisive smiles at the sound of its stodgy and morally inflexible tone. Throughout the film, George epitomizes the prurient moral censor who cares more about image than substance, and who sees more dirt and debauchery in the world than even exists. When, in his final moments on screen, he tells Tracy that "it didn't take much imagination" for him to interpret her drunken swim with Mike in a sexual manner, she cuttingly observes, "Not much, perhaps, but just of a certain kind."

In an exchange that I consider to be central to the thematic structure of the film, George's sense of morality is specifically contrasted with that of the film's other, more likable characters in terms of its lack of "sophistication." After observing Tracy and Mike in their post-swim, ostensibly post-coital state, Dexter and George discuss what the ramifications of the untoward scene should be:

> Dexter: You won't be too hard on her, will you?
> George: I'll make up my own mind what I'll be!
> Dexter: We're all only human, you know.
> George: You . . . all of you . . . with your sophisticated ideas!
> Dexter: (*smiling wryly*) Ain't it awful?

George means here to be critiquing the profligate ways of the upper class—the upper class has immoral, "sophisticated" ideas whereas he, proudly, does not—but his critique is undermined by the fact that the particular immoral idea he is bristling against is Dexter's innocuous, democratizing remark about everyone being "only human" after all. In this sequence and in the film as a whole, George's unsophisticated censoriousness is portrayed as the unappealing antithesis to Dexter's sophisticated humanity. To object to "sophisticated ideas" is, within the slanted moral universe of *The Philadelphia Story*, deemed to be "most objectionable" indeed.

By contrast, Austen's moral universe appears to be much more conventional in nature, as Emma's moral "education" is typically read in terms of her learning to be less egotistical, less snobbish, less oblivious to the emotional truths of the people around her. But I contend that it is also possible to read *Emma* as a *bildungsroman* of sophistication. For as much as Emma may view herself as the epitome of the cultured sophisticate at the outset of the novel—"handsome, clever, rich"—we are repeatedly shown otherwise. The pre-educated Emma is, in fact, both bad at speaking in a successfully "sophisticated" dialect and at being an astutely "sophisticated" listener. This can be seen as early as the first time she engages in (supposedly sophisticated) banter with Mr. Knightley, in response to his comment that "poor Miss Taylor" must necessarily be happier in her newly married state than she had been in her position as Emma's governess because, as he puts it, "it must be better to have only one to please, than two." "Especially," Emma responds playfully, "when *one* of those two is such a fanciful, troublesome creature! . . . That, is what you have in your head, I know—and what you would certainly say if my father were not by" (4–5). In this "playful" remark, Emma thinks she is demonstrating her prowess both at unearthing the hidden meaning of Mr. Knightley's words and at framing her own barb in such a way that her father will not quite be able to follow it, so that he will not be hurt or offended by it. But her "sophisticated" comment backfires on both fronts. Mr. Woodhouse is even more offended by it than he would have been if he had understood its true import ("I believe it is very true, my dear," he says with a sigh. "I am afraid I am sometimes very fanciful and troublesome"), while Mr. Knightley insists that she has read more insult into his comment than was there ("I meant no reflection on any body.

Miss Taylor has been used to have two persons to please; she will now have but one. The chances are that she must be a gainer" [5]).

This one small example of unsuccessful discursive sophistication on Emma's part is, of course, highly representative of the kinds of misinterpretations and miscommunications—with Mr. Elton, with Frank Churchill, with Harriet Smith, among others—that will constitute the bulk of the diegetic tension throughout the narrative. The tension culminates at the pivotal group outing to Box Hill, where Emma commits her most egregious "crime" of the novel, a crime that arises from yet another failed attempt at sophisticated conversation—though this time her attempt fails in a very different way. Perhaps out of frustration with her tendency to err on the side of under-communication (meaning that her intended subtext is misunderstood or ignored by those to whom she is directing it), Emma errs at Box Hill on the side of over-communication, by leveling a "subtextual" insult at the benign and pitiable Miss Bates that is really not subtextual at all. In response to Miss Bates's self-effacing claim that she will "be sure to say three dull things as soon as ever I open my mouth," Emma replies, "Ah! ma'am, but there may be a difficulty. Pardon me—but you will be limited as to number—only three at once" (239). In the wake of this exchange, Mr. Knightley reproaches Emma more heatedly than he does anywhere else in the novel—for being so "insolent," so "unfeeling," and so ethically "wrong" (241). But if we look carefully at the way Mr. Knightley's lecture is framed—at what exactly he is saying Emma has done "wrong"—we find that Austen's system of ethics is not quite as simple as it might at first seem to be, either. For Emma's real crime is not that she has been witty at someone else's expense, but that her wit has not been *sophisticated* enough to escape the comprehension of even her least perspicacious of listeners (in this case, Miss Bates, who has, as Knightley assures her, "felt your full meaning" [241]). In other words, the problem is not that Emma has been cruel, but that she has been obvious.

Mr. Knightley has, it should be noted, earned the right to lecture Emma about the importance of sophisticated discourse, being one of Austen's best employers of it himself. Consider, for example, the scene in which he is stopped on the street by Miss Bates, who calls to him from her mother's bedroom window while Emma, Harriet Smith, Jane Fairfax, Frank Churchill, and Mrs. Weston are gathered in the "little sitting-room" adjacent. After Miss Bates has finished gushing about Emma and Frank's "delightful" dancing at the party the night before, Knightley gives a typically, because subtly, humorous response:

> "Oh! very delightful indeed; I can say nothing less, for I suppose Miss Wood-house and Mr. Frank Churchill are hearing every thing that passes. And (rais-ing his voice still more) I do not see why Miss Fairfax should not be men-tioned too. I think Miss Fairfax dances very well; and Mrs. Weston is the very best country-dance player, without exception, in England. Now, if your friends have any gratitude, they will say something pretty loud about you and me in return; but I cannot stay to hear it." (157)

In this passage, Mr. Knightley is finding humor in the unwieldy nature of certain forms of discourse (gossip, eavesdropping, etc.) that are so deeply woven into the fabric of village life. But he is also, significantly, finding humor in the foolishness of Miss Bates for not realizing that her "pretty loud" compliments can and must be audible to all of her guests in the other room. He is, in other words, just as willing to mock the "poor," "degraded" Miss Bates as Emma later will be at Box Hill, with the im-portant distinction that he knows how to calibrate his insult correctly, in such a way that his sophisticated listeners (Emma, Mrs. Weston, Jane Fairfax, etc.) can be in on the joke while his more naïve listener (again, Miss Bates) cannot. Knightley as a moral censor is, then, less Joseph Breen, more Jason Joy; what he really wants is for Emma to speak in that Joy-ian language "from which conclusions might be drawn by the so-phisticated mind, but which would mean nothing to the unsophisticated and inexperienced." And if, as so many critics maintain, Knightley serves as the "normative and exemplary figure" of the novel,[61] then his stance on sophistication would seem to be Austen's stance on sophistication, even if she never uses that particular term to discuss the conversational politics at play.

Interestingly, meanwhile, if we look at the negotiations between Joseph Breen and George Cukor regarding the content of *The Philadel-phia Story*, we find that Breen himself was more "Joy-ian" in his censor-ship approach than tends to be imagined. In his first "recommendation" letter to MGM that discusses the film, Breen opens with a predictably conservative list of four specific items that he deems to be absolutely "*not* acceptable, and which must be corrected in the finished picture." They are: (1) "It will be not be acceptable to suggest that Tracy and Mike go swimming in the nude," (2) "It will have to be definitely established that there has been no actual adultery between Seth Lord and the dancer," (3) "Some of the dialogue is not acceptable, either from the standpoint of sex suggestiveness, or because of containing a condonation of illicit sex," and (4) "There is too much display of liquor and drinking, in certain scenes."[62] But as forcefully dogmatic as his initial demands may have been, something clearly altered his attitude toward these four elements between his perusal of the screenplay and his signing off on the final cut of the film. The fact that Tracy and Mike so obviously *have* gone swimming in the nude, that Tracy's father so clearly *has* had an affair with the dancer, that so much of the dialogue *does* either contain sexual innuendo or a condonation of illicit sex, and that so many characters *do* drink to excess throughout the film raises serious questions about the strength and viability of "post-Code" film censorship. If, in 1934, the Production Code really became as powerful as so many film historians have claimed, then how could *The Philadelphia Story* have managed in 1940 to evade each and every one of Breen's preliminary prohibitions with such seemingly carefree aplomb?

The answer to this question can, in my opinion, be found in the film's "sophisticated" mystique. For as much as Breen may have objected to *The Philadelphia Story*'s risqué content in theory, the glamorously high-brow atmosphere of the final product seems to have drastically modified his sense of what was "acceptable" for the film to show and suggest after all. Breen can forgive the film for its excessive "display of liquor and drinking" because of the sophisticated, black-tie attire of the characters doing the drinking and the sophisticated bubbles of the champagne being drunk. He can forgive Seth Lord for his implied philandering because of the sophisticated, "high society" status of the fictitious family to which he belongs. He can forgive Tracy Lord and C. K. Dexter Haven (or, perhaps more accurately, Katharine Hepburn and Cary Grant) for the "sex suggestiveness" of their banter because of the sophisticated tone in which the lines are spoken. When, for instance, Tracy answers her mother's rhetorical question, "Is there no such thing as privacy anymore?" with the salty reply, "Only in bed, mother, and not always there," it is Hepburn's upscale Bryn Mawr accent that moves the remark from the category of "dirty joke" to the category of "witty repartee."

This sophisticated sleight of hand did not go unnoticed by *The Philadelphia Story*'s reviewers in 1940. According to the film critic for *Variety*, who specifically pointed out the fact that the movie "is highly sophisticated, and gets a champagne-sparkle, jewel-polish job of direction by George Cukor" and that "some of its cracks are faintly bawdy, some not so faintly, but laughter glosses them over—and the way they're delivered," the combination of directorial polish and bawdy sexuality was almost sure to guarantee an enormous female following for the film: "Women patronage—they came out of the previews with tears in the eyes as well as laughter on the lips—will insure smash business as far down the line as the femme customers know what time it is."[63] Even more enthusiastic was the reviewer for the *Hollywood Reporter*, who declared *The Philadelphia Story* to be "one of those rare pictures that has everything—everything that any fan could want for his or her money. It's the type of entertainment that will set a box office on fire." The *Reporter* reviewer, however, credited the film's appeal more to Hepburn's acting than to Cukor's direction; in violently effusive language, he (or she) insisted that Hepburn's "banter of words, the toss of her head, the fire in her eyes, the twists of her luscious mouth, cause about as much excitement as any performance that has ever been given in a screen presentation. She looks ravishingly beautiful, and in her big scenes . . . you almost feel as if you would like to tear up the seats in an effort to reach the screen to grab her."[64] Ironically, then, the very attribute of sophistication that had condemned Katharine Hepburn to the "box-office poison" list of 1938 is what allowed her comeback vehicle to be as provocative and explicit and, ultimately, as successful as it turned out to be. By the end of the film's first three weeks in circulation, the trade papers' financial predictions had been proven right: Cukor's "thoroughly sophisticated comedy" broke the all-time box-office record that had previously been held by Walt Disney's *Snow White and the Seven Dwarfs* (1937).[65]

Hence even in the middle of the famously strait-laced, post-Code era, it must be conceded that there were acceptable exceptions to the censorship rules. Lea Jacobs, who is generally one of the stronger proponents of differentiating between pre-1934 and post-1934 censorship, has made precisely this concession: "It should be noted that ambiguity in the treatment of detail did not always work in the interests of censorship. The screwball comedies of the late thirties and early forties proved to be a constant source of irritation and complaint for the MPPDA precisely because they were so adept at exploiting the sorts of denial mechanisms typically favored by the Production Code Administration"—especially, she points out, "insofar as the plots revolved around misinterpretations, around the difficulty of knowing the truth about the heroine's putatively guilty past."[66] *The Philadelphia Story* certainly follows this pattern, with its plot revolving around the misinterpretation of Tracy's putatively guilty late-night swim. But it also does more than just follow the pattern; it explicitly comments upon the hypocritical censoriousness of the pattern by condemning George for even thinking about calling off his marriage to Tracy on the basis of her ostensible sexual guilt. Whereas the plot of a more typical screwball comedy (*The Awful Truth* [1937], for instance, or *My Favorite Wife* [1940]) merely requires the man to realize that he has been mistaken about his wife's apparent infidelity and to forgive her accordingly, *The Philadelphia Story* requires its hero to love and respect its heroine whether the more illicit interpretation of her behavior proves to be true or false.[67] In other words, Dexter does not win Tracy's hand because he is the only man sophisticated enough to interpret the extent of her sexual deviance correctly, but because he is the only man sophisticated enough not to care whether she has been deviant or not.

The plot of *Emma*, meanwhile, is even more interested in questions of interpretation and misinterpretation. How do games of interpretation reflect the moral and intellectual faculties of the players involved? What are the potential pleasures and dangers of reading between the lines? To what extent are interpretations influenced by emotions such as pride, anger, jealousy, and love? Although Austen addresses these questions in each of her novels, *Emma* is unique in its physicalization of the game play: in it, the grown-up characters put together books of riddles, fashion words out of alphabet blocks, and come up with verbal conundrums just to pass the time of day. The characters believe, of course, that they are being clever and cunning by engaging in all of this linguistic sophistry, and that they are transmitting socially forbidden messages with anonymity and impunity. But they could not, for the most part, be more wrong. Hidden meanings are misconstrued, misdirected, and intercepted at almost every turn. While this could be read as Austen's way of critiquing the entire enterprise of indirect discourse, her own persistent use of indirection at the authorial level would seem to undermine such a reading. For, as critics such as John Dussinger have observed, the narrative of *Emma* "insinuates itself like a crossword puzzle, providing just enough information to stir the reader's interest in filling in the empty spaces"—or, as Virginia Woolf more succinctly put it, Austen "stimulates us to supply what is not there."[68]

A frequently cited example of this kind of narrative interpretability can be found in Mr. Woodhouse's partial recollection of David Garrick's dirty riddle, "Kitty, a fair, but frozen maid," which was originally printed in the scandalous 1771 publication *The New Foundling Hospital for Wit* (and not, as the text of *Emma* claims, in the conservative and morally instructive *Elegant Extracts*). The riddle, whose first stanza tells us that "Kitty, a fair, but frozen maid, / Kindled a flame I still deplore; / The hood-wink'd boy I call'd in aid, / Much of his near approach afraid, / So fatal to my suit before," is now understood to have been alluding to the subject of venereal disease, which the narrator of the riddle is hoping to cure by having sexual intercourse with a virgin.[69] It has been much debated "[p]recisely what kind of game Jane Austen is playing with Mr. Woodhouse and her readers" by putting a poem about syphilis and prostitution into such a feeble, seemingly sexless character's mouth.[70] But however the riddle of Mr. Woodhouse's riddle may be solved, what does seem clear is that Austen the novelist was actively engaging in the same kind of teasingly ambiguous wordplay as Emma the matchmaker, Mr. Elton the suitor, or Frank Churchill the secret fiancé—so that, in Dussinger's words again, "the charades in *Emma* function reflexively as a play-within-a-play, imitating in miniature the whole enterprise of constituting the text of the novel."[71]

Emma is not, of course, the only Austen novel about which this observation could be made; a much more literal example of a "play-within-a-play" can be found in *Mansfield Park*, when the Bertrams and their friends decide to put on their own amateur stage production of *Lovers' Vows* (1798). The play, which is Elizabeth Inchbald's adaptation of August von Kotzebue's *Natural Son* (1780), deals quite explicitly with the subjects of extramarital fornication and illegitimacy, and raised its share of contro-versy when it was first brought to the English stage. Within the context of *Mansfield Park*, the performance of the play is controversial on several different levels: because Sir Thomas would so clearly disapprove of his children's theatrical experimentation, because of the specific content of the play itself, and because the play is so clearly being used as an outlet to express the actors' true and forbidden emotions. As Lionel Trilling has put it, "The impropriety lies in the fact that they [Maria and Henry, Mary and Edmund] are *not* acting, but are finding an indirect means to gratify desires which are illicit, and should have been contained."[72] As we continue to read the novel, moreover, we learn of one additional motive for Austen's inclusion of Inchbald's play: it serves to foreshadow the most controversial episode of Austen's own story, Maria Bertram's adulterous and irretrievably ruinous affair with Henry Crawford.

For it must be remembered that, as prim and proper as Austen's work is so often presumed to be, each of her first three published novels contains one episode of sexual scandal that fundamentally alters the course of the narrative—John Willoughby's seduction of Colonel Bran-don's ward Eliza in *Sense and Sensibility*, Mr. Wickham's unwedded elopement with Lydia Bennet in *Pride and Prejudice*, and Maria's fall from grace in *Mansfield Park*. Part of the reason that Austen's reputation for respectability has not been sullied by her inclusion of these episodes is that she makes sure her protagonists loudly and preemptively vocal-ize the moral censor's disapproving point of view—just as Dexter slugs Mike in the jaw in order to prevent the morally outraged George from doing the same, Elinor Dashwood, Elizabeth Bennet, and Fanny Price all beat Austen's anticipated objectors to the morally indignant punch. But there is one important difference between the moral indignation of Austen's heroines and that of the implied moral censor. Where the moral censor, like nineteenth-century British society itself, was much more apt to place the blame of an indecent affair squarely upon the shoulders of the woman involved, Austen's heroines are more judgmental of the male participants: Elinor, for example, feels pity for Eliza but outright contempt for Willoughby, while Elizabeth considers Lydia to be foolish but Wickham to be really cruel. Even Fanny, who has the most conser-vatively censorious reaction to the news of scandal, is at least equally appalled by the conduct of Maria and Henry. Fanny does not, in other words, have the sexist response to adultery that the narrator of *Mansfield Park* specifically bemoans: "That punishment, the public punishment of disgrace, should in a just measure attend *his* share of the offence, is, we know, not one of the barriers, which society gives to virtue. In this world, the penalty is less equal than could be wished."[73]

In *Emma*, Austen chooses to deviate from the formula established in her prior three novels, inasmuch as the one scandalous relationship that Emma believes to exist (that between Jane Fairfax and her best friend's husband, Mr. Dixon) turns out to be a figment of her imagination. But the false scandal in *Emma* is, in a way, more audacious than the real scandals in *Sense and Sensibility*, *Pride and Prejudice*, and *Mansfield Park*, precisely because Emma does not react to the thought of it with shock or disgust—it is, after all, a fiction that she has created in order to fulfill the latent desires of her own psyche. Emma may not express those desires as transparently as the Bertrams do in their drawing-room production of *Lovers' Vows*, but she does write and direct a series of theatrical fictions of her own. As Marilyn Butler has pointed out, the "masterstroke" of these fictions, from a censorship perspective, is that Emma does not cast herself as the romantic heroine of them: "Social taboos would have prevented any young woman from taking so commanding a role in pursuing a man for herself. But Emma is unhampered by propriety when she takes the initiative in choosing a husband for Harriet."[74] By marking the text's most sexual material as the "fanciful" product of Emma's "imaginist" mind, Austen effectively holds that material out of the censor's reach—in much the same way that Joseph Breen cannot object to Tracy's ostensible affair with Mike after it is diegetically declared to be fictitious, Austen's moral censors are stripped of their power by the very "vicariousness" of Emma's "promiscuity," to borrow D. A. Miller's terminology.[75]

Emma's active imagination also challenges the assumptions of moral censorship in another pivotal way: as clearly as the text defines her to be an elegant, well-bred lady, it also repeatedly shows her indulging in the "unladylike" habit of reading sexual motives into ostensibly innocent behaviors (Mr. Elton's interest in Harriet's portrait, Jane Fairfax's refusal to visit her friend Miss Campbell after she has married Mr. Dixon, Frank Churchill's rescue of Harriet from a band of gypsies, etc.). If Emma is an "imaginist," she is a markedly prurient one, contrary to the expectations—or, at least, the wishes—of the moral censor. Of course, Emma is ultimately proven to be wrong in the majority of her prurient suspicions. But she is almost never wrong about the *existence* of underlying sexual motives behind the actions of the other characters, just about the identities of the sexual partners involved. She is right, for example, that Jane Fairfax has received her pianoforté as a romantic gift from a forbidden lover, and that Mr. Elton's desire to watch Harriet's portrait being drawn and to contribute a charade about "courtship" to Harriet's compilation of riddles are signs of a passionate flirtation on his part. The fact that she mistakes Mr. Dixon for Frank Churchill and Harriet for herself does not mean that she is mistaken in her overall perception of the world as an excessively sexual place.

In *The Philadelphia Story*, Tracy demonstrates some of Emma's prurient imaginative tendencies; she automatically assumes, for instance, that the relationship between her father and the Broadway dancer Tina Mara is a sexual one, even though he, unconvincingly, insists that it is not. But the character in the film who possesses the most prurient mind is not Tracy or even the priggishly censorious George; it is Tracy's precocious, thirteen-year-old sister Dinah (Virginia Weidler). Although Dinah is both young and female—two characteristics that should, according to the precepts of moral censorship, mark her as an innocent, "unsophisticated" reader—she is persistently shown to derive great, energetic pleasure from picking up as much grown-up "innundo" (*sic*) as she possibly can, be it about her father ("I'll bet it's on account of father and that dancer in New York!"), her sister ("Did [Dexter] really sock her? Did he really?"), or about the tawdry world at large, as covered by the fictitious scandal sheet *Spy Magazine* ("I love it. It's got pictures of *everything*!"). In spite of all her family's attempts to shield Dinah from the sordid details of adult life—"I can tell there's something in the air, because I'm being taken away," she observes at one point—they cannot take away her fervent desire to know those details (see fig. 6). The prepubescent Dinah, then, epitomizes the kind of "woman" to whom the aforementioned *Variety* article of 1931 was referring in its dramatic opening claim that "Women love dirt. Nothing shocks 'em."

But Dinah also epitomizes the kind of feminine/feminist reading of events that Elinor Dashwood, Elizabeth Bennet, and Fanny Price point

FIGURE 6 *Dinah loves dirt. Mary Nash, Katharine Hepburn, Virginia Weidler, and Cary Grant in* The Philadelphia Story.

to in their respective stories. When Dinah observes through her window the sight of Mike carrying Tracy from the pool to her bedroom, she jumps to the same illicit conclusion that George does, but reacts to that conclusion in a very different way. Instead of reproving Tracy for failing to live up to the "ideals of womanhood," Dinah directs all of her indignation at Mike instead for exposing her beloved sister to the ignominy of a public disgrace—upon first seeing him the following morning, she stonily sneers, "How *do* you *do*?" and does not stop scowling at him until she departs the scene. What Dinah's response demonstrates is that women (even the young, impressionable women whose "innocence" the moral censor believes it is his sacred duty to protect) are not afraid of sexuality or of scandal; they are afraid of the social suppression that tends to occur in the wake of sexual scandal. As soon as Dinah sees that Tracy will be marrying Dexter instead of George, all of her concerns about Mike and Tracy's late-night swim fly out the window, even though she has not yet learned—as the other characters and the audience have—about the "perfect innocence" of that swim. Watching Tracy stand in front of a minister next to the morally imperfect but also morally tolerant man that she has been rooting for all along, Dinah is able to read, with a sharply "sophisticated" eye, that her sister will be safe from censure, and will enjoy the kind of happy ending that has nothing to do with "moral improvement" or "compensating moral values."

The marriage between Emma and Mr. Knightley may, meanwhile, appear to fit more neatly into the code of conduct prescribed by moral censorship: Emma is rewarded with the love of a good man only when she has learned how to be more humble, respectful, and "good" herself. But, again, this seeming conventionality is undermined if we look at the specific dynamics of their relationship. One particularly revealing comment comes near the end of the novel, when Emma and Mr. Knightley are discussing whether or not his lifelong habit of lecturing her has, in fact, changed her for the better. She insists that it has, but he is not so sure:

> "My interference was quite as likely to do harm as good. It was very natural for you to say, what right has he to lecture me?—and I am afraid very natural for you to feel that it was done in a disagreeable manner. I do not believe I did you any good. The good was all to myself, by making you an object of the tenderest affection to me. I could not think about you so much without doating on you, faults and all; and by dint of fancying so many errors, have been in love with you ever since you were thirteen at least." (298)

The implications of this statement are radical indeed. Mr. Knightley is admitting not just that moral instruction can be and often is a self-defeating enterprise, but that his (near-pedophiliac) romantic interest in Emma was inspired, increased, and inflamed by the moral flaws in her budding character. As Joseph Litvak has argued of this same moment, Mr. Knightley's confession turns our entire notion of his function in the novel on its head: "If the narrative has traditionally been conceived as a linear development whereby Emma, changing under Knightley's influence, moves gradually toward a welcoming recognition of that influence, now the Pygmalion myth gets a new twist: Knightley is interested less in perfecting the 'object of [his] tenderest affection' than in 'fancying'—at once imagining and liking—her charming imperfections."[76] What makes

Knightley so different from the typical romantic hero of Austen's day is, then, his lack of interest in a more typical (because more docile) romantic heroine: he considers Jane Fairfax to be too "reserved," Harriet Smith to be "too young and too simple," and Emma's sister Isabella to be "too much like Emma—differing only in those striking inferiorities, which always brought the other brilliancy before him" (185, 38, 279). Emma is strong-willed, self-centered, and hot-tempered, and Mr. Knightley clearly would not want her any other way. The goal of the narrative, then, is *not* to rob Emma of her most dominant and domineering attributes, as some critics have argued, but rather to make sure that she winds up with the one character who can and will appreciate them properly.

Just as Austen ends her novel with a promise of "the perfect happiness of the union" between Emma and Mr. Knightley (313), so too does Cukor conclude his story with a visual representation of promised marital bliss: a glamorized still photograph of Tracy and Dexter as they are about to kiss their way back into the married state (fig. 7). And yet,

FIGURE 7 *Eyes wide open. Cary Grant and Katharine Hepburn in* The Philadelphia Story.

there is something fundamentally unromantic about this photograph. It is, in the first place, a shot that we know to have been underhandedly captured by the noxious editor of *Spy Magazine*, Sidney Kidd. But what is most noticeable—and least romantic—about the image is the fact that it shows us Tracy entering into the state of matrimony with her eyes, quite literally, wide open. No longer consumed by her puritanical ideas of what married life "should" be, Tracy is, in the film's closing moments, finally able to see the complicated moral world around her. By the time, then, that we reach these two seemingly conventional endings of the romantic comedy form, we have come to realize that "perfect happiness," for Emma and Knightley and Tracy and Dexter, is not found in the censor's conventional vision of moral perfection. It is found, instead, in the never-ending circuit of moral slips and fumbles that necessarily belong to any life worth living—and in the kind of love that is "sophisticated" enough to travel that circuit without judgment and without fear.

3

Beyond Censorship
Charles Dickens and Frank Capra

> Vices are sometimes only virtues carried
> to excess.
> —*Charles Dickens*

> Whenever a situation develops to its
> extreme, it is bound to turn around and
> become its opposite.
> —*Frank Capra*

NOTHING IS PURER THAN CHRISTMAS. Flakes of pure white snow fall upon the Christmas ground. Carolers sing out pure, familiar Christmas songs. Rosy-cheeked children clap with pure delight at the sight of Christmas feasts and presents. But it is more than that: the Christmas season also brings about a mystical social transformation. Greed is replaced by generosity. Cynicism is replaced by sympathy. Corruption is replaced by righteousness. We know this is true because we have been told it is true, year in and year out, ever since we were rosy-cheeked children ourselves. We have heard about a crotchety old miser transformed overnight into the most munificent of givers, and about a tiny, crippled child whose life is saved by the Christmas miracle of charity. We have seen a man who is on the brink of suicide realize that the unglamorous, small-town life he leads is in fact a wonderful life, and his friends and neighbors amiably empty their pockets to rescue him from financial ruin. We have seen and read and learned all this from two of our culture's most beloved and most perennial of classics, Charles Dickens's *A Christmas Carol* (1843) and Frank Capra's *It's a Wonderful Life* (1946). Christmas simply would not be "Christmas" without them.

What, then, can such revered and sacred texts possibly have to do with the issue at hand, the issue of moral censorship? Who, in other words, would ever want to censor Christmas?

Interestingly, the holiday of Christmas has played an influential role in the histories of both English literary and Hollywood film censorship. As Frank Fowell and Frank Palmer describe in their detailed study of *Censorship in England*, the office of English Dramatic Censor originated in the figure of the Lord of Misrule who, in medieval times, was put in charge of selecting entertainment for the Royal Court to be performed in the weeks leading up to Christmas. Over time, the "ephemeral and irresponsible powers" that belonged to the Lord of Misrule became more structured and official in nature, and the post was provided with a less anarchic-sounding name: Master of Revels. It was in this incarnation that the post began to take on a more directly censorious role; according to Fowell and Palmer, "The Master of Revels was held responsible for the inoffensiveness and general success of these court entertainments, and for his own credit's sake it was necessary for him to discriminate between good and bad plays."[1] Eventually, too, the Master of Revels was put in charge of licensing the printed versions of the plays in question, thereby making him a direct ancestor of the modern literary censor. Tony Tanner has remarked upon the inherently paradoxical nature of this censorship ancestry: "Titles like Lord of Misrule and Master of Revels suggest a responsibility which looks two ways. The 'Master' must make sure that the 'Revels' take place, thus he has (originally) to organize them and help them into expressive form; at the same time he must 'master' them, control and delimit the form they take."[2] Plays produced specifically for medieval Christmas festivities were, then, the first English narratives on record to be influenced by the simultaneously productive and repressive powers of moral censorship.

In the world of film, meanwhile, there is a clear and much-analyzed link between the implementation of Hollywood's Production Code and the pressures of Christian (and, in particular, Catholic) morality groups. In fact, the issue of film censorship first gained national attention in the United States during the Christmas boycott of 1908, when a coalition of New York ministers pressured Mayor George B. McClennan into closing down all New York movie theaters on Christmas Day in order to make the statement to moviemakers that, as Gregory Black has put it, "[u]nless they took some action to clean up their image, improve the physical condition of the theaters, and, most important, address the concern of critics that movies were corrupting children and adults, they could expect continued attacks by moral guardians, who would continue to press for restrictive legislation."[3] Ironically, Christmas also played a role in the groundbreaking Supreme Court decision of 1952 that finally gave movies protection under the First Amendment and paved the way for the dissolution of Hays Code censorship. The decision was made in response to a legal dispute over the banning of *The Miracle* (1948), Roberto Rossellini's allegedly "sacrilegious" film about a peasant woman who is seduced and impregnated by a vagrant stranger but convinces herself that she is experiencing a modern-day version of Mary's immaculate conception.

The two Christmas stories that I will be examining in the course of this chapter do not have such a direct connection to the legal history of artistic censorship. In fact, as we shall see, their authors were two of the most popular, least "objectionable" artists of their respective eras. The stories themselves, meanwhile, have become so much a part of our cultural consciousness that they have, to borrow Paul Davis's terminology, reached the seemingly untouchable status of "culture-texts."[4] Though there is certainly much in the writing and filming of *A Christmas Carol* and *It's a Wonderful Life* that warrants the critical and popular acclaim they have achieved, I would argue that the reason they, out of all of Dickens's and Capra's works, have reached *such* a lofty status lies in their inescapable association with the holiday of Christmas. Yet it is precisely because of this association that I have chosen to examine the texts under the thematic lens of censorship. My goal is to determine the role that censorship plays in the production and reception of even the most mainstream, family-friendly, respectable of texts—texts that appear to be beyond reproach, beyond censorship.

· · ·

Charles Dickens's relationship with censorship was undeniably shaped by his desire to be popular, accepted, and widely read. As Joss Marsh has aptly put it, "Dickens never 'despaired' of 'pleasing,' and was determined that no 'prejudice' should stand in the way of thoroughly respectable and remunerative success."[5] Though this determination on Dickens's part could be construed as a form of pandering to his audience (as well as to the moral censors of his time), it could also be seen as a reflection of his lifelong efforts to increase the status of the literary profession in terms of its social respectability. Sambudha Sen has recently argued that Dickens's "deepening commitment to respectability" over the course of his career led to a gradual softening of the political satire in his work, but also that this softening allowed his satire to "cater not only to a radical artisanal community but to the middle classes as well."[6] To a certain extent, of course, Dickens's desire to appeal to as broad an audience as possible was selfishly motivated—as the son of a debt-ridden navy payroll clerk, Dickens wanted his own role as a highly successful professional writer to provide him with that much-coveted treasure in the Victorian world, upward social mobility—but that desire was also tied into a larger philanthropic vision that Dickens had for the artistic community as a whole. Indeed, at an elegant society soirée held in his honor toward the end of his life, Dickens confessed that one of his greatest hopes was that he had left the "social position [of art] in England something better than I found it."[7] If art was ever going to be seen as truly "dignified," in Dickens's mind, it simply could not afford to be regarded as immoral or obscene.[8]

But this is not to say that Dickens's desire for social acceptability was the only motivating force that informed his art. He was also, as Edgar Johnson has pointed out, "deeply sceptical of the whole system of respectable attitudes and conventional beliefs that cemented all of society into a monolithic structure stubbornly resistant to significant change."[9] To a writer who considered psychological and social "truth" to be essential ingredients of any novel worth reading, this system posed a very real threat indeed. While residing in Paris in 1855 and 1856, Dickens confessed to his friend John Forster some of the frustrations he felt about the current state of the arts in England: "Don't think it a part of my despondency about public affairs," he wrote, "when I say that mere form and conventionalities usurp, in English art, as in English government and social relations, the place of living force and truth."[10] Even when describing the works of some of his closest friends, his complaint remained intact: "There is a horrid respectability about most of the best of them—a little, finite, systematic routine in them, strangely expressive to me of the state of England itself."[11] Although Dickens refrained from voicing these particular complaints too directly in his public speeches regarding the literary profession, he did allow them to work their way into certain key moments and key elements of his literary texts.

In a way, the most severe of Dickens's attacks on the "horrid respectability" that he considered to be plaguing his nation appeared in the form of several scathingly derisive character depictions, ranging from Mr. Pecksniff in *Martin Chuzzlewit* (1844)—"Perhaps there never was a more moral man than Mr. Pecksniff: especially in his conversation and correspondence"—to Mrs. General in *Little Dorrit* (1857)—"Mrs. General was not to be told of anything shocking. Accidents, miseries, and offences, were never to be mentioned before her. Passion was to go to sleep in the presence of Mrs. General, and blood was to change to milk and water"—to the character whose very name came to symbolize the hypocrisies of Victorian morality, Mr. Podsnap in *Our Mutual Friend* (1865).[12] "Podsnappery," as Dickens originally conceived it, had as much to do with self-satisfied jingoism as with moral prudery (one of Podsnap's most prominent character traits is his tendency to dismiss all foreign art and politics with the stiff observation, "Not English!"[13]), but it is the latter feature for which it is most remembered. In particular, literary scholars have repeatedly used the Podsnappian concept of "the cheek of the young person" as a metaphor for the repressive limitations imposed upon Victorian artists.[14] It is easy to understand why—Dickens's metaphor is not, as we may see, a particularly subtle one:

> A certain institution in Mr. Podsnap's mind which he called "the young person" may be considered to have been embodied in Miss Podsnap, his daughter. It was an inconvenient and exacting institution, as requiring everything in the universe to be filed down and fitted to it. The question about everything was, would it bring a blush into the cheek of the young person? And the inconvenience of the young person was, that, according to Mr. Podsnap, she seemed always liable to burst into blushes when there was no need at all. There appeared to be no line of demarcation between the young person's excessive innocence, and another person's guiltiest knowledge. Take Mr. Podsnap's word for it, and the soberest tints of drab, white, lilac, and grey, were all flaming red to this troublesome Bull of a young person.[15]

This passage can be used to demonstrate several things: that censorship creates the censorable as much as it condemns it, that censorship equates both youth and femininity with impressionable, corruptible innocence, that the moral censor reveals the guiltiness of his own knowledge by dint of his very censoriousness. For it is, of course, Mr. (not Miss) Podsnap who selfishly "files" the world down to "fit" his purposes; he, not she, who reads the color "red" into the mildest of "grey" matters; he, not she, who functions as the "troublesome Bull" of Victorian society.

Although Dickens waited until the penultimate novel of his career to introduce the character who most overtly lampooned his culture's prudishly censorious mentality, his most blatant authorial attack on that mentality occurred nearly three decades earlier, in his preface to the third edition of *Oliver Twist* (1839). Barbara Leckie has recently shown how certain prefaces to controversial novels published in the 1880s were used as pulpits from which the authors could decry the hypocritical tendencies of their censorious critics.[16] In 1841, Dickens anticipated this later trend by speaking directly to those members of *Oliver Twist*'s original reading public who were morally offended by its "coarse and shocking" depiction of thieves, murderers, and prostitutes. As his speech progresses, his tone toward these hypothetical readers becomes more and more petulant, ultimately reaching a pitch of unadulterated and undisguised contempt:

> I will not, for these readers, abate one hole in the Dodger's coat, or one scrap of curl-paper in the girl's dishevelled hair. I have no faith in the delicacy which cannot bear to look upon them. I have no desire to make proselytes among such people. I have no respect for their opinion, good or bad; do not covet their approval; and do not write for their amusement. I venture to say this without reserve; for I am not aware of any writer in our language having a respect for himself, or held in any respect by his posterity, who ever has descended to the taste of this fastidious class.[17]

The Dickens of this passage is as full of bravado as any Victorian narrator (including the Thackerayan narrator to whom I directed my attention in chapter 1), though if Dickens had actually followed through with his proclaimed indifference to his readers' "fastidious" sensibilities, *Oliver Twist* would probably have felt a bit more like Thackeray's decisively raunchier take on the Newgate novel, *Catherine: A Story* (1840).

The difference is that, in the midst of all the boldness that Dickens displays in refusing to excise so much as a single descriptive detail in the name of narrative "delicacy," he freely admits to censoring his characters on a conversational level. He will, he tells us, show us "the very dregs of life," but only "so long as their speech [does] not offend the ear."[18] His reason for adopting this paradoxical attitude toward censorship, he claims, has as much to do with his own personal sense of moral decency as it has to do with his hypothetically offended readers': "No less consulting my own taste, than the manners of the age, I endeavoured, while I painted in all its fallen and degraded aspect, to banish from the lips of the lowest character I introduced, any expression that could by possibility offend; and rather to lead to the unavoidable inference that its existence was of the most debased and vicious kind, than to prove it elaborately by words and deeds."[19] The paradox of Dickens's censoring tendencies has been duly noted by several critics; Tony Tanner, for example, has raised the question of "[j]ust why Dickens felt so ready, indeed eager, to describe dirty clothes while absolutely refusing to transcribe 'dirty' words."[20] The answer to this question lies, I would argue, in Dickens's keen awareness that the usage of certain red-flagged words was one of the easiest ways to have a text banned or boycotted in Victorian England (and, a century later, in classical Hollywood). The censorship of profane words is a quick, straightforward, precise science; the censorship of artistic imagery and thematic content is, decidedly, not.

So Dickens first eliminates the dirty words from his text, then justifies the dirty clothes (and the dirty characters who inhabit those clothes) by invoking a strategy of excessive purity. Dickens does not, of course, put it quite this way; instead, he tells us that he "wished to show, in little Oliver, the principle of Good surviving through every adverse circumstance, and triumphing at last" and assures us that "a lesson of the purest good may . . . be drawn from the vilest evil."[21] But, as many critics have pointed out, throughout the novel it feels much more as if we are following Oliver's story so that we can be exposed to the seedy but exciting underworld of Fagin, Sikes, and the Artful Dodger than as if we are being exposed to their crimes and debaucheries so that we can appreciate Oliver's moral sanctity all the more. Even the preface supports this view; in it, Dickens spends far more time discussing why he felt artistically compelled to go into all of the dirty details about his lowlife characters, particularly Nancy, than he does discussing why his depiction of sweet, innocent little Oliver might be important or interesting. As much as he defends the authenticity of his depiction of Nancy's miserable depravity, Dickens does not make the same claim about Oliver's wide-eyed innocence. And, indeed, many readers have complained about Oliver being unconvincing as a character; about his moral purity being laid on rather too thick; about that purity feeling exaggerated, excessive, and overblown. In the end, the novel (like so many of Dickens's other works) seems less to defend the existence of unadulterated goodness in the modern world than to call that goodness into serious question.

. . .

Frank Capra's most celebrated films—which borrow so much from Dickens in terms of style, theme, and tone[22]—are similarly accused of being implausibly innocent and excessively pure. The same cannot be said, however, of Capra's lesser-known pre-Code films; in these earlier works, Capra repeatedly and unapologetically pushes the boundaries of moral and social acceptability. Witness, for example, the content of his three pre-Code Barbara Stanwyck vehicles: *Ladies of Leisure* (1930), in which Stanwyck plays a strong-willed hooker who comes across as far more likeable and sympathetic than her hypocritically "respectable" costars; *Forbidden* (1932), in which she plays a librarian who has an affair and an illegitimate child with a well-respected politician; and *The Bitter Tea of General Yen* (1933), in which she plays an American missionary who falls in love with a suicidal Chinese warlord. But in the years that followed Joseph Breen's ascension to the PCA throne, moral purity quickly began to play a more prominent role in Capra's work, as more and more of his films' plots began to revolve around the struggle between his protagonists' wholesome idealism and the greed and corruption of the powers that be. Although these later films are often praised for being Capra's most overtly and daringly political work, they are also the films that elicit the most derision for being overly sentimental and cloyingly melodramatic—for being, as so many critics have quipped, "Capracorn."

In his autobiography, Capra attributes the shift in his films' tone and theme that occurred right around 1934 not to the sudden tightening of the Production Code, but rather to an anonymous visitor who came to see him while he lay fighting for his life after an acute bout of appendicitis.[23] According to Capra's rendition of the story, this mysterious "little man" calmly but forcefully accused him of being a "coward," even an "offense to God," because of his failure to use his directorial power to convey morally responsible messages to his vast moviegoing audience. The little man even went so far as to compare Capra's influence to the influence of Adolf Hitler: "That evil man is desperately trying to poison the world with hate. How many can he talk to? Fifteen million—twenty million? And for how long—twenty minutes? You, sir, you can talk to *hundreds* of millions, for two hours—and in the dark."[24] That, according to Capra, was all the epiphany he needed; from that day forward, "my films had to *say* something. . . . From then on my scripts would take from six months to a year to write and rewrite; to carefully—and subtly—integrate ideals and entertainment into a meaningful tale."[25]

As neat and dramatic as this anecdote may be, its authenticity has often been questioned. Capra biographer Joseph McBride, in particular, has adamantly determined "most, if not all, of this fantastic story [to be] an invention."[26] McBride comes up with several potential motives that Capra may have had for creating the fiction of the little man, none of which are particularly flattering to Capra (for instance: "the 'little man' incident provided Capra's readers with an explanation for his transformation into a socially conscious director without giving any credit for it to [his most frequent collaborator, screenwriter Robert] Riskin"[27]). I would like to add to McBride's string of conjectures the possibility that Capra's fierce sense of creative independence made him want to deny any influence that the tightening of the Production Code might have had upon his work. For even though Capra was not a writer/director in the same sense that Preston Sturges was, he certainly considered himself to be the one in control of his own artistic vision. In his autobiography, he describes how, as a young filmmaker, "that simple notion of 'one man, one film' (a credo for important filmmakers since D. W. Griffith) . . . became for me a fixation, an article of faith. In my subsequent forty years of film directing, I never forgot it, nor compromised with it—except once. I walked away from the shows I could not control completely from conception to delivery."[28]

Like Dickens, then, Capra prided himself on being an uncompromising artist; but, also like Dickens, Capra made sure that his popular appeal and economic success were not too compromised by the proclivities of his artistic vision, either. As a Sicilian-born peasant who immigrated to America when he was six and maneuvered his way up the social and financial ladder by sheer force of will and hard work, Capra valued success with a passion that bordered on obsession. As he says in the first lines of the preface to his autobiography, "I hated being poor. Hated being a peasant. Hated being a scrounging newskid trapped in the sleazy Sicilian ghetto of Los Angeles. My family couldn't read or write. I wanted out."[29] And out he got: by the 1930s, Capra was one of the best-paid, most popular, most reliable makers of Hollywood smash hits. Paradoxically, then, Capra's burning desire for creative autonomy ("I take a very dim view of authority of any kind; I don't like anybody telling me what to do"[30]) was consistently tempered by his overall willingness to follow the dictates of social decorum ("In short: 'The audience is always right' is a safe bet"[31]). Not surprisingly, both of these conflicting drives played an important role in the development of Capra's complex relationship with moral censorship.

Relatively little has been written on Capra's dealings with the Production Code, and for good reason: the most trouble Capra ever got into for one of his works occurred when the U.S. Congress was treated to an early screening of *Mr. Smith Goes to Washington* (1939) and shortly thereafter threatened to pass an Anti–Block Booking Bill (which would have caused a great deal of financial hardship for the studio system) if Capra chose to release the film in an unaltered state. Ironically, the PCA was one of *Mr. Smith*'s most adamant supporters in the wake of the controversy; in a letter to Will Hays, Joseph Breen adamantly defended the film on the grounds that it "splendidly emphasized the rich and glorious heritage which is ours and which comes when you have a government of the people, by the people, and for the people."[32] This view of the film is, however, a far cry from Breen's initial opinion of the novel *The Gentleman from Montana* on which the screenplay was based. After MGM first submitted the novel to Breen for his Code's consideration in 1938, he "most earnestly" urged the studio to "take serious counsel before embarking on the production of any motion picture based on this story," largely because of its "generally unflattering portrayal of our system of Government, which might well lead to such a picture being considered, both here, and more particularly abroad, as a covert attack on the Democratic form of government."[33] The difference between Breen's two very contradictory takes on the film was almost certainly a result of Capra's dexterously "delicate" handling of the material. Breen had, in fact, been impressed by Capra's artistic delicacy ever since he first took office at the PCA: in response to an early draft of *It Happened One Night* (1934), Breen remarked that, "While a few of the situations will need careful handling, we feel sure that under Mr. Capra's direction, they will be treated in such a way in the finished picture as to be not only satisfying under the Code, but free from danger of censorship."[34] The few critics who have discussed the Code's uncharacteristically lenient treatment of Capra's work have hypothesized that the popular and critical success of his early films were so impressive to the PCA that it consciously chose to treat his later work "with particular favor," as Richard Maltby has put it.[35]

But it is also important to note that the trust that Breen placed in Capra's sense of delicacy was, to a large extent, justified. The self-proclaimed goal of the PCA was, after all, to object solely to that which the American public would find objectionable; so the fact that Capra reliably and unabashedly catered to the dictates of public opinion must surely have gone a long way in quelling the PCA's fears. Indeed, as a *Los Angeles Times* writer concluded after an interview with Capra in June 1934, "One of the prime Capra tenets is to keep a film clean; smut, he insists, is the way of the lazy writer, the slothful director, the misguided producer."[36] This is not to say, however, that Capra was exactly on the side of censorship. Within the same *Los Angeles Times* interview, he also makes it clear that he "holds no brief for censorship, believing that the industry at large should not be made to suffer for the sins of the few."[37] In fact, it was only a few months after that interview that Capra shot the famous "walls of Jericho" scene in *It Happened One Night*—a scene that has been read as a shrewd metaphor for the self-defeating nature of censorship by, for example, Stanley Cavell:

In one camera set-up we watch the blanket-screen with the man as it is rippled and intermittently dented by the soft movements of what we imagine as the woman changing into pajamas in cramped quarters. The thing that was to "make everything all right" by veiling something from sight turns out to inspire as significant an erotic reaction as the unveiled event would have done. . . . The barrier works, in short, as sexual censorship typically works, whether imposed from outside or from inside. It works—blocking a literal view of the figure, but receiving physical impressions from it, and activating our imagination of that real figure as we watch in the dark—as a movie screen works.[38]

Like other film scholars who have examined this scene, Cavell considers it to be an intentional indictment of Code censorship on Capra's part: "I cannot doubt that the most celebrated Hollywood film of 1934 knows that it is, among other things, parodying the most notorious event of the Hollywood film's political environment in 1934, the acceptance of the motion picture Production Code."[39]

If we return, then, to the issue of the shift in Capra's tone that took place around the time of *It Happened One Night*, there does seem to be some indirect evidence that Capra was responding to the intensification of Code enforcement that was occurring at roughly the same historical moment. One of the most striking differences between Capra's pre-Code and post-Code work is the altered persona of his male protagonist; whereas most of the "heroes" in Capra's early films are either dishonest (*Forbidden*), manipulative (*Platinum Blonde* [1931]), or even outright violent (*The Bitter Tea of General Yen*), the heroes of his mature works tend to be sweet, simple, and wholesome to a fault. The most obvious examples of this kind of hero can be found in Capra's enormously successful "Mister" films, *Mr. Deeds Goes to Town* (1936) and *Mr. Smith Goes to Washington*; in each of these works, the excessive innocence of the male protagonist serves as a central narrative concern. Both Longfellow Deeds (Gary Cooper) and Jefferson Smith (James Stewart) are small-town heroes who are thrust overnight into the lair of urban corruption, where they are mercilessly mocked for their extreme artlessness and naïveté. But as the films progress, the authenticity of Deeds's and Smith's artlessness is called into serious question by a world that simply cannot comprehend how anyone could be that "good." Deeds is put on trial for insanity simply because he wants to give away his twenty million dollar inheritance "to people who need it," while Smith is accused of wanting to pass his National Boys Camp bill for his own personal profit rather than for the sake of the "boys of America" he claims to hold so dear. Although Capra's Mister films do officially allow their wholesome protagonists to thrive and triumph in the end, that triumph is only achieved when the heroes learn to shake off some of their small-town innocence and play by the big city's (or the big Senate's) slicker, more cynical rules.

As a result, there are two potential ways to read the role that innocence plays in the moral landscapes of these films. On one hand, both films paint innocence as a valorous, appealing, heroic trait; on the other hand, they both expose the rarity of that trait within the modern world and portray it as something that must ultimately be outgrown and overcome. In the case of *Mr. Smith*, the offended U.S. Congress obviously chose to read the film in the latter light, while the contented PCA chose to read it in the former. In the letter from Breen to Hays defending the film, in fact, Breen is so satisfied with what he perceives to be the film's "morally pure" message that he predicts it "will do a great deal of good for all those who see it and, in my judgment, it is particularly fortunate that this kind of story is to be made at this time."[40] In Breen's eyes, then, the excessiveness of the male protagonist's innocent idealism effectively overshadows and excuses what he had once determined to be the story's problematically "unflattering portrayal of our system of government." And Breen was certainly not alone in his attitude toward the film: many of its contemporary reviewers made some sort of reference to the "redemptive light" that "Jimmy Stewart's boyishly sincere performance" was able to cast in the midst of Capra's otherwise scathing "one-man campaign against crooked politics."[41]

.   .   .

Seven years and a world war would pass before Capra would have the opportunity to collaborate with his "boyishly sincere" *Mr. Smith* star again, on a film that they would both consider to be the pinnacle of their Hollywood careers, *It's a Wonderful Life*. Out of all of Capra's films, *Wonderful Life* is, of course, the one that is most frequently and most facilely compared to a specific work of Dickens's. To cite a small sampling: James Agee refers to it as "one of the most efficient sentimental pieces since *A Christmas Carol*"[42]; Paul Davis hails it as "the apotheosis of the American

Carol"[43]; and David Mamet condemns it as a "warped," "populist" version of the "old-world vision [of] Charles Dickens's *A Christmas Carol*."[44] The reasons for such comparisons are fairly obvious: both texts' plots revolve around the education and, ultimately, the moral redemption of their erring protagonists. Both contain the unwanted intrusions of supernatural spirits. Both rely on the machinery of retrospection (Scrooge looks back over the course of his own life, Clarence looks back over the course of George Bailey's) followed by the machinery of counterfactuals (Scrooge gets to see what life will be like if he does not change his miserly ways, George gets to see what life would be like if he had never been born). And, most obviously of all, both are proudly and ostentatiously set during the Christmas holiday season.

Less well known, perhaps, is the fact that both *A Christmas Carol* and *It's a Wonderful Life* were conceived at particularly uneasy moments of their authors' careers. Dickens was in the middle of serializing his least financially successful work, *Martin Chuzzlewit*, which was doing so poorly that it suddenly became "the rage," according to a review in *The Critic*, "to decry Dickens, by pronouncing his *Chuzzlewit* a failure, and his writings vulgar, and whispering 'Boz is going down.'"[45] One reason that Dickens was having more trouble than usual in winning over his reading public was, perhaps, that his new novel lacked a sufficiently sympathetic, innocent protagonist; *The New World*, for one, felt that the novel suffered from its author's "mistake of supposing that a tale can be perfectly successful without the impersonation of a single character worthy of, or capable of exciting, the reader's sympathy. In *Martin Chuzzlewit* we are introduced to a world of knaves and fools, destitute of any one quality that could command respect."[46] Dickens was not quite so indifferent to the public's moral criticism of his work as he professed himself to be in his *Oliver Twist* preface—he referred in his letters to his "*Chuzzlewit* agonies,"[47] and was both mortified and enraged when his publishers threatened to reduce his monthly payment by fifty pounds as a result of the book's disappointingly sluggish sales.

Capra, meanwhile, was newly returned from his four-year tour of duty in World War II, and was extremely nervous that he would not be able to regain the directorial glory of his prewar years: "There's no denying that butterflies began putting on their own private air show in my stomach," he confesses in his autobiography. "How would a Ruth, Gehrig, or DiMaggio feel if he hadn't swung a bat for four years and was suddenly asked to hit a home run in Yankee Stadium?"[48] Capra's sense of trepidation was, moreover, compounded by the fact that his first postwar film would inaugurate the independent production company that he had recently formed with William Wyler, George Stevens, and Samuel Briskin, causing him to feel that "I was not only carrying the load of making *Wonderful Life* a successful picture. I had to make a success out of Liberty Films. We were the bellwether of the post-war independents."[49] For both Dickens and Capra, then, there was an enormous pressure to come up with stories that would appeal to a wide audience and reconfirm their status as major "box-office" draws.

At the same time, however, we must bear in mind that the years of 1843 and 1946 were periods of intense social reflection for Dickens and Capra, respectively. The plight of the poor weighed very heavily on Dickens's mind in 1843, thanks largely to two parliamentary reports issued by the Children's Employment Commission that publicly exposed the appalling conditions of child labor in England.[50] In response to these reports, Dickens told friends that he planned to write "a very cheap pamphlet, called 'An appeal to the People of England, on behalf of the Poor Man's Child.'"[51] Although this pamphlet never materialized, Dickens explained his decision not to write it by assuring his social reformer friends that "when you . . . see what I do, and where, and how, you will certainly feel that a Sledge hammer has come down with twenty times the force—twenty thousand times the force—I could exert by following out my first idea."[52] Several months after making this assurance, just after giving a rousing speech at the Manchester Athenaeum about the need for educational reform for the poor, Dickens finally conceived of a very different way to "hammer" home his political message: by dressing it up and serving it as a crowd-pleasing Christmas treat.

In 1946, Capra was emotionally preoccupied with what he perceived to be "the cataclysmic aftermaths of war—hunger, disease, despair—[that] would breed gnawing doubts in man. Why? Why? Why did my wife and children have to be blown to bits? Where is God now?"[53] But, like Dickens, Capra came to realize that the best way to address the world's "gnawing doubts" would be in an indirect fashion; when contemplating what the subject matter of his first postwar film should be, he says that he specifically "knew one thing—it would *not* be about war."[54] Instead, Capra chose to adapt a short story by Philip Van Doren Stern—a story so short, in fact, that it had originally been circulated as Stern's 1943 Christmas card to his friends and family. The story is certainly not about war, but it is important to note that it is not too much about Christmas, either. The opening lines of the story are indicative of the peripheral role that the yuletide setting plays in both Van Doren Stern's Christmas card and Capra's filmic adaptation of it: "The little town straggling up the hill was bright with colored Christmas lights. But George Pratt did not see them. He was leaning over the railing of the iron bridge, staring down moodily at the black water."[55] Ironically, then, the modern world's two most celebrated Christmas narratives are a ghost story and a suicide story that do not deal, in any direct way, with the biblical birth of Christ.

Despite the fact that both texts have garnered a certain amount of criticism for their secular natures—criticism along the lines of Margaret Oliphant's gripe that the *Carol* promoted only "the immense spiritual power of the Christmas turkey"[56]—the reality is that the forces of moral censorship worked to minimize the texts' religiosity rather than to augment it. Indeed, with the exception of the opening set of prayers that serve as the expository foundation of the film, Joseph Breen's string of recommendation letters ask Capra to cut out almost all of *Wonderful Life*'s most direct references to God and Jesus (in phrases such as "I wish to God," "Thank God," "A, Dio Mio," and a comment made by Uncle Billy to George about "the place your father used to try to run like he thought Jesus would run it") for fear that they were not being used "reverently" enough.[57] Following a similar logic, the London Censorship Board even attempted to make Capra remove all references to "heaven," "wings," and "angels" before the film was released in England.[58] But, after pleading with the censors "not to ruin our first independent production" and assuring them that "all United States censor boards have hailed picture as just the type of clean wholesome entertainment they all cry for,"[59] Capra was able to get most of his wings and angels through to the British public after all.

Even before these official objections were raised, however, Capra's desire to obtain his audience's moral stamp of approval had a strong impact on the way he chose to present the film's religious content. As he explained to a reporter later on:

> For a long time we were worried about how to show heaven. . . . I knew we wouldn't please everybody, and I knew we'd probably get some laughs with the thing that we naturally didn't want. So rather than getting laughs that we didn't want, I used laughs we did want. . . . This was, in a way, a way out of a difficulty. But a conscious way. When a thing gets tough, try to make it funny and it'll go over. It's like Mae West with her sex. If you make it funny, you can get away with murder. So heaven was humorous this way and it didn't offend anybody.[60]

As little as *Wonderful Life*'s divine moments may seem to have in common with the saucy, bawdy humor of Mae West, Capra does manage to portray heaven in a relatively unholy, unspiritual way without raising objections from even his most devoutly religious viewers. Capra's angels do not talk about the Pearly Gates. Or eternal salvation. Or Jesus or Mary or God, for that matter. Instead, they focus on what the audience is focusing on: sitting back and watching a good movie. ("Sit down," Joseph instructs Clarence. "If you're going to help a man, you want to know something about him, don't you?") Interestingly, Joseph Breen appears to have had no problem with Capra's secular approach to representing the afterlife; the scenes in heaven are not so much as mentioned in any of the five recommendation letters that Breen wrote in response to early drafts of the film. Apparently, the Catholic-based Production Code considered it to be more acceptable for a film to avoid religious discourse altogether than to contain discourse that might be considered blasphemous by any of the members of its audience.

Although we do not have quite such formal evidence of censorship's influence on the secularization of the *Carol*, we do know that Dickens made several last-minute textual changes to the galleys that seem to have been based on his fear of offending his audience's sense of religious decorum (i.e., the Ghost of Christmas Present's reason for sprinkling his spirit-lifting incense upon the dinner of poor men "the most" is changed from "Because my eldest brother took them especially under his protection" to "Because it needs it most"[61]). In addition to excising some of his most direct references to religious subject matter, Dickens also relied on the "heavenly" strategy outlined by Capra: he sprinkled his account of spirits and spiritual salvation with a hearty dose of genial Dickensian humor. (This can be seen as early as the second paragraph of the text, when Dickens abruptly turns his discussion of Marley's death into a comic discussion of the ineptness of the simile "as dead as a door-nail."[62]) This strategy did not work on everyone, of course. In response, for example, to the *Carol*'s light-hearted assertion that "it is good to be children sometimes, and never better than at Christmas, when its mighty Founder was a child himself" (89), a reviewer in the Anglican periodical the *Christian Remembrancer* criticized "the extreme irreverence of this way of speaking" and advised Dickens that "his expunging, or altering, the sentence in the next edition, will give general satisfaction."[63] Such complaints notwithstanding, the vast majority of Dickens's readers were more than satisfied with his "way of speaking" in the *Carol*, as irreverent and/or irreligious as it may have been. In fact, as critics like Paul Davis have pointed out, Dickens's Christmas stories seem to have been specifically catered toward the secularized sensibilities of his Victorian London reading public: "Writing for these new urban readers," Davis asserts, "Dickens sought to express spiritual truth in the humanized language of the self-mirroring secular city."[64] In a way, then, the secular nature of Dickens's and Capra's seminal "Christmas" texts can be understood less as a form of rebellion against the conservatively religious ethos of Victorian and Hays Code–era systems of censorship than as a paradoxical result of that ethos: ultimately, the moral censor's fear of blasphemy both promoted and provoked the secularization of Dickens's and Capra's narrative art.

But what, we might ask, is the secular message that is being promulgated in these texts in place of a religious one—and what role does censorship play in that message's creation and repression? As Mrs. Oliphant's quip about Dickens's undue emphasis on "the Christmas turkey" implies, the most obvious thematic statements being made by the texts are socioeconomic in nature; and yet, the exact nature of those statements is anything but obvious. Both works spend a great deal of narrative energy pointing out and bemoaning the economic injustices of the modern world's capitalist system, and cast as their villains characters who personify the cutthroat potential of that system (the unreformed Scrooge, the never-reformed Potter). At the same time, however, some recent critics have begun to argue that the texts actually work to reinforce an "essentially conservative" capitalist ideology. J. Hillis Miller, for instance, has commented upon the fact that at the end of the *Carol*, "Scrooge is not supposed to give up his business, nor is he to cease to go daily on 'Change, nor is the capitalist system of getting, spending, production and exchange supposed to be altered in any basic way,"[65] while David Mamet has criticized *Wonderful Life* for being a "self-deluded" proponent of "un-selfinterested capitalism, [which] is of necessity an oxymoron."[66] Because Dickens's and Capra's resolutely mainstream texts participate so conspicuously in the commodity culture of literary and cinematic production, such critics argue, their authors cannot help but have a personal investment in making the economic system at the heart of that culture look good. And what better way to cast a positive light upon the buying and selling of goods than by broaching the subject of Christmas—that "phantasmatic" season during which, to borrow Audrey Jaffe's phrase, "laissez-faire economics is happily wedded to natural benevolence."[67]

That wedding is carried out by the stories of spiritual transformation that these scripts tell—but they do not tell them easily or outside the forces of the marketplace of ideas. Christmas is, after all, the most manufactured of spiritual holidays, both in terms of its endlessly regenerated representation in popular culture and in terms of its pronounced connection to raw commercialism. The Christmas fantasy that plays out in the lives of Ebenezer Scrooge and George Bailey is also, therefore, an "ideological project," as Jaffe has called it. "A capitalist sensibility is perhaps most evident," Jaffe argues, "in the story's external and internal refusals of temporality: in the identification with a time of year that ensures its annual return and in its offer to Scrooge, to its readers or viewers, and, theoretically, to the poor themselves of an endlessly repeatable cycle of failure and recovery."[68] Jaffe's words could, of course, apply just as easily to Capra's seasonal tale of financial ruin followed by redemption; in both *A Christmas Carol* and *It's a Wonderful Life*, the holiday of Christmas is used to demonstrate (and, in the minds of most Marxists, to grossly exaggerate) the warmer and friendlier side of capitalism.

This dynamic of dressing capitalism in the red and white robes of Father Christmas intriguingly reflects the role of the censor in shaping novels and films—like the Lord of Misrule, both inviting and restraining merriment. Just as Dickens and Capra clearly had a personal and professional stake in the success of capitalism, so too did the system of moral censorship under which they were forced to operate—the censorship of the marketplace. This can, as usual, be seen most explicitly in the case of the Production Code; as is outlined in my introduction, Hollywood's decision to adopt the 1930 Production Code only a few months after the stock market crash of 1929 was unmistakably influenced by the economic ramifications of that crash. If Hollywood wanted to keep as much of its box-office revenue as possible in the face of the Depression, the thinking went, it had better start trying to offend as few of its potential viewers as possible. Because the very genesis of the Code was so market-driven in nature, it is no surprise that classical Hollywood filmmakers consistently found themselves being "encouraged" by Code administrators to create works that would defend and uphold the capitalist status quo.

This type of encouragement gained new momentum when the infamous House Un-American Activities Committee (HUAC) began to question Hollywood's relationship to communism in the years following World War II. Throughout this postwar/Cold War era, the PCA attempted to suppress any messages that they thought HUAC would consider to be communist or anticapitalist in nature, suddenly subjecting filmmakers to even stricter censorship policies than the Production Code had originally established. As many film scholars have noted, one of the primary ways that the PCA believed it could control the messages of Hollywood films was by forcing filmmakers to *conclude* their narratives on ideologically conservative notes.[69] This pressure came under the heading of the "rule of compensating moral values"—a rule that never technically appeared in the Production Code but that was cited time and time again by Code administrators in their recommendation letters to filmmakers over the years. According to this rule, filmmakers were permitted to portray morally objectionable behavior if, and only if, that behavior was criticized, vilified, and punished in the end. Depravity must be defeated; goodness (and capitalism) must prevail.

The respective endings of *A Christmas Carol* and *It's a Wonderful Life* certainly appear to satisfy the censor's demand for compensating moral values, particularly when it comes to their depiction of capitalism in a morally complimentary light. Both endings hinge, of course, on the psychological transformation and moral salvation of their stories' misguided protagonists. But if we look closely at what each protagonist is called upon to do in his text's final moments—at how he is called upon to change—we can see the ideological imprint of the moral censor: in order to become better men, both protagonists must learn to become better capitalists. Scrooge's redemption manifests itself in his newfound appreciation for the "spending" side of the economic equation (exemplified, famously, by his purchase of "[n]ot the little prize Turkey: the big one" [112]—the more money Scrooge spends, the better and purer we know he has become), while George's salvation comes when he learns to participate in the "profit" side of the equation (after a lifetime of "not making a dime" out of his family's successful Building and Loan, George must ultimately give in and allow his customers to pay him a proper monetary compensation for his efforts). In the end, then, the Christmas "miracles" depicted in *A Christmas Carol* and *It's a Wonderful Life* are not religious but economic in nature. In the former, the miracle is that Scrooge finally gives his clerk a raise; in the latter, the miracle (as Mary Bailey [Donna Reed] even explicitly calls it—"I hear them now, George, it's a miracle! It's a miracle!") is that George's friends pile into his living room and hand him a basketful of cash.

And yet, as much as the happy endings of the texts may appear to serve as ringing, Christmas-card endorsements of capitalist consumerism, it is important to note that they are not the only "endings" that Dickens and Capra provide for us. Because the texts employ the machinery of the counterfactual conditional, each of them is given the opportunity to depict two alternative endings, only one of which need paint capitalism in a glowingly optimistic light. The alternate ending of *It's a Wonderful Life* can, of course, be found in the dark and seedy "Pottersville" dream sequence that shows George what life would have been like if he had never been born. Although the dialogue used in the sequence never addresses the issue of capitalism or consumerism in a direct manner (the most it even refers to banking is when George is informed that his family's Building and Loan "went out of business years ago"), the message of the sequence is as glaringly obvious as the flashing neon signs of the nightclubs, liquor stores, pool halls, and pawn shops that line Pottersville's Main Street. If Potter's brand of no-holds-barred, purely profit-based economics is allowed to triumph over George's more community-based brand, then the moral fabric of Bedford Falls society will utterly and irrevocably disintegrate. This is, in fact, precisely the if-then scenario that George has been warning his friends and neighbors about throughout the film: "This town needs this measly one-horse institution if only to have some place where people can come without crawling to Potter"; "If Potter gets hold of this Building and Loan there'll never be another decent house built in this town." But it is only in the Pottersville dream sequence that we are able to follow George's premonitions to their darkest and most disturbing economic conclusions.

Everything in Pottersville is, crudely, for sale. Nick the bartender (now turned bar-owner) sells hard-core inebriation: "We serve hard drinks in here for men who want to get drunk fast." George's mother (now the coldly suspicious proprietor of Ma Bailey's Boarding House) sells her home. Violet Bick (now an out-and-out prostitute) sells her body. Those who do not or cannot participate in the sales game, moreover, are brutally punished for it: Uncle Billy, the epitome of the inept businessman, has "been in the insane asylum ever since he lost his business," while Mary, who refuses to marry for money (as is seen in her rejection of the exceptionally wealthy Sam Wainwright), has become a meek and pitiable "old maid." As George stumbles through this nightmarish revision of the life he once knew, Capra emphasizes the disparity between the world of Bedford Falls and the world of Pottersville by abruptly switching into an entirely new cinematic genre—as Robin Wood has put it, "the iconography of small-town comedy is exchanged, unmistakably, for that of film noir, with police sirens, shooting in the streets, darkness, vicious dives, alcoholism, burlesque shows, strip clubs, and the glitter and shadows of noir lighting"[70] (see fig. 8). Under the glare of this new lighting, Potter's fairly standard capitalist ambitions—to make more and more money, to own more and more property, to achieve greater and greater socioeconomic success—are suddenly made to look monstrous, lurid, and morally unsound.

The *Carol's* alternate ending, meanwhile, occurs in its bleakly futuristic fourth stave, as Scrooge is guided through the terrifying landscape of what his "end" will be if he does not change his miserly ways. Although the section of this stave that is most remembered—and most often dramatized in film and television versions of the tale—is the section that

FIGURE 8 *Capra's film noir. James Stewart in* It's a Wonderful Life.

shows the Cratchits mourning the death of Tiny Tim, there are several lesser known, less reenacted episodes that lead up it, each of which paints a rather grim portrait of the inner workings of capitalism. Scrooge starts his Christmas Yet To Come journey by finding himself "on 'Change, amongst the merchants; who hurried up and down, and chinked the money in their pockets, and conversed in groups, and looked at their watches, and trifled thoughtfully with their great gold seals; and so forth" (96). These business merchants are depicted, for the most part, as unappealing ogres: one is "a great fat man with a monstrous chin," another is "a red-faced gentleman with a pendulous excrescence on the end of his nose, that shook like the gills of a turkey-cock" (96). But they are also, more importantly, portrayed as heartless, callous individuals who can yawn and laugh about a man's death, and focus more on the economics of the situation than on anything else: "What has he done with his money?" asks one. "It's likely to be a very cheap funeral," remarks another. "I don't mind going if a lunch is provided," chuckles a third (96–97).

As grotesque as the businessmen's financial discussion of Scrooge's death may be, however, their grotesqueness is one-upped by the scene that follows. In it, Scrooge watches his servants pawn the possessions of his that they have managed to steal away from his death chamber (and, indeed, from his dead body—the charwoman has gone so far as to rob him of the clothes that he had been dressed in for his burial). Scrooge regards the actions of these servants as examples of profiteering taken to a diabolic extreme. "[H]e viewed them," we are told, "with a detestation and disgust, which could hardly have been greater, though they had been obscene demons, marketing the corpse itself" (102). To soothe his sense of moral revulsion, Scrooge asks the Ghost of Christmas Yet To Come to take him to see "any person in the town, who feels emotion caused by this man's death" (103). In response to this request, the Ghost brings Scrooge to the home of a kind young couple and their children, who have nothing "monstrous" or "demonic" about them. But even in this house of warmth and goodness, the pressures imposed by Victorian England's economic system cause the family to have a reaction to death that is no less callous than the business merchants' or less profit-driven than the servants'. Because it means a timely delay in the repayment of their debt, the family morbidly delights in the news of their creditor's passing. "Soften it as they would, their hearts were lighter. The children's faces, hushed and clustered round to hear what they so little understood, were brighter; and it was a happier house for this man's death! The only emotion that the Ghost could show him, caused by the event, was one of pleasure" (106).

In both the Pottersville section of *It's a Wonderful Life* and the futuristic fourth section of *A Christmas Carol*, then, we are shown the darker, seedier, uglier results of capitalism. Interestingly, however, neither section aroused much disapproval from the moral censors of its time. Indeed, when looking through the pages and pages of objections that Joseph Breen raised in response to the various drafts of *Wonderful Life* that were submitted to his office, one is struck by the near-total absence of complaints directed toward the content of the Pottersville sequence. (Breen's very first letter warns that any "indication of Violet as a street walker is unacceptable,"[71] but the objection is never mentioned again, in spite of the fact that Capra did nothing to alter Violet's Pottersville dialogue or characterization between the screenplay's first draft and the film's final cut.) Similarly, one would be hard-pressed to find so much as a sentence written by one of Dickens's contemporaries that finds fault with the sociopolitical implications of his Christmas Yet To Come. All in all, both Dickens and Capra seem to have been extremely successful in achieving the goal of inoffensiveness that Dickens specifically describes in his pithy preface to the *Carol*: "I have endeavored in this Ghostly little book," he writes, "to raise the Ghost of an Idea, which shall not put my readers out of humour with themselves, with each other, with the season, or with me. May it haunt their house pleasantly, and no one wish to lay it" (29).

The reason, I would argue, that the social criticism of the *Carol* and *Wonderful Life* so successfully avoids putting readers, viewers, and censors "out of humour" with the texts lies largely in the counterfactual positioning of that criticism. According to the *official* plotline of each narrative, it is, after all, the unrelenting bleakness of the alternate universe that is the fiction, the fabrication, the hallucination, while the reassuring optimism of the happy ending is the diegetic reality. Understanding the importance of this fiction/reality distinction from a censorship perspective, both Dickens and Capra take great pains within their texts to prove to us that their final moments are, in fact, real. George has to make sure that he has "really" woken up from his Pottersville nightmare by verifying the empirical evidence of his bloodied lip, his smashed-up car, Zuzu's petals in his pockets, and the corporality of his non-librarian wife ("Mary! Let me touch you! Are you real?"). Scrooge, meanwhile, has to keep insisting to the people he encounters that *he*, in his reformed state, is real—when he asks the Cockney boy beneath his window to go buy the prize turkey for him, the boy exclaims in disbelief, "Walk-ER!" (113); when he makes a shockingly large donation to the poor, the "portly gentleman" to whom he makes it breathlessly replies, "My dear Mr. Scrooge, are you serious?" (114); and when he gives Bob Cratchit the raise that he has deserved for so long, the bewildered Cratchit responds by trembling and considering "knocking Scrooge down with [a ruler]; holding him; and calling to the people in the court for help and a strait-waistcoat" (116). Moreover, in the case of *A Christmas Carol*, the omniscient narration works to reinforce our sense of what is real and what is not, for even though the Ghost of Christmas Yet To Come refuses to tell Scrooge whether or not his reformed actions will be able to alter the tragic future events that he has witnessed,

Dickens's narrator does specifically tell us that "Scrooge was better than his word. He did it all, and infinitely more; and to Tiny Tim, who did NOT die, he was a second father" (116). In this one, capitalized phrase, the question of diegetic reality is flatly answered for us—if Tiny Tim does NOT die, then we know once and for all that Stave Four is merely a dream sequence and that goodness and innocence do, really, prevail.

Yet in spite of all of this textual insistence that we can and should believe in the stories' happy endings, many readers and viewers over the years have had a hard time doing so. Some of these disbelievers have chosen mentally to rewrite the ending of the particular text in question in a more plausible fashion; see, for example, Edmund Wilson's famous *New Yorker* article from 1939, in which he tries to imagine "what Scrooge would actually be like if we were to follow him beyond the frame of the story" and comes to the conclusion that "he would relapse when the merriment was over—if not while it was still going on—into moroseness, vindictiveness, suspicion. He would, that is to say, reveal himself as the victim of a manic-depressive cycle, and a very uncomfortable person."[72] Others, meanwhile, have chosen simply to disregard their story's ending, or to push the ending back to what they would consider to be a more believable point in the story; see William S. Pechter's essay from 1962, in which he insists that "for those who can accept the realities of George Bailey's situation—the continual frustration of his ambitions, his envy of those who have done what he has only wanted to do, the collapse of his business, a sense of utter isolation, final despair—and do not believe in angels, . . . the film ends, in effect, with the hero's suicide."[73]

But it is not only the presence of supernatural angels and ghosts in the texts that prevents these readers and viewers from trusting fully in the happy endings that are provided for them. There is, I would argue, one other major element of those endings that distinctly stands in plausibility's way: the element of excess. Scrooge, for instance, does not simply transform into a kinder, less miserly old man—he transforms into "as good a friend, as good a master, and as good a man, as the good old city knew, or any other good old city, town, or borough, in the good old world" (116). He does not simply buy the Cratchits a turkey—he buys them a turkey so improbably large that "[h]e never could have stood upon his legs, that bird. He would have snapped 'em off short in a minute, like sticks of sealing wax" (113). He does not simply make a charitable donation to the poor—he makes a donation so overwhelmingly "munificent" that it takes the charity worker's breath away (114). And Scrooge is not the only one who can be accused of excessiveness in the *Carol*'s fifth stave; Dickens, too, employs many linguistic techniques that serve to inflate the narrative's sense of urgency and intensity—such as, for example, his extensive use of superlatives, exclamation points, and repeated words or repeated rhythms. To give just a few illustrations: "He was checked in his transports by the churches ringing out the lustiest peals he had ever heard. Clash, clang, hammer; ding, dong, bell. Bell, dong, ding; hammer, clang, clash! Oh, glorious, glorious!" (112). Or: "The chuckle with which he said this, and the chuckle with which he paid for the Turkey, and the chuckle with which he paid for the cab, and the chuckle with which he recompensed the boy, were only to be exceeded by the chuckle with which he sat down breathless in his chair again, and chuckled till he cried" (113). Or: "Let him in! It is a mercy he didn't shake his arm off. He was at home in five minutes. Nothing could be heartier. His niece looked just the same. So did Topper when *he* came. So did the plump sister, when *she* came. So did everyone when *they* came. Wonderful party, wonderful games, wonderful unanimity, won-der-ful happiness!" (115). The desperation of Scrooge's conversion—the sense that he must continually come up with new and more emphatic ways to demonstrate the change in his spirit, that he cannot express that change nearly *enough*—is mirrored in the excessive desperation of Dickens's prose.

A similar type of excess marks the end of *It's a Wonderful Life*, particularly when it comes to the over-the-top emotion of its male protagonist. Indeed, George Bailey's "light as a feather, happy as an angel, merry as a school-boy, giddy as a drunken man" actions and demeanor in the film's final sequence constitute the most direct link between his character and the character of Ebenezer Scrooge (111). On a narrative level, meanwhile, Capra mimics many of Dickens's excessive linguistic maneuvers, from his abundant use of exclamation (more than half of the screenplay's "happy ending" lines are punctuated with exclamation points) to his saccharine use of one particularly memorable superlative ("To my big brother, George—the richest man in town!") to his frequent use of repeated sentences (i.e., "My mouth's bleeding, Bert! My mouth's bleeding!") and repeated rhythms (i.e., George's friends and neighbors each making their little explanatory speech of gratitude as they give him their money). But Capra's cinematic excess does not stop there: the last few minutes of his film also bombard us with an excessive amount of snow falling to the ground, an excessive number of Christmas lights lining Bedford Falls's Main Street, an excessive amount of holiday decorations adorning the Bailey's living room, an excessive number of friendly neighbors piling into that living room, an excessive amount of cash accumulating on the living room table, an excessive number of voices crooning one yuletide song after another, an excessive amount of cheering and laughing and crying and hugging—an excessive amount, in other words, of heart-warming, wholesome *Christmas*.

For in spite of Capra's repeat casting of the "boyishly sincere" Jimmy Stewart in the film's leading role, it is not *Wonderful Life*'s male protagonist who embodies the trait of excessive innocence, as was the case in the earlier Mister films—it is, instead, the setting of proverbially pure Christmas itself. Interestingly, only a small percentage of the story actually takes place during the Christmas season, since Capra does not limit his detailing of George's personal history to moments from his "Christmases past" in the same way that Dickens does. Still, thanks largely to the excessive vigor with which Capra portrays George's miraculously Merry Christmas in the film's final moments, *It's a Wonderful Life* has come to be identified not only as a Christmas movie but also as an intrinsic part of the modern world's Christmas tradition. Yet I would also argue that the excessive "Christmassiness" of the closing sequence serves another specific narrative purpose: it gives Capra's story an overall impression of joyfulness, hopefulness, and family-friendly inoffensiveness, while drawing the moral censor's attention away from the darker, bitterer sentiments that lie at the heart of the film—or, to put it more precisely, *in* the heart of the film's protagonist.

For, again, as much as the character of George Bailey may physically look like the character of Jefferson Smith, it is important to acknowledge how little the two actually have in common. Where Jefferson Smith cherishes the small-town life he lives before being whisked off to Washington, George Bailey detests all of Bedford Falls's homey conventionalities and yearns desperately to escape them; where Jefferson Smith blushes and stammers every time a pretty girl talks to him, George Bailey vehemently resists giving in to the matrimonial advances of his town's resident pretty girl, Mary Hatch;[74] where Jefferson Smith fights with every honorable fiber of his being to clear his name after being wrongly accused of large-scale political corruption, George Bailey cravenly plans to commit suicide after being wrongly accused of misappropriating $8,000. But the biggest difference between George Bailey and Jefferson Smith (and Long-fellow Deeds, and John Doe, and most of Capra's other prewar heroes) can be found in the way that they "triumph" in the end. Where the typical Capra protagonist triumphs by defeating vice and exposing villainy, George Bailey never even realizes that Mr. Potter is the one who has gotten hold of his $8,000, and therefore never achieves the satisfaction (for himself or the audience) of making the antagonist pay for his sins. As it turns out, snapping George out of his suicidal funk has relatively little to do with the missing money at all, and much more to do with convincing him that his small-town, domesticated existence is not as claustrophobically dismal as he has been making it out to be.

The scene that best depicts George's sense of claustrophobia is, significantly, the one other scene of the film that is as steeped in the trappings of Christmas as is its happy ending. The scene takes place just after George and Uncle Billy have unsuccessfully scoured the town looking for their missing $8,000—at a point when George is, as he later puts it, "at the end of his rope." Upon arriving home, George is confronted with a barrage of what *should* be the comforts and joys of the holiday season: a Christmas tree so tall that Mary must stand on a chair to trim it; a "Merry Christmas" banner running across the entire living-room ceiling; a table piled high with wrapping paper, bows, and half-wrapped presents; a fire burning brightly in the fireplace; a son enthusiastically working on his own Christmas play; and a daughter diligently practicing "Hark, the Herald Angels Sing" on the piano (see fig. 9). Yet instead of finding solace in his family's excessive hominess and holiday spirit, George finds them rather to be overwhelming ("You call this a happy family? Why did we have to have all these kids?"), overbearing ("Janie, haven't you learned that silly tune yet? You've played it over and over again. Now stop it! Stop it!"), and, ultimately, profoundly alienating ("George, why must you torture the children? Why don't you . . .").

FIGURE 9 *Christmas with all the trappings. James Stewart, Larry Simms, Jimmy Hawkins, Donna Reed, and Carol Coombs in* It's a Wonderful Life.

Although Mary does not finish her accusatory reprimand, George is so stung by her tone, and the disappointed looks on his children's faces, that he begins to think quite seriously about committing suicide. As much, then, as *Wonderful Life* may leave us with the impression that it has depicted Christmas as a warm and winsome symbol of conventional domestic bliss—fitting neatly into the nostalgic tradition of such holiday films as Ernst Lubitsch's *The Shop Around the Corner* (1940), Mark Sandrich's *Holiday Inn* (1942), and Vincente Minnelli's *Meet Me in St. Louis* (1944)—the truth is that it gives us one of classical Hollywood's starkest portrayals of the desolate feeling a man may get when the spirit of Christmas has left him out in the cold. And this portrayal was no accident on Capra's part, as he makes clear in an interview from the early 1980s. When explaining why two of his most emotionally powerful works, *Meet John Doe* (1941) and *Wonderful Life*, just so happen to pair the setting of Christmas with the theme of suicide, Capra points out that "Christmas makes people vulnerable, brings out deep feelings. No one is neutral. People either feel more joyous or sadder. It's a time when some people feel lonelier, more abandoned. There are many suicides that time of year."[75]

Capra is, here, echoing a sentiment that is briefly but emphatically expressed within the text of the *Carol*; as one of the "portly gentlemen" who is soliciting Christmas donations for the poor explains to Scrooge, "We choose this time, because it is a time, of all others, when Want is keenly felt, and Abundance rejoices" (39). Even though Dickens, like Capra, makes sure that the most memorable moments of his Christmas story serve to illustrate how "abundantly joyful" the holiday can be (think, for example, of the Cratchits' jovial Christmas Day dinner, or of the Fezziwigs' jubilant Christmas Eve ball that Dickens chose to serve as the frontispiece illustration for the original edition of his text [fig. 10]), he finds many other ways of conveying a less sanguine view of the season as well. One of the most interesting ways he does this is through his creation of a distinctly unwholesome, un-joyful, un-Christmassy protagonist—if George Bailey is no Jefferson Smith, Ebenezer Scrooge is certainly no Oliver Twist. By casting such a character as his story's hero, Dickens is able to include in his text a great deal of anti-Christmas sentiment with utter impunity. Indeed, who but Dickens could pen lines such as "every idiot who goes about with 'Merry Christmas' on his lips, should be boiled with his own pudding, and buried with a stake of holly through his heart" (36) and still be regarded as the literary incarnation of good Father Christmas himself?[76]

Of course, the reason that Scrooge's ornery, atheistic sentiments are excused is that they are so emphatically recanted after his conversion has taken place. But if we consider the root cause of Scrooge's initial yuletide animosity, we find a very different way in which Dickens chips away at the Merry Christmas myth. When the Ghost of Christmas Past takes Scrooge to the first stop on his trip down memory lane, we are immediately confronted with a scene of excessive Christmas gaiety: "Some shaggy ponies now were seen trotting towards them with boys upon their backs, who called to other boys in country gigs and carts, driven by farmers. All these boys were in great spirits, and shouted to each other, until the broad fields were so full of merry music, that the crisp air laughed to hear it!" (57). But then, standing in stark contrast to these "jocund travellers," we are shown one other figure: "'The school is not quite deserted,'

FIGURE 10 *Abundance rejoices. Illustration from* A Christmas Carol.

said the Ghost. 'A solitary child, neglected by his friends, is left there still.' Scrooge said he knew it. And he sobbed" (57). In this moment, Dickens simply but devastatingly portrays one type of "Want" that can be "keenly felt" during the holiday season—not the type meant by the *Carol*'s portly gentlemen, perhaps, but a very tender type nonetheless.

This is not to say, however, that Dickens disregards the type of Want that *is* meant by his portly gentlemen; as we have already seen, his text is extremely interested in depicting and decrying the economic injustices felt by London's poor. The way that Dickens manages to impart this kind of social criticism while still maintaining the *Carol*'s aura of benign holiday cheer is by stressing the fact that the Merry Christmases portrayed within it are merry *in spite of* his characters' wretched financial situations. This is most obviously true in the case of the Cratchits, but the Ghost of Christmas Present shows us many other cheery-in-spite-of-everything Christmas celebrations as well—celebrations of lowly miners, lighthouse attendants, sailors, all of whom are able to enjoy the warmth of Christmas even in the midst of their "bleak," "desolate," "dreadful" surroundings. How do they do it? Dickens specifically tells us: it is a feat of Christmas magic, in the form of laced incense sprinkled by the Ghost upon poor men's Christmas dinners. "The Spirit stood beside sick beds, and they were cheerful; on foreign lands, and they were close at home; by struggling men, and they were patient in their greater hope; by poverty, and it was rich" (91). The problem with this kind of Christmas miracle is, of course, that it is so short-lived; the Ghost can only work his wonders but one day a year. By turning hope and patience and wealth and good cheer into gifts that are artificially and temporarily bestowed, Dickens reveals Christmas to be a bright and shiny façade that merely cloaks the social, moral, and economic failures of his society. At the end of the third stave, in fact, Dickens goes so far as to literalize this rather cynical view of Christmas: hidden beneath the skirts of the "genial," "unconstrained," "joyful" Ghost of Christmas Present, we discover two children, "a boy and girl," who are described in the most pejorative language Dickens can muster: "wretched, abject, frightful, hideous, miserable," as well as "yellow, meagre, ragged, scowling, wolfish" (92). They are the human incarnations of Ignorance and Want, and even though we are specifically told that they belong to Man, we can see that they cling, steadfastly, to Christmas (fig. 11).

The image of these horrifying creatures skulking behind the curtain of the Spirit's rich and plenteous robes stands as an excellent metaphor for the thematic double standard being practiced in *A Christmas Carol* and *It's a Wonderful Life*: in both texts, we are left with enough diegetic wiggle-room to interpret the morals of the stories as we see fit. Because the texts were required, by the forces of moral censorship, to adhere to

FIGURE 11 *Beneath the robes of plenty. Illustration from* A Christmas Carol.

certain well-known structural rules (e.g., the rule of compensating moral values), Dickens and Capra were able to infuse them with ordinarily censorable sentiments—distrust of capitalist ideology, bitterness toward the confinement of domestic life, antipathy toward Christmas—without inciting too much shock or controversy. But if censorship, in this way, allows for powerful social criticism to enter into the most family-friendly of popular entertainment, it also allows for a formidably affirmative power to reach even the most sophisticated of cynics. For as much as the skulking horrors of humanity may haunt these texts, theirs are not the voices that carry. Far more resonant, on a cultural level, are the sounds of tender, childish optimism (Tiny Tim's "God bless Us, Every One!" [116]; Zuzu Bailey's "Every time a bell rings, an angel gets his wings!") with which each author chooses to end his narrative. When taken out of context, these lines smack of a mawkish sentimentality. But when, after having plunged with George Bailey into the abyss of suicide and with Ebenezer Scrooge into a spectral sea of crime and punishment, we are finally permitted to come gasping back up for air, we find that the cloyingly sentimental has transmuted into the authentically euphoric. Whether we choose to read these euphoric endings as the fantasy or the reality of the counterfactual stories we are being told, it is difficult to resist their urgent pull toward a brand of joy that manages to lie just outside the reach of censorship—improper in its exorbitance, indecorous in its immoderateness, indecent in its unapologetic excess.

4

The Thrill of the Fight
Charlotte Brontë and Elia Kazan

> It is vain to say human beings ought to be satisfied
> with tranquility: they must have action; and they
> will make it if they cannot find it.
> —*Charlotte Brontë*

> Breen is a hell of a guy, and I'm just tickled he's in
> the business.
> —*Elia Kazan*

PERHAPS MORE THAN any other Victorian novelists or classical Hollywood directors, Charlotte Brontë and Elia Kazan considered themselves to be artists of "passion," and belittled the creative contributions of those novelists and filmmakers whose work they dismissed as dispassionate. Brontë, for example, famously complained of Jane Austen that "the Passions are perfectly unknown to her . . . what throbs fast and full, though hidden, what blood rushes through, what is the unseen seat of Life and the sentient target of Death—*this* Miss Austen ignores," while Kazan brusquely wrote off Alfred Hitchcock as an "artificial" filmmaker who was merely a "master of stunts and tricks."[1] In contrast, Brontë spoke frequently in her letters about the importance that she placed on raw emotional truth in her own writing, and Kazan peppered his autobiography with allusions to his own creative intensity, integrity, and fervor. These were, of course, no empty boasts on Brontë's or Kazan's parts; both artists have been repeatedly hailed for their ardent and visceral portrayals of the complex drama of human desire. Yet as ostentatiously impassioned as the majority of their works may be, the specific plots of those works almost always revolve around the seemingly antithetical impulse of repression. Uncompromising ardor, in Brontë and Kazan, is persistently coupled with sexual and emotional compromise and restraint. It is the goal of this chapter to demonstrate why.

A good place to begin my discussion of repression is, not surprisingly, with Freud. Ever since Freud first directed his psychoanalytic gaze at the complicated sexual lives of his patients, the concept of repression has been central to the way the modern Western world has perceived itself. According to Foucault, as we may recall, there arose in Freud's wake a "repressive hypothesis" that specifically cast Victorian sexual repression as the cold and ruthless enemy of truth, freedom, and personal fulfillment. Although there is much in Freud's writing that does point to repression as a psychologically debilitating force (e.g., "The commonest cause of anxiety neurosis is unconsummated excitation. Libidinal excitation is aroused but not satisfied, not employed; apprehensiveness then appears instead of this libido that has been diverted from its employment"[2]), there are many other moments that point in precisely the opposite direction. In one of the essays from his "Contributions to the Psychology of Love," for example, Freud starts off arguing that "the injurious results of the deprivation of sexual enjoyment at the beginning manifest themselves in lack of full satisfaction when sexual desire is later given free rein in marriage," but then immediately backtracks:

> But, on the other hand, unrestrained sexual liberty from the beginning leads to no better result. It is easy to show that the value the mind sets on erotic needs instantly sinks as soon as satisfaction becomes readily obtainable. Some obstacle is necessary to swell the tide of the libido to its height; and at all periods of history, wherever natural barriers in the way of satisfaction have not sufficed, mankind has erected conventional ones in order to be able to enjoy love.[3]

As much, then, as Freud may attribute such psychological neuroses as hysteria, masochism, and impotence to the cultural prohibition against premarital sexual experiences, he also acknowledges the eroticizing power of externally imposed "obstacles" and "barriers," otherwise known as the pleasure of the forbidden fruit.

At more or less the same time that Freud was inventing psychoanalysis in Vienna, Havelock Ellis was conducting his own "investigation into the psychology of sex" on British soil.[4] Ellis's studies are equally, if not more, concerned with the effects of repression on people's sexual lives, though they are framed in what now feels like outdated and rather sexist language. Instead of "repression," he traces the evolution of "modesty," which he sees as being the major libidinal tool that the female of the species uses to attract her male prey: "It is," Ellis argues, "the spontaneous and natural instinct of the lover to desire modesty in his mistress."[5] Although he insists that "there is no such instinctive demand on the woman's part for innocence in the man," he does find there to be "an allied and corresponding desire which is very often clearly or latently present in the woman: a longing for pleasure that is stolen or forbidden." Ultimately, Ellis concludes that "both male and female are instinctively seeking the same end of sexual union at the moment of highest excitement," meaning that, even when there is no "real" conflict, there must always be "the semblance of a conflict, an apparent clash of aim, an appearance of cruelty" in order for both partners to feel sexually and emotionally satisfied.[6] Despite the fact that contemporary psychology has, in many ways, moved beyond the findings of Freud and Ellis, their basic theories on the paradoxical relationship between sexual passion and sexual repression are quite helpful to our understanding of repression's close artistic relation, censorship.

Both Brontë and Kazan have been frequently held up as exemplars of "psychological" artistry. John Lahr, for example, has observed that "Kazan's particular gift was to highlight and to release the interior drama of conflicting desires" and that his "great contribution was to discover a theatrical vocabulary that turned psychology into behavior,"[7] just as Joseph Boone has argued that Brontë's work "anticipates the attempts of its modern and modernist successors to convey in fictional form those elusive psychosexual and libidinal currents that, since the advent of turn-of-the-century sexological theory and psychoanalytic discourse, have increasingly come to be seen as constitutive of human subjectivity."[8] Particularly relevant to my discussion is John Kucich's chapter on Brontë in his careful analysis of *Repression in Victorian Fiction*. For Kucich, there is little difference between the ways that Brontë's characters express and repress their libidinal desires. (He cites, for example, Rochester's perverse courtship of Jane Eyre in which he pretends that he is not attracted to her at all and would rather marry Blanche Ingram, followed by Jane's equally perverse "confession" of her love for Rochester that "takes the form of a threat to leave him."[9]) By recasting repression as an "intensifying" and "destabilizing" force within Brontë's fiction, Kucich attempts to free her from the stigma of being thought to have succumbed to the "tragic," "unhealthy" emotional injunctions of self-denial and self-restraint. Much as this line of thinking has in common with my own destigmatizing work throughout this study, Kucich establishes at the outset of his argument that his "repression" is *not* Freud's "repression," the repression that "censors, displaces, and condenses dangerous material, driving it from the conscious into the unconscious, and producing the distortions of neurosis"; instead, Kucich's focus is on "the nineteenth-century cultural decision to value silenced or negated feeling over affirmed feeling."[10] Where Kucich eschews a psychological reading of repression in Brontë's novels in favor of a more socio-ideological one, I want to conflate the two approaches. In my view, the private act of "censoring" and "distorting" one's sexual urges is both a product of and a helpful metaphor for the larger "cultural decision" to censor and modify works of art.

I am also, therefore, more interested than Kucich is in the ways in which censorship and repression play out, for Brontë, on a more biographical level—the ways in which the "dialectic of repression and expression" in her works reflect the battle with the moral censor that she waged throughout her life.[11] This battle has, to a large extent, been either discounted or disregarded by literary scholars in the past: "Though she had her skirmishes with prudes," writes one such scholar, "Brontë was not able in her time to make the direct challenge to the public standards for publishing on sexual subjects that her successors, with such battle and such wounds, were able to."[12] Brontë's "skirmishes" may not have been quite so visibly or publicly bloody as those of such "successors" as Thomas Hardy, D. H. Lawrence, and James Joyce, but they were, as we shall see, just as central to her work.

Elia Kazan, on the other hand, did engage in a series of very vocal, very well-known bouts with the moral censor over the course of his cinematic career. Some of the elements of Kazan's films that the Production Code Administration (PCA) found most objectionable were the interracial romance in *Pinky* (1949), the rape in *A Streetcar Named*

Desire (1951), the depiction of the inside of a brothel in *East of Eden* (1955), and the erotic impulses of high school students in *Splendor in the Grass* (1961). But it was the condemnation of his Southern gothic sexual farce *Baby Doll* (1956) by the Catholic Legion of Decency—and the relative success of the film in spite of that condemnation—that played the most visible role in the process of censorship erosion that gradually took place over the course of the 1950s and 60s.[13] According to Vincent Brook, Warner Brothers' decision to release the film in the midst of the Legion's fierce opposition to it "signaled a radical shift in Hollywood's relations with the Catholic Church. The fact that Cardinal Spellman's condemnation of *Baby Doll* not only failed to kill the film at the box office but may even have helped it turn a slight profit showed that while defiance of the Church was no guarantee for success, neither did it necessarily spell financial ruin nor public relations disaster."[14] Although Kazan does complain in his autobiography about the injurious blackballing of his film ("People were reading that the film was breaking box office records. This was not true; the cardinal's attack hurt us"), he also acknowledges that those blackballing efforts were, to a large extent, what gave the film its forbidden allure: "It took Cardinal Spellman to make [*Baby Doll*] famous."[15] As much, then, as Kazan may have declared himself to be "the victim of a hostile conspiracy" when it came to his dealings with censorship,[16] the degree of his true victimization remains questionable.

Indeed, as Kazan's candid descriptions of his own directorial efforts make clear, he took great pleasure in manipulating various forms of emotional conflict for the benefit of his "art." In discussing the antipathy between James Dean and Raymond Massey while shooting *East of Eden*, for example, Kazan admits that "[t]his was an antagonism I didn't try to heal; I aggravated it. . . . The screen was alive with precisely what I wanted; they detested each other."[17] But Kazan did not reserve this sadistic push toward conflict for his actors alone; he always maintained an ample supply of conflict within his own life as well. "I really enjoy being in battle," he would boast; "I love fighting out of a hole. It's exhilarating to me. And I like to get people angry because they should be angry."[18] Although this kind of comment on Kazan's part is usually read in terms of the most infamous fight of his life—the controversy surrounding his decision to

name names during the McCarthy blacklisting trials of the 1950s—I believe it can be applied just as easily to the battle that he enjoyed waging
with the moral censor throughout his cinematic career.

To explore the interplay of repression, conflict, and pleasure in the
works of Brontë and Kazan, I will concentrate on texts from very different points in the arcs of their respective careers: Brontë's *Villette* (1853),
which was the final novel that she completed before dying abruptly at the
age of thirty-eight, and Kazan's *A Streetcar Named Desire*, which is generally considered to be the first film to demonstrate his directorial powers
in full.[19] My decision to focus on *Streetcar*—a text that is more strongly
associated with its writer, Tennessee Williams, than with its director—
will necessarily raise questions of authorship that I have, for the most
part, been able to bypass in my other chapters. I could have looked at one
of the films that Kazan did write entirely himself (i.e., *America, America*
[1963]), or at one that is taken to be more representative of his own life
struggles (i.e., *On the Waterfront* [1954]). But I have chosen to look at
Streetcar instead for two reasons: because it was the first film over which
Kazan had to fight vigorously with the moral censor, in ways that have
been much (though, to my mind, somewhat faultily) analyzed, and because so many of the repressive psychological elements of *Streetcar* seem
to me to be strongly connected to the psychology of moral censorship.
Through examining *Streetcar* alongside *Villette*—simultaneously Brontë's
most repressed and most erotic novel—I hope to reveal the hidden, forbidden pleasures that can be aroused by the imposition of private obstacles and public prohibitions.

.   .   .

Villette is widely perceived to be Brontë's most autobiographical
book, based upon her experiences at a girls' pensionnat in Brussels where
she studied and taught between 1842 and 1844. But the "authenticity"
with which her fiction is so often credited ("The most obvious of all remarks about Miss Brontë is the close connection between her life and her
writings," observed Leslie Stephen[20]) can also be seen as a thinly veiled
artistic critique, a questioning of her ability to write anything outside
of her small realm of personal knowledge. Brontë was not oblivious to
the fact that her works were narrower in scope than many of the other

successful novels of her day, but she chose to write about more internal than external subjects nonetheless. In a letter that accompanied the first two volumes of *Villette* that she sent to her publisher in October 1852, she explained the rationale behind this choice:

> You will see that "Villette" touches on no matter of public interest. I cannot write books handling the topics of the day—it is of no use trying. Nor can I write a book for its moral—Nor can I take up a philanthropic scheme though I honour Philanthropy—And voluntarily and sincerely veil my face before such a mighty subject as that handled in Mrs. Beecher Stowe's work—"Uncle Tom's Cabin."
>
> To manage these great matters rightly they must be long and practically studied—their bearings known intimately and their evils felt genuinely—they must not be taken up as business-matter and a trading-speculation.[21]

But even if Brontë did deliberately limit herself to writing what she knew, part of what she knew by the time she was working on *Villette*—"intimately" and "genuinely"—was the cultural pressure of censorship, particularly as that pressure was directed toward female writers.

At the age of twenty, Brontë sent samples of her writing to poet laureate Robert Southey and asked for his opinion of their merit. In response, Southey advised her to give up her hopes of ever publishing her work, not because it was poorly written, but because "Literature cannot be the business of a woman's life: & it ought not to be. The more she is engaged in her proper duties, the less leisure will she have for it, even as an accomplishment and a recreation."[22] Brontë was dismayed but not surprised by Southey's counsel, since, as she explained to him in a follow-up letter, she was accustomed to hearing such talk: "Following my Father's advice who from my childhood has counselled me just in the wise, and friendly tone of your letter; I have endeavoured not only attentively to observe all the duties a woman ought to fulfil, but to feel deeply interested in them—I don't always succeed, for sometimes when I'm teaching, and sewing I'd far rather be reading or writing; but I try to deny myself."[23] The fact that Brontë was told in no uncertain terms to deny and repress her literary desires both by the symbolic patriarch of English literature and by her own familial patriarch demonstrates the intense social opposition that faced women writers of her day. At the same time, the fact that Brontë—

along with two of her sisters—ultimately refused to follow this patriarchal advice demonstrates the ferocity of her, and their, artistic passion.

The creative utopia of the household in which Brontë was raised is by now a fixture of Victorian folklore: cordoned off from the rest of the world in their father's small Yorkshire parsonage, siblings Charlotte, Branwell, Emily, and Anne devoted the majority of their childhood and adolescent energies to the detailed chronicling of two imaginary kingdoms, Gondal and Angria. These chronicles, referred to as the "juvenilia," are the Brontës' most unapologetically passionate and salacious fictions, precisely because they were written for private, rather than public, consumption. When Brontë first attempted to get her work published, however, she consciously chose to rein in some of that passion in an effort to make her writing more palatable to the world at large. As she would later describe in a letter to George Henry Lewes, "I restrained imagination, eschewed romance, repressed excitement: over-bright colouring too I avoided, and sought to produce something which would be soft, grave and true." The result of such restraint and repression was *The Professor* (published posthumously in 1857), which was rejected by "six publishers in succession," each of whom told her the work was "deficient in 'startling incident' and 'thrilling excitement'" and therefore simply "would not sell."[24] Dejected but not defeated, Brontë immediately began work on her next novel, this time coming up with the far more "startling" and "thrilling" *Jane Eyre* (1847), which immediately became an enormous popular success.

Ironically, though, Brontë's fulfillment of the publishers' (and the public's) wishes brought her precisely the kind of moral criticism that she had been trying to avoid by taming her "romantic" and "imaginative" impulses in *The Professor*. As John Maynard has put it, "Brontë found that her society rewarded and punished her relative boldness at one and the same time. As [*Jane Eyre*] was making Currer Bell a household name, critics were as quickly warning readers about the dangers of bringing this man's work into one's home. When it appeared that this was no male but a female writer, the fear grew in proportion to the relative danger."[25] Much as she may have claimed to have a thick skin about this kind of negative publicity ("You do very rightly and very kindly," she assured her publisher, "to tell me the objections made against 'Jane Eyre'; they are more essential than the praises"[26]), the defensive tone taken in many of her subsequent letters signals that she was in fact deeply hurt by the various attacks lodged against her novel on moral grounds.[27] Three months after the initial release of her "godless" and "pernicious" book, as some critics called it, Brontë wrote to Lewes that she was determined to alter her writing style once again: "I mean to observe your warning about being careful how I undertake new works. . . . If I ever *do* write another book, I think I will have nothing of what you call 'melodrame.'"[28] By the time Brontë got around to writing *Villette*, therefore, the course of her artistic career had already been subtly but decisively influenced by the silent specter of moral censorship.

When critics talk about the influence that moral censorship had upon the film version of *A Streetcar Named Desire*, meanwhile, what they are usually discussing are the four minutes that were excised from the final cut of the film, without Kazan's knowledge or consent, in order for it to avoid a "C" (Condemned) rating from the Catholic Legion of Decency.[29] I will briefly consider the impact of those excised minutes at the end of this chapter, but the majority of my textual analysis will concentrate on the footage that Kazan assembled prior to the intervention of the Legion— the "director's cut," as it is now marketed on DVD. By restricting myself to a reading of this restored version, I will be able to focus on the censorship changes that Kazan *chose* to make over the course of adapting and shooting the film, as opposed to the censorship changes that were thrust upon him. In some critics' eyes, even the changes that Kazan allowed were so damaging to the integrity of Williams's original play that the film must be labeled an adaptive failure—see, for example, Ellen Dowling's "The Derailment of *A Streetcar Named Desire*," in which she criticizes the film's "blatant bowdlerization" and "general whitewashing" of Williams's controversial material, and calls for "a new film version of Tennessee Williams's masterpiece which would, indeed, be a faithful adaptation of the stage play."[30] While Dowling's opposition to the principle of censorship is, of course, understandable, her implied belief that there exists one "correct" version of Williams's story that Kazan's film simply failed to tell is somewhat misguided. The truth is that all plays—and particularly ones as complex and nuanced as *Streetcar*—are vulnerable to change every time that they are restaged, reproduced, redesigned, or recast.

This theatrical malleability is well illustrated by the fact that there are several competing versions of Williams's original play currently in print: the "acting edition" that was prepared directly from the stage manager's script for Dramatists Play Service, the "reading edition" that Williams prepared for publication by New Directions (making slight changes to the script each time a new edition was released), and other British editions that take their own approach to transcribing the text. In all published versions, however, Kazan's handprint on the material can quite clearly be seen—in the form of stage directions, set descriptions, and various bits of "business" that Kazan devised during the course of the initial Broadway run. Indeed, as Brenda Murphy explains in her analysis of the dramatic partnership of Williams and Kazan, "A director who works with a playwright on the first production of a play is a full collaborator in the work that is eventually described in the published script."[31] The more that Williams and Kazan worked together, the more collaborative their work became, leading many critics of the 1950s to question "whether Williams was a 'weak' playwright who allowed his director to 'tamper' with his plays, or whether Kazan was an overbearing director who violated the writer's artistic integrity, or both."[32] Regardless of what the dynamics of Williams and Kazan's creative relationship within the confines of the theater may have been, the movement of *Streetcar* from stage to screen necessarily granted Kazan a new form of power over Williams's artistic vision since, in Kazan's words, "The director tells the movie story more than the man who writes the dialogue. . . . The director tells the essential story with pictures. Dialogue, in most cases, is the gravy on the meat."[33] What Kazan decided to do with the additional power afforded him by the movie medium was to rebalance the viewer's sympathies. Indeed, according to Kim Hunter (the actress who first played Stella on both stage and screen), the primary reason that Kazan agreed to do the film was "because he felt that he had laid too much emphasis on the character of Stanley in the play. Otherwise I don't think he would have wanted to direct it because he wasn't one who wanted to repeat anything, ever. . . . But he wanted to make the focus more on Blanche."[34] This assessment of Kazan's motivations is also borne out by several of the notes that he made in the margins of his final draft of the screenplay: "There is no use in the world in doing *Streetcar*," he reflected, "unless you really make work your idea about 'subjective photography,' using the camera to penetrate Blanche and then showing the SUBJECTIVIZED source of the emotion. . . . So crawl into her with your camera. Be free. . . . This will make for a new kind of storytelling. You tell not the literal facts, as an observer might see them. You bring directly to the screen BLANCHE'S WORLD!!!"[35]

One way that Kazan planned to shift our focus away from Stanley and onto Blanche was by starting the film off with her backstory; "by putting on screen everything that Blanche describes in dialogue about Belle Reve and her last days there."[36] To that end, Kazan worked closely with script adapter Oscar Saul to create a more visually explicit, more "opened up" screenplay. But when he returned to the draft after a brief vacation from it, he discovered that it was, to his mind, a complete "fizzle": "The force of the play had come precisely from its compression, from the fact that Blanche was trapped in those two small rooms. . . . Everything we'd done to 'open up' the play diluted its power."[37] While Kazan is certainly right to locate a great deal of the play's emotional power in its claustrophobic compression, I would argue that the other main reason for the failure of his revised script was that it stripped Williams's story of its equally powerful tendency toward narrative *re*pression. Just as Blanche tries to keep the secret of her sullied past hidden from Stella, Stanley, and Mitch as long as she possibly can, so too does Williams repress that information on a narrative level until it violently bursts forth. Importantly, then, Kazan's initial impulse to show Blanche's sexual past in vivid, lurid detail—an impulse that would, no doubt, have encountered serious objections from Code censors—was not a better choice simply because it was a bolder choice. Repression is one of *Streetcar*'s central narrative concerns, but it is also one of its most potent narrative techniques.

Villette is even more obviously a text of repressed narration. Far from being candid or forthcoming, Lucy Snowe is one of the most perversely private first-person narrators in all of English literature. She refuses to tell us anything, really, of her family history ("It will be conjectured that I was of course glad to return to the bosom of my kindred. Well! the amiable conjecture does no harm, and may therefore be safely left uncontradicted"[38]). She refuses to tell us what becomes of her at the end of the narrative ("Here pause: pause at once. There is enough said"

[596]), and concludes instead by cursorily letting us know the fates of her worst enemies ("Madame Beck prospered all the days of her life; so did Père Silas; Madame Walravens fulfilled her ninetieth year before she died. Farewell" [596]). Perhaps most eccentrically of all, she refuses, for six chapters, to tell us that two of the text's central characters—Graham Bretton and Dr. John—are in fact the same person. In describing why she has chosen not to reveal her awareness of this small identificatory detail to Graham/John himself, she explains:

> To *say* anything on the subject, to *hint* at my discovery, had not suited my habits of thought, or assimilated with my system of feeling. On the contrary, I had preferred to keep the matter to myself. I liked entering his presence covered with a cloud he had not seen through, while he stood before me under a ray of special illumination, which shone all partial over his head, trembled about his feet, and cast light no farther. (248)

For Lucy, repression—which must surely rank at or near the top of her "system of feeling"—serves as a narrative tool that allows her to gain a certain sense of subversive control. Although this passage is officially discussing the pleasure that she takes in gaining such control over Graham, the reader has been deprived of the same critical information for the same period of time, and is therefore equally subordinated by Lucy's (and Brontë's) willful act of narrative repression. In a variation on Thackeray's "tail below the water" metaphor from *Vanity Fair* that Brontë specifically praised in a letter to one of her publishers,[39] Brontë is telling her readers here that she will *not* be telling us everything; if Thackeray can submerge some of his meaning under the water, she can "cover" some of hers with a "cloud."

In addition to the formal similarities between *Villette* and *A Streetcar Named Desire*, which lie in their mutual penchant for repressed narration, there are other significant attributes that the two seemingly disparate texts have in common. Both are about women from comfortable, even affluent backgrounds who have tragically but mysteriously lost everything—home, family, friends—and must try to negotiate their way through the world on their own. To do so, both women become English teachers; one of them unexpectedly thrives in the occupation, one of them flounders (though more for personal than professional reasons) and must attempt to start her life over yet again. They both move to big, unfamiliar cities where they take up residence in tight, claustrophobic quarters. They are both treated as dangerous outsiders within their new homes and are, ultimately, expelled from them. For Lucy, this expulsion feels much more like a desirable release—Kate Millett has, famously, described *Villette* as "one long meditation on a prison break"[40]—whereas the expulsion in *Streetcar* is quite literally an act of incarceration, as Blanche is brutally shuttled off to the insane asylum. But the risk of mental breakdown is as real for Lucy as it is for Blanche, and both texts are equally concerned with the threatening and potentially self-destroying role that passion plays in their heroines' lives.

In *Villette*, Lucy labors intensively to keep her passions in check and stages lengthy internal debates between "Feeling" and its archrival "Reason." After she has reconnected with Graham and Mrs. Bretton and tasted the fruit of human kindness for the first time in her adult life, for example, she calls on her sense of Reason to calm her Feelings down: "Do not let me think of them too often, too much, too fondly," she implores, "let me be content with a temperate draught of this living stream: let me not run athirst, and apply passionately to its welcome waters: let me not imagine in them a sweeter taste than earth's fountains know" (251). As masochistic as such an inner monologue may sound, Lucy's life experiences have given her good cause to fear her own emotionalism—she has, after all, just recuperated from "a strange fever of the nerves and blood," which, she believes, brings her to the brink of "Death" (231), and whose origins lie entirely in the "despairing," "hopeless" mental wanderings that besiege her during her solitary stay at the pensionnat through its eight-week holiday vacation (228). If she does not find a way to repress the ardent longings of her passionate heart, Lucy reasons, they very well might kill her.

Although Reason never fully triumphs over Feeling within Lucy, it does convince her to strike an external compromise:

> These struggles with the natural character, the strong native bent of the heart, may seem futile and fruitless, but in the end they do good. They tend, however slightly, to give the actions, the conduct, that turn which Reason approves, and which Feeling, perhaps, too often opposes: they certainly make a

difference in the general tenor of a life, and enable it to be better regulated, more equable, quieter on the surface; and it is on the surface only the common gaze will fall. As to what lies below, leave that with God. (252)

What is important to Lucy, then, is not that she can eliminate her own passions, but that she can successfully hide them from the world at large in an attempt to live a more socially acceptable life. It is here that Lucy's emotional "struggles with [her] natural character" begin to feel distinctly metaphoric of Brontë's artistic struggles with the moral censor. For here, again, we are reminded of Thackeray's differentiation between what floats above the water and what lies below, as we hear Brontë endorsing a strategy of subterfuge that will satisfy the "common gaze" of the Moral World. The metaphor becomes even more apparent as Brontë changes the terms of combat from Reason versus Feeling to Reason versus Imagination: "Reason might be right; yet no wonder we are glad at times to defy her, to rush from under her rod and give a truant hour to Imagination—*her* soft, bright foe, *our* sweet Help, our divine Hope" (308). Reason is no longer simply fighting Lucy's desire to feel; it is fighting her desire to imagine, to invent, and, even, to write.

Before Lucy receives the letter from Graham Bretton that will set her sexually and emotionally aflame, she begins to debate with Reason about whether or not she is "allowed" to reply to it. "Do you meditate pleasure in replying?" scoffs Reason. "Ah, fool! I warn you! Brief be your answer. Hope no delight of heart—no indulgence of intellect: grant no expansion to feeling." "But," Lucy protests, "if I feel, may I *never* express?" to which Reason callously insists, "*Never!*" (307). Prohibited from expressing what is in her heart or in her mind, Lucy finds herself in much the same position that Brontë was in after writing to Robert Southey for professional advice. Lucy's response to this prohibition is to split herself in two, by first writing a lengthy letter to Graham that boldly and poetically "give[s] expression to a closely-clinging and deeply-honouring attachment—an attachment that wanted to attract to itself and take into its own lot all that was painful in the destiny of its object; that would, if it could, have absorbed and conducted away all storms and lightnings from an existence viewed with a passion of solicitude," but then promptly tearing that letter up and replacing it with a "terse, curt missive of a page" that she actually sends out (335). In this moment, sexual repression is intrinsically equated with literary censorship, as Lucy represses her physical and emotional attraction to Graham through the act of mercilessly censoring her own writing.

Like Lucy, Williams and Kazan's Blanche (Vivien Leigh) works hard to keep the "strong native bent of [her] heart" in check, because, as she describes to Mitch (Karl Malden) on one of their dates, "A single girl, a girl alone in the world, has got to keep a firm hold on her emotions, or she'll be lost!" This statement is meant, on one hand, to refer to the social prejudice against women who give in to their sexual desires and lose their chance of ever capturing a good man. (To Stella, Blanche makes this point even more bluntly when she declares that she hasn't given Mitch anything beyond a goodnight kiss, since she "want[s] his respect, and men don't want anything they get too easily.") But it is also meant to refer more specifically to Blanche's fear of her own emotions, and to the possibility that, if she does not rein them in, they too will lead to her social destruction. Just as Lucy consciously strives to present a false front of self-regulation and equanimity to the world at large, Blanche tries desperately to maintain the image of a prim and proper (and young) Southern belle in the face of a very different physical reality. Although Blanche first defends her ruse in pragmatic terms, telling Stella that she "want[s] to deceive [Mitch] just enough to make him want me," she later defends her motivations more poetically, in a speech that is often taken to describe Tennessee Williams's own aesthetic approach: "I don't want realism, I want magic! . . . Yes, yes, magic! I try to give that to people. I do misrepresent things, I don't tell truths, I tell what ought to be true. And if that is sinful, then let me be punished for it. *Don't turn the light on!*" But it is not only our playwright who practices Blanche's brand of deception on an artistic level; we must remember that our director, too, freely admitted in his script notes that he did not feel bound to tell "the literal facts, as an observer might see them" (a.k.a.: realism) but would instead perform the magic trick of "crawl[ing] into [Blanche] with [his] camera" in order to show "the SUBJECTIVIZED source of the emotion."

There is, of course, one major difference between Blanche's cover-up and Lucy's cover-up, which is that Blanche has so much more to conceal—not simply that she feels more than she "should," or that she is physically attracted to others, but that she has already *acted* on those feelings and attractions, quite prolifically, in the past. "Yes," she finally confesses, "I have had many meetings with strangers. After the death of Allan, meetings with strangers was all I seemed able to fill my empty heart with." During this earlier period of her life, Blanche uses casual sex in the same way that Lucy uses her fertile Imagination: to fill a deep and painful emotional void. (By the end of the film, it should be noted, Blanche does discover the "sweet Help" and "divine Hope" of her own imaginative powers that Lucy has been extolling all along, and retreats into the fantasy plot of receiving a telegram from a rich, well-intentioned suitor who wants to whisk her away from her misery and keep her as his platonic companion on his Caribbean yacht.) But as promiscuous as Blanche's behavior may have been prior to her arrival in New Orleans, we must remember that all we get to see within the confines of the film are demonstrations of sexual repression and restraint: Blanche rebuffing Mitch's too-familiar advances, Blanche sending away the young collector for the *Evening Star* after one brief kiss because she knows she has to "keep [her] hands off children," Blanche fighting off Stanley (Marlon Brando) with the broken end of a bottle. The Blanche that *we* meet, in other words, is living as chaste a life as that of Lucy Snowe, and is actively suppressing all of her "natural" romantic impulses in a similar manner.

The buried nature of Blanche and Lucy's feelings stands in stark contrast to the unapologetic expressions of love and passion voiced by their respective sister-figures, Stella and Polly Home (or, at least, the childhood version of Polly that we meet at the outset of the novel). Polly and Stella shock Lucy and Blanche with their fearless willingness to give into desire so completely, to declare their emotions so openly. After hearing young Polly tell Graham point-blank that she loves him—that, "if [he] were to die . . . [she] should 'refuse to be comforted, and go down into the grave to [his] mourning'"—Lucy watches in awe as the audacious child gathers Graham in her arms, "drawing his long-tressed head towards her" (87). The action excites in Lucy "the feeling one might experience on seeing an animal dangerous by nature, and but half-tamed by art, too heedlessly fondled. Not that I feared Graham would hurt, or very roughly check her; but I thought she ran risk of incurring such a careless, impatient repulse, as would be worse almost to her than a blow" (87).

Even though the relationship between Polly and Graham is, at this stage, officially presexual (she is a child of six in "love" with a young man of sixteen), the fact that the two do marry at the end of the novel retroactively marks this moment as the first physical manifestation of their courtship, with Polly quite brazenly being the one doing the courting.

The relationship between Stella and Stanley, meanwhile, is most certainly sexual, with Stella taking as active a role in the romantic interplay as Polly does. We need only think, for example, of the famous scene where Stella slowly, lustfully descends the staircase to return to Stanley's arms after he has gotten drunk and beaten her. As I will discuss later on, Stella's descent was one of the most offensive elements of the film to the Catholic Legion of Decency, which demanded that Warner Brothers significantly trim it down before the film's initial release. But in either its edited or restored form, the scene exudes a sense of raw female desire that is more or less unheard of in classical Hollywood cinema. Blanche is, of course, awestruck by Stella's visceral—and publicly visible—demonstration of her passion, and chastises her the following morning for giving in so easily to her "desire—just brutal desire!" Much as Lucy mentally compares Graham to a "dangerous animal," Blanche tells Stella that Stanley "acts like an animal, has an animal's habits" and beseeches her sister not to "hang back with the brutes!" The reason that Blanche and Lucy are so judgmental about Stella and Polly's emotional availability stems at least partially from a sense of jealousy. Lucy quite obviously envies Polly's ultimately successful pursuit of Graham, since he is the man with whom she first falls in love as well, and it does not take much reading between the lines to hear the echo of covetousness in Blanche's vehement disapproval of Stanley the Beast.

But in spite of all the textual evidence that seems to label Lucy and Blanche as a pair of frustrated, green-eyed, "old-maid school-teacherish" women who are driven to the brink of insanity by the unhealthy suppression of their sexual urges, there is also an important undercurrent in both texts that tells a much different story about their erotic lives. For in addition to all the externally imposed barriers that stand in the way of Lucy and Blanche's sexual fulfillment—the social expectation that they will be good, modest girls who never reveal their interest in sex unless and until they are safely confined in the state of wedlock; Lucy's unappealing plainness, Blanche's unappealing age—there are multiple ways in which the heroines can be seen to create *further* romantic obstacles for themselves in order to heighten and enhance their own sensations of desire.

One obvious way that Lucy and Blanche do this is by falling for men who are somehow unattainable or marked as forbidden to them. Lucy falls in love first with Graham, or "Dr. John" as all the girls and women of the pensionnat swooningly call him. Aside from the fact that he is the tallest, handsomest, most desirable man that enters the small world of the Rue Fossette and is, therefore, hopelessly out of poor, plain Lucy's league, Graham comes with the additional hindrance of being ardently smitten with someone else—the younger, prettier, more vivacious Ginevra Fanshawe—before Lucy even has the opportunity to enter his adult life. We have already seen some of Lucy's attempts to "reason" her way out of her "feelings" for Graham, but what is also apparent in her interior monologues is the perverse pleasure that she derives from her romantically unsuccessful dealings with him. When he fails to acknowledge or understand her true feelings, for example, she reflects that "[t]here is a perverse mood of the mind which is rather soothed than irritated by misconstruction; and in quarters where we can never be rightly known, we take pleasure, I think, in being consummately ignored" (164). When he falls into the habit of confiding to her his romantic thoughts about Ginevra, we are told that, "In a strange and new sense, I grew most selfish, and quite powerless to deny myself the delight of indulging his mood, and being pliant to his will" (267). And, when he subsequently transfers his feelings from the undeserving Ginevra to her superior cousin, Countess Paulina de Bassompierre (née Polly Home), Lucy's perverse enjoyment only seems to be amplified, in spite of all her forlorn protestations to the contrary. She specifically chooses, after all, to spend countless hours in the presence of the nascent lovebirds, vigilantly observing (and, later, meticulously recording) the minute details of their idyllic romance. She refuses to accept a position as Polly's paid companion, but that does not stop her from unofficially serving as personal confidante and trusted adviser to both Polly and Graham throughout their courtship. During one such confidence session, Graham inflicts a particularly vicious brand of pain upon his "inoffensive shadow," as he calls her, by reflecting that "if you had been a boy, Lucy, instead of a girl—my mother's godson instead of her god-daughter—we should have been good friends: our opinions would have melted into each other" (403, 401). Yet as much as it may pain Lucy to hear herself being relegated to the realm of platonic fraternity, it is, in her words, a "pain which thrilled my heart" (401). Indeed, had another, even more forbidden love object not entered into Lucy's line of vision to supplant the unattainable Graham, one could quite easily imagine her drawing a lifetime of masochistic pleasure from the well of unrequited love.

Lucy's next love interest, M. Paul, is forbidden to her on several different levels. He is, in the first place, a devout Catholic, she an unflinching Protestant, and for a time their religious differences do manage to erect a significant philosophical barrier between them. He is morally appalled by her "strange, self-reliant, invulnerable creed," her "terrible, proud, earnest Protestantism" (512); she is sickened by the legends of his Catholic saints that are, to her mind, impious "nightmares of oppression, privation, and agony" (184). Eventually, though, Lucy and M. Paul come to accept and forgive each other's spiritual "eccentricities," but the obstacles between them do not end there. Lucy learns (or thinks she learns) about two daunting rivals for M. Paul's heart: his young, wealthy ward Justine Marie, and the memory of his beloved, deceased fiancée after whom his ward was named. It turns out, of course, that a triumvirate of M. Paul's closest connections, Madame Beck, Père Silas, and Madame Walravens, has conspired to squelch Lucy's feelings for its financial provider by thrusting the threat of the two Justine Maries before her. But Lucy's sexual attraction to M. Paul—a man she had once considered to be disagreeably "dark," "little," "pungent," and "austere" (197)—is enflamed, not extinguished by the image of this romantic competition (in much the same way that M. Paul only begins to show a real interest in Lucy when he starts seeing her out in public with Graham). "Was I, then," Lucy thinks to herself, "to be frightened by Justine Marie? Was the picture of this pale dead nun to rise, an eternal barrier? . . . Madame Beck—Père Silas—you should not have suggested these questions. They were at once the deepest puzzle, the strongest obstruction, and the keenest stimulus, I had ever felt" (491). For both Lucy and M. Paul, then, enticement and impediment are two deeply and inextricably interdependent forces.[41]

This interdependency can be seen even more clearly in the ways that they stage their social interactions with one another. From the time M. Paul first begins to pay any attention to Lucy, his discourse is marked more by frustration, ferocity, and fuming than by anything resembling flirtation or affection. He even, in the midst of their "courtship," makes a long, eloquent speech denying that there can ever be anything like a romance between them: "Don't suppose that I wish you to have a passion for me, Mademoiselle . . . —the thing, I assure you, is alien to my whole life and views. It died in the past—in the present it lies buried—its grave is deep-dug, well-heaped, and many winters old" (433). One of the rougher instances of his unromantic conduct toward her occurs late in the novel, when he physically drags her, along with her chair and desk, into the middle of a large interrogation room where he forces her to write an impromptu essay on "Human Justice" in front of two of his colleagues to prove to them that she is capable of intellectual thought. Although Lucy is at first so offended by these dictatorial proceedings that she can "neither write nor speak," she soon finds inspiration in her outrage, and composes an inventively sardonic essay in which Human Justice is personified as "a red, random beldame" who smokes and drinks and ignores the melancholy pleas of the "suffering souls" around her (495–96). In this moment of expository triumph, Lucy proves the point that she had earlier made about the paradoxical effect of M. Paul's malice: "Yet, when [he] sneered at me . . . his injustice stirred in me ambitious wishes—it imparted a strong stimulus—it gave wings to aspiration" (440).

Lucy's treatment of M. Paul, meanwhile, is willfully "perverse," as she herself repeatedly puts it. When the thing that she "most wishe[s] to do in the world" is talk to him, she finds herself running away from him and hiding in one of the schoolrooms (477); when she makes a lavish watchguard to present to him on his fête-day, she finds herself holding it in her lap and pretending she has nothing for him, merely to see him "vexed" (427). He calls her "vain," "unpleasant," and "intractable," she calls him "stern," "dogmatic," and "imperious." Yet as little as this may sound like the language of love, there is more passion in their petty bickering than in all of Lucy's conversations with Graham put together. Take, for example, one of Lucy and M. Paul's most heated exchanges, in which anger and ardor are volatilely mixed: "You alluring little coquette!" he hisses at her in French. "You seem sad, submissive, dreamy, but you aren't really: it is I that says this to you: Savage! with a blazing soul and light in your eyes!", to which Lucy just as vehemently hisses back, "Yes, I have a blazing soul, and the right to have one!" (404). M. Paul is, in this moment and throughout the text, both Lucy's lover and her moral censor, admiring and judging her in the same breath.

"Censor" is, in fact, a term that is directly applied to M. Paul several times in the novel. After he lectures Lucy about the risqué turn her wardrobe has lately taken (denouncing in particular an offensive "scarlet" dress that is, in truth, a modest "pale pink"), she mentally calls him "[t]his harsh little man—this pitiless censor" (421). After he cuts out some pages from a book he is giving to her, she explains to us that "he generally pruned before lending his books, especially if they were novels, and sometimes I was a little provoked at the severity of his censorship" (434–35). Some feminist critics have taken M. Paul's moral censoriousness to be Brontë's subtle way of hinting to us that he is not really the romantic hero that the structure of the text declares him to be. To Kate Millett, M. Paul is a "jailer" and pedagogical "tyrant" from whom Lucy cannot wait to "escape" at the novel's end. As soon as she has "beguiled" him into setting her up in her own school and giving her social and financial freedom, Millett rejoices, "she's gone. The keeper turned kind must be eluded anyway; Paul turned lover is drowned," and Lucy, at last, "is free."[42] Along similar lines, Sandra Gilbert and Susan Gubar see in Brontë's depiction of M. Paul's suffocating pedantry an indictment of the patriarchal convention of heteronormative romance: "As if to emphasize the false expectations created by romantic enthrallment, Brontë has Lucy set the glamour of the 'romantic' courtship against her own growing friendship with M. Paul, who is emphatically an anti-hero—small, dark, middle-aged, tyrannical, self-indulgent, sometimes cruel, even at times a fool."[43]

But what if Brontë's strange conflation of the roles of lover and censor in the character of M. Paul points to something more complicated than a judgment against the entire male sex? What if it points, instead, to the inadvertently stimulating, perversely arousing effect of moral censorship itself? What if Lucy is inspired to use her imagination to fill in the pages that M. Paul excises from her books, and what if the pages she envisions are more tantalizing and liberating than those which have been cut? What if Lucy never feels sexier than when M. Paul pruriently sees in her demure pink dress an indecent scarlet gown? And what if Brontë the novelist never felt more emotionally or artistically fired up than when her moral censors tried to tell her what and what not to do—when Robert Southey advised her not to publish and to know her "womanly" place, when the critics of *Jane Eyre* called her "godless" and "pernicious" and demanded that she improve her "low moral tone," when G. H. Lewes suggested that she rely less on "melodrame" and write more like Jane Austen? *Villette* has been viewed as the story of a woman learning how to write, how to voice the "heretic narrative" that she has within her, how to rebel against the impulse of censorship. Patricia E. Johnson, for example, has argued that, predominantly due to her work in *Villette*, Brontë "will continue to be signally important to female writers and readers: first, because she struggles with cultural prohibition, but second, and more essentially, because she discovers her pleasure and power in writing despite it."[44] But *Villette* is also, to my mind, the story of a woman who thrives on her own heresy, and who experiences "pleasure and power" not only in spite of her moral censors but also, paradoxically, because of them.

Blanche DuBois's story, though vastly different in many respects, has this same basic perversity at its core: like Lucy, Blanche is continually attracted to men she cannot or should not have. Most blatantly prohibited are the string of male strangers—and, in particular, young male strangers—with whom Blanche holds so many illicit "meetings" at the Tarantula Arms in her pre–New Orleans life. We are given a glimpse of how such meetings were orchestrated in the brief scene where she starts to seduce the collection boy for the *Evening Star*. Nowhere in the film does Blanche appear more charged up or turned on than during this triply forbidden encounter—forbidden because the boy is so young, forbidden because Mitch is due to arrive any moment for their date and might catch her in the act, forbidden because she is living in a narrow-minded world that expects her to be chaste and virginal until she marries or dies. Interestingly, this was the one scene that Kazan himself chose to cut down (meaning: censor) after it elicited nervous, "bad" laughter from the test audiences who initially screened it. To spare the character of Blanche from this humiliating reaction to her sexuality, Kazan edited the scene in a more dreamlike way, using more shots of her looking at the boy and fewer shots of the boy himself (see fig. 12). Without altering any of the dialogue or belittling the import of the scene, Kazan managed to make the audience judge Blanche less severely for her sexual "misconduct;" to show us the

FIGURE 12 *Keeping the focus on Blanche. Vivien Leigh and Wright King in* A Streetcar Named Desire.

"SUBJECTIVIZED source of the emotion" that is underlying her controversial compulsion to seduce someone so obviously forbidden to her.

Of course, the man that Blanche spends much more time and energy trying to seduce over the course of the film is Mitch. Although it might appear that Blanche sets her sights on him precisely because he is not forbidden or unattainable—"Is he married?" she checks with Stella before allowing herself to get too interested, "Is he a wolf?"—the fact that he is *not* a wolf, that he is visibly "superior to the others" in terms of manners but, also, in terms of morals, means that he is the suitor who is most likely to be shocked and offended by the truth of her sordid past. He is, in other words, the one who is most likely to reject her. And reject her he ultimately does: in the film's most cruelly moralistic line, Mitch tells Blanche that he no longer wants to marry her because she is "not clean enough to bring in the house with Mother." For all his seeming sweetness, then, Mitch turns out to be a variation on the "harsh" and "pitiless" censor/lover that M. Paul embodies in *Villette*. Yet it is, I would argue, this very character trait of Mitch's—his upright, unforgiving censorious-ness—that makes Blanche "want him, very badly."

It is, though, Blanche's relationship to the other major male charac-ter of the film, Stanley, that paints the most complex portrait of the nature of human desire. Critics have had many different opinions over the years about what exactly is going on between Blanche and Stanley, but the opin-ion that I would like to begin by considering is that of the Production Code Administration. When Joseph Breen was first sent a script of the sa-lacious Broadway hit that was trying to make its way to Hollywood, he did not know what to object to most. The four major issues that he had with the play were the homosexuality of Blanche's husband (what he called "the element of sex perversion"), Stanley's act of raping Blanche (and the fact that "this particularly revolting rape goes unpunished"), Blanche's sexual-ity (referred to, alternately, as her "nymphomania," her "promiscuity," and her "prostitution"), and Stanley's "unacceptable vulgarities."[45] Importantly, however, the only one of these eliminations that was fully realized in the film adaptation was the first: Blanche's husband still commits suicide when she tells him how disgusted she is by him, but in the film her disgust stems not from finding him in bed with another man but from a vaguer objection to his sensitivity and weakness. ("Oh my god," Vivien Leigh re-portedly groaned when she first read the censored version of her backstory, "You mean I have to say, 'You disgust me because you're a poet?'"[46]) Other, though, than this one rather ludicrous change—which did not, ultimately, do particularly much good, since so many moviegoers of 1951 were familiar enough with the major plot points of *Streetcar* to know full well why Allan "really" killed himself—the majority of the revisions made to the script to satisfy Breen's demands were minor in nature and did not alter the crucial facts of the story. Blanche in the film still clearly has had sex with many strangers, Stanley in the film still clearly is vulgar, and the climax of the film still lies in Stanley's brutal act of raping Blanche.

What the interloping of the Hays Office did force Kazan to do was to present the play's most controversial elements in a more ambiguous, in-direct manner, so that our character perceptions are less reliant on lines of actual dialogue and more reliant on camera angles, staging, tone of voice, and musical cues. Let us take, as our primary example, the excision of one of the play's best-known lines, muttered by Stanley just before he carries

Blanche off to his bed to rape her: "We've had this date with each other from the beginning!" Even though the line, in its immediate context, is certainly meant to come across as an abuser's disturbing rationalization of an unforgivable crime (along the lines of "Come on, you know you want it"), the fact that Blanche plainly does *not* want it in that moment should not nullify the complexity of her feelings about Stanley leading up to that point. Her feelings of repugnance are repeatedly verbalized throughout the film, but her feelings of attraction, because the PCA considered them to be a further demonstration of the "nymphomaniacal" tendencies that needed to be deemphasized, are relegated to a subverbal realm: to the shots of her watching him when he doesn't know he is being watched, to the moan of the background music when they carry on a seemingly innocent conversation, to the expression of her face, the tenor of her speech, the import of her movements. In all of these subtle ways, Kazan allows us to see what he perceived to be the central moral complexity of the drama: the fact that Blanche is, in spite of everything, "drawn" to Stanley. In a 1971 interview, Kazan described this element of the story in biographical terms: "I wanted to show exactly what Williams meant, which is that he, as a homosexual, is attracted to the person he thinks is going to destroy him—the attraction you have for someone who's on the other side, supposedly dead against you, but whose violence and force attract you."[47] Similarly, in his notes to the final draft of the *Streetcar* screenplay, he concludes, "There is no doubt [Blanche] is drawn to what will kill her. She has a death wish. She is drawn to her 'executioner.' It is suicide."[48]

In these comments, Kazan is specifically referring to yet another pivotal line that was expunged from the film (but whose content is also nonverbally transmitted to us), Blanche's declaration to Mitch that "[t]he first time I laid eyes on [Stanley], I thought to myself, that man is my executioner! That man will destroy me!" Part of what Blanche means by this, I would argue, is that she can tell from the outset that Stanley will be the "harshest" and most "pitiless" moral censor ever to cross her path. For as much as he may appear to be the very opposite of a censorious prig—crude, crass, unapologetically sexual—Stanley has a fierce, primitive sense of right and wrong, and is, ultimately, the one who makes the life-ruining decision to announce Blanche's past indiscretions to all his friends so that she is forced to pay for her sins. This first stage of Blanche's punishment is very much in line with the mandates of the Production Code, which would clearly expect the wanton seductress of teenage boys to receive some kind of severe moral retribution for her crimes. The problem, from a Code perspective, is that Stanley then continues to mete out Blanche's punishment in a way that is deeply immoral in its own right—by raping her. This action fundamentally disturbs some of the Code's most basic tenets: that the "presentation of crimes" must never throw sympathy "with the criminal as against those who punish him," that the audience must always "feel sure that evil is wrong and good is right."[49] If, as John Roderick has argued, "The sexually healthy marriage that [Stanley] shares with Stella" is meant to "stand as the sacred arena defiled by the profane intruder Blanche with her sexual perversity,"[50] then how is the audience supposed to respond to the "defiled" becoming the "defiler"?

It was a question whose answer Joseph Breen did not want to learn. Out of all the play's objectionable elements, Kazan had to fight hardest to convince Breen to allow Stanley's act of raping Blanche to remain in the film. There were numerous memos and countless conversations in which the viability of "the rape scene" was heatedly discussed; Code administrators wanted it to be cut entirely or, perhaps, made out to be a figment of Blanche's imagination, while Kazan kept insisting that the fact of the rape was crucial to the emotional fabric of the film and threatened to walk out on the production if it was eliminated. Ultimately, Kazan wound up winning the battle of the rape sequence by promising to present it "by suggestion and delicacy."[51] On film, we do not see Stanley "start[ing] towards the bed" with Blanche in his arms as per the stage directions of the play, but we do still see Stanley attacking Blanche physically, grabbing her by the arms and pushing her into a mirror to the point where it smashes and she is left unconscious in his grasp, after which we cut directly to a none-too-subtle shot of a hose spurting water onto the dirty New Orleans pavement outside (see fig. 13). Regardless of all the pent-up attraction that Blanche may feel for Stanley throughout the film—the perverse attraction to her moral censor who, she knows, will be her executioner—the metaphoric, shattered-mirror staging of the scene that Kazan had to devise in order to satisfy Breen's demands works, in fact, to emphasize the unadulterated tragedy and injustice of the fate that befalls her. Blanche on screen is not "just" defiled and injured; she is, irrevocably, broken.

FIGURE 13 *Broken. Vivien Leigh in* A Streetcar Named Desire.

In an essay linking Blanche's story to that of her author, Nancy Tischler contends that Tennessee Williams has Stanley rape Blanche because "[r]ape is an effective term for what the Romantic believes the world does to him and his art. It robs the artist of his dreams and then uses him for its own diversion."[52] Although this morbid and somewhat hystericized outlook on life and art was not, on the whole, Kazan's way of thinking about things, there is one section of his autobiography in which he does seem to consider rape to be an appropriate description of what was happening to him artistically. It is the section that discusses the postproduction "moral improvements" to *Streetcar* that were forced upon him by the Legion of Decency, amounting to four minutes of deleted footage: the scene of Stella descending the staircase was significantly shortened; a shot of Blanche sighing, moaning, and arching her body as she sits alone in the Kowalskis' apartment was excised; and various "overly suggestive" lines were eliminated ("You know, if I didn't know that you was my wife's sister, I would get ideas about you," "It would've been nice to keep you, but I've got to be good and keep my hands off children," "Well, maybe you wouldn't be bad to interfere with," etc.). Even though Kazan ultimately came to believe that the cuts imposed by the Legion failed to make any real difference ("You still get it, don't you?" he would comment late in his life[53]), in 1951 the cuts made him feel small, hurt, and powerless: "The plain fact was—and I had to recognize it—the picture had been taken away from me, secretly, skillfully, without a raised voice. I discovered I had no rights."[54] But it is important to note that Kazan only develops this victimized, wounded tone when he is talking about the "conspiratorial" censorship practices of the Legion of Decency, *not* the practices of the PCA. Kazan's dealings with Breen, as antagonistic as they sometimes were, felt to him like a "fair fight" and were, therefore, a source of pleasure for him rather than strife. After he finished editing the film (but before he found out about the Legion's additional excisions), Kazan wrote a very friendly note to Breen letting him know that he was pleased with the final cut and "thanking" him for all his "cooperation and help on this picture."[55] Breen may have been the artistic "enemy," but he was an enemy that Kazan could enjoy tussling with, just as Blanche enjoys tussling with Stanley until he, like the Legion of Decency, becomes conspiratorially vindictive and "deliberately cruel." Or, to draw an intertextual analogy, Kazan appears to have resented the silent, collaborative scheming of the Catholic Legion in much the same way that Lucy resents the Catholic "junta" of Madame Beck, Madame Walravens, and Père Silas for stealthily conniving to keep her away from M. Paul.

At the end of *Villette*, the Catholic junta is as unsuccessful in its attempts to keep Lucy and M. Paul apart as the Legion of Decency was in its attempts to purify Kazan and Williams's *Streetcar*. But Lucy and M. Paul face a far more formidable opponent in the form of their literary creator, who makes the brutal authorial choice to conclude the story of their romance with a shipwreck. This brutality is tempered, of course, by the notorious narrative elision that allows Brontë's readers to envision a pleasanter ending than the tragic one implied: "Here pause: pause at once. There is enough said. Trouble no quiet, kind heart; leave sunny imaginations hope. Let it be theirs to conceive the delight of joy born again fresh out of great terror, the rapture of rescue from peril, the wondrous reprieve from dread, the fruition of return. Let them picture union and a happy succeeding life" (596). Significantly, however, we know that Brontë did not originally plan to conclude her story with such evasiveness; the ending was, instead, a compromise that she came up with in order to satisfy the demands of her first and most influential "censor," her father. As Elizabeth Gaskell describes in *The Life of Charlotte Brontë*,

> Mr. Brontë was anxious that her new tale should end well, as he disliked novels which left a melancholy impression upon the mind; and he requested her to make her hero and heroine (like the heroes and heroines in fairy-tales) "marry, and live very happily ever after." But the idea of M. Paul Emanuel's death at sea was stamped on her imagination till it assumed the distinct force of reality; and she could no more alter her fictitious ending than if they had been facts which she was relating. All she could do in compliance with her father's wish was so to veil the fate in oracular words, as to leave it to the character and discernment of her readers to interpret her meaning.[56]

In this, arguably the most direct act of censorship imposed on Brontë during her writing career, we find one of the clearest illustrations of the paradoxical effects of the word "no." Because she is explicitly forbidden to write one sentence—"M. Paul died in a shipwreck"—the substance of that sentence is forced to surface throughout the text in subtler, darker, more insidious ways.

For we must remember that the entire story of *Villette* is told to us in retrospect, from the distanced perspective of Lucy's old age—"I speak of a time gone by," she confesses, "my hair which till a late period withstood the frosts of time, lies now, at last white, under a white cap, like snow beneath snow" (105). What this means is that the Lucy who is narrating our story has been through all of it already, and that each of her acts of narrative self-censorship is performed in the shadow of the nautical disaster that we only learn about at the novel's close. If we go back and reread the book with this disaster as our underlying subtext, we see that turbulent oceans and raging storms are everywhere, as if Lucy can only view the world through the lens of the focal trauma of her life. Some of these storms are presented to us as being physically "real" (the squall on the night that Lucy visits the confessional before collapsing on the street; the downpour that traps her in Madame Walravens's house while Père Silas tells her the story of Justine Marie), but the majority of them are, more powerfully, consigned to the figurative realm. Indeed, at almost every textual moment when Lucy is discussing something too "painful" for her to describe in detail, she relies on the forbidden metaphor of the sea storm to suture the break in her narrative.[57] Metaphor works in *Villette* the way the visual works in *A Streetcar Named Desire*: as a means of speaking the unspeakable. And, just as Kazan appears to have been creatively energized by the challenge of having to communicate so many of his text's most important ideas through his camera, Brontë appears to have relished the indirection and ambiguity that her father's injunction had, in effect, required of her. When her publisher suggested that she fill in some of *Villette*'s "morbid" narrative gaps, Brontë flatly refused to do so, explaining that "it would be too much like drawing a picture and then writing underneath the name of the object intended to be represented."[58] For both Brontë and Kazan, censorship was an integral part of the artistic process—more inspiring than limiting, more productive than destructive.

In *The Interpretation of Dreams*, Freud uses the analogy of a writer facing censorship to explain why the human psyche chooses to distort its most forbidden desires into dreams that must be deciphered in order to be understood. Initially, Freud paints this analogous picture in primarily constrictive terms: "The writer stands in fear of the censorship; he therefore moderates and disguises the expression of his opinions. He finds himself compelled, in accordance with the sensibilities of the censor, either to refrain altogether from certain forms of attack, or to express himself in allusions instead of by direct assertions; or he must conceal his objectionable statement in an apparently innocent disguise."[59] It is not long, however, before Freud changes the tenor of his argument and points out that the censored writer, like the repressed sexual being, can paradoxically benefit from the constrictions placed upon him. "The stricter the domination of the censorship," he acknowledges, "the more thorough becomes the disguise, and, often enough, the more ingenious the means employed to put the reader on the track of the actual meaning."[60] What Freud makes it possible for us to imagine, and what these two challenging works make even clearer, is that "the actual meaning" is finally inseparable from the ingenuity of the means of representation; repression and artistry are, in the end, impossible to tell apart.

Postscript
Oscar Wilde and Mae West

MY USE OF EVALUATIVE WORDS throughout this study—"subtler,"
"richer," "more effective," "more powerful"—necessarily exposes my personal preference for the literary and cinematic styles of the works I have
been discussing. And, indeed, I will confess that there is no book with
which I would rather curl up on a Sunday afternoon than a Victorian
novel, and no network that I watch with more frequency than Turner
Classic Movies. From my biased perspective, therefore, the underlying
contention of *Better Left Unsaid* is precisely what its title implies: that
censored works of art are better, more enjoyable works of art. But even
if my predilection for Victorian literature and classical Hollywood film
is not quite as universal as I might privately desire it to be, I am hope-
ful that my illustration of censorship's favorable effects upon these two
genres will encourage a more complex and nuanced view of censorship
practices across the artistic spectrum. Perhaps, in the end, it may be said
that the "joy of censorship" belongs more to the outside observer than to
either of the participants in the never-ending volley for creative control.
For whatever "moral of the story" the censor *or* the artist may wish for a
given text to impart, it is always the reader or viewer who takes from the
story what he or she will, unpredictably and ahistorically. If censorship is
a gift, it is a gift that keeps on giving, defining its powers anew each time
that a book is opened or a film lights up a screen.

To put all of this joy and positivity into perspective, however, I would like to conclude with a brief glance at the lives and works of two figures from the time periods in question who benefited enormously from the constraints of moral censorship—until, abruptly, they did not. The first of these figures is Oscar Wilde, an artist who officially counts as a Victorian novelist even if he is more frequently classified as a *fin-de-siècle* playwright. The second is Mae West, the only Hollywood artist explored in this project who served as writer and actor rather than director (though, in fact, there were a few years in the early 1930s when her extreme popularity granted her a degree of creative control over her films that effectively put her *above* the director). As dissimilar as the shapes of their respective careers may be, Wilde and West have both achieved a specific brand of notoriety that is firmly rooted in their dealings with the moral censor; in strikingly parallel language, recent critics have pointed out that "Oscar Wilde is commonly considered to be the iconic victim of Victorian puritanism" and that "Mae West is best remembered as Hollywood's most colorful victim of censorship."[1]

What this language of victimization glosses over is the extent to which Wilde and West succeeded, prior to their personal and professional defeats, in their censorship-evasion efforts—efforts that were characterized by wordplay, double entendres, and insouciant, incalcitrant wit. Wilde's artistic heyday took place during the first half of the 1890s, when his series of social comedies (*Lady Windermere's Fan* [1892], *A Woman of No Importance* [1893], *An Ideal Husband* [1894], and *The Importance of Being Earnest* [1895]) brought him both great critical acclaim and enormous popular appeal, in spite of all the morally controversial ideas contained within them. As Peter Raby has put it, "Wilde, with one eye on the dramatic genius of Ibsen, and the other on the commercial competition in London's West End, targeted his audience with adroit precision."[2] And while West's films may have had little of Ibsen about them, she too was a censorship manipulator par excellence when at her prime. In an essay that bears much in common with the overarching premise of this project, Marybeth Hamilton specifically makes the claim that, in the best of West's films, "censorship actually enhanced her appeal. Not only West, but also her censors, sought to mediate sex so as to appeal to the widest range of viewers. And it is hard not to argue that, though West had done it well on Broadway, in Hollywood the Hays Office did it even better."[3]

Collectively, the works of Oscar Wilde and Mae West exemplify a wide array of "mediation" strategies, including all of the major ones I have explored in the preceding chapters: the strategy of scandal, the strategy of sophistication, the strategy of excess, and the strategy of restraint. The fact that these two particular artists were struck down by the forces of censorship at the very pinnacles of their strategizing careers should not make us disregard what they were able to achieve before their respective downfalls. It should instead remind us that the game of censorship circumvention is necessarily a dangerous one, with very high stakes indeed. For West, the game began several years before she arrived in Hollywood, when obscenity charges were brought against her for "corrupting the morals of youth" with her prostitution-themed first Broadway hit, *Sex* (1926). West spent ten days in prison for her crime, a sentence that was just scandalous enough to enhance, rather than ruin, her reputation. Significantly, however, West believed that the city officials' real objection was to her gay-themed second venture, *The Drag* (1927), which was going through a trial run in New Jersey at the time of her arrest. Due to threats from the Society for the Prevention of Vice that the production would be loudly and vigorously boycotted, *The Drag* never made it to the Broadway stage.

West's early struggles against the constraints of theatrical censorship were a precursor to the troubles that she would experience in Hollywood, with partly productive but ultimately injurious results. By 1934, thanks to the unparalleled success of her brazenly bawdy first two starring vehicles, *She Done Him Wrong* (1933) and *I'm No Angel* (1933), the very name "Mae West" had become a catchphrase for everything that was "wrong" with the motion picture industry. "There must," lamented one Presbyterian protester, "be tens of thousands of high school girls all over the United States reading, hearing, and seeing all they can of this particular star and her wanton heroines, imitating them so far as they can."[4] Hence when Joseph Breen took charge of the Production Code Administration (PCA), Mae West was one of the first problems that he intended to fix. Initially, he tried to clean up her act by insisting that she eliminate all of her trademark double entendres and that the storylines of her films be exaggeratedly "moral" in nature. (The plot of *Klondike Annie* [1936], for example, transforms West from a dance-hall singer to an Alaskan missionary by the story's end.) But Breen soon realized that the Mae West dilemma was harder to solve than he had originally anticipated; in a private memo from 1936, he admitted that "[j]ust so long as we have Mae West on our hands . . . we are going to have trouble. Difficulty is inherent in a Mae West picture. Lines and pieces of business, which in the script seem to be thoroughly innocuous, turn out when shown on the screen to be questionable at best, when they are not definitely offensive."[5] The only solution was to get West off of Hollywood's hands altogether, a feat that was accomplished within a few short years. By 1938, West's popularity had waned so dramatically that her movies began losing money, at which point Paramount promptly canceled her contract and her career was, more or less, over. Even though, as Leonard Leff and Jerold Simmons have noted, West's rapid fall out of favor cannot be attributed to Breen's efforts alone—it was also due to the "throwback" style of her "burlesque blue humor," which dated quickly[6]—it is difficult to deny that the films made after the Production Code unleashed its full wrath of censorship upon them are, to their detriment, less brash, less roguish, and significantly less fun.

Like West, Wilde was introduced to the caprices of censorship at the very outset of his career. His first play, *Vera; or, The Nihilists* (1881), was canceled before rehearsals were even allowed to begin, due entirely to unlucky timing: its plot revolved around an aborted assassination attempt on a Russian Czar, which suddenly became forbidden subject matter in the wake of the successful assassinations of Czar Alexander II and President James Garfield. Though this early example of censorship was, as Richard Ellman has put it, "no less infuriating because [it] was unofficial,"[7] the best-known case of Wilde's work being explicitly censored involved his 1892 retelling of the story of *Salome*. Rehearsals had, this time, already gotten underway (with the legendary Sarah Bernhardt slated to play the title role) when Wilde was informed that E. F. S. Pigott, the Lord Chamberlain's licensor of plays, would be banning the theatrical performance of *Salome* on the grounds that it was illegal to depict biblical characters on stage—a ban that would not be lifted in England for almost forty years.

Wilde's one foray into novel writing, meanwhile, was also influenced by censorship, though in somewhat subtler ways. First published in

Lippincott's Monthly Magazine in 1890, *The Picture of Dorian Gray* aroused a flurry of moral criticism that was as much about Wilde's own persona as it was about the dangers of his "unmanly, sickening, vicious" tale.[8] In response to the barrage of insults, Wilde made a series of changes to his text before publishing it in book form a year later. Gone, for example, were some of the lines with the most overtly homoerotic overtones: "There was something in his nature that was purely feminine in its tenderness," "It is quite true that I have worshipped you with far more romance of feeling than a man usually gives to a friend," and so on. Wilde's exercise in self-censorship was, to a large extent, successful: the literary reviews were significantly less condemnatory the second time around, and certain critics who had considered it to be "too dangerous" to comment positively about the work after its initial magazine release now came forward to express their admiration.[9] Still, the major circulating libraries refused to carry the "dirty" novel, and conservative moralists lamented the enormous level of popularity that it managed to gain in spite of all their best efforts to see it (and its "profligate" author) flounder.

It would take a series of legal trials, the first of which was instigated by Wilde himself, to fulfill his moral adversaries' ill wishes. In 1895 Wilde filed a libel suit against the father of his longtime lover, Lord Alfred Douglas, for leaving a calling card at Wilde's social club that was addressed to "Oscar Wilde, posing somdomite" (*sic*). By taking the matter of his sexuality to court, Wilde opened the door for legal proceedings against himself. After Douglas's father was acquitted on all counts, Wilde was immediately arrested for "gross indecency" and eventually found guilty of the charge. His last words in the courtroom were, famously, "And I? May I say nothing, my lord?"—words that were drowned out by the crowd's pitiless, censorious cries of "Shame!"[10] Wilde was sentenced to two years of hard labor, after which he moved to the Continent where he would spend the last three years of his life in relatively penniless exile. He died on November 30, 1900, less than two months before the death of Queen Victoria—the death which marked the official endpoint of the Victorian moral culture that had, in effect, destroyed him.

As the observant reader may have noticed, Oscar Wilde and Mae West are the only featured artists of this study whose words were not elevated to the stature of an epigraph. This is not because it was difficult to find statements made by the pair on the subject of moral censorship, however. To the contrary: Wilde and West have had so *much* to say on the subject, and have said it with such inimitable, quotable panache, that I have chosen (in what may be described as my own version of "compensating moral values") to give these two improvidently stymied artists the final word in my discussion of censorship. I will close, therefore, with a list of Wilde-isms and West-isms which, taken together, say almost everything that I have been trying to say about the perverse relationship between censorship, morality, and art. Positioned in this way, the statements serve more as epitaphs than epigraphs, gesturing at once to the possibilities and the limitations of prohibitive practices and cultural taboos.

I like restraint, if it doesn't go too far.

Virtue has its own reward, but no sale at the box office.

Every man that I meet wants to protect me. I can't figure out from what.

It's not what I do, but the way I do it. It's not what I say, but the way I say it.

Those who are easily shocked should be shocked more often.

When I'm good, I'm very good. But when I'm bad, I'm better.

I believe in censorship. I made a fortune out of it.

—Mae West

The books that the world calls immoral are books that show the world its own shame.

Moderation is a fatal thing. Nothing succeeds like excess.

The only thing worse than being talked about is not being talked about.

A man cannot be too careful in the choice of his enemies.

An idea that is not dangerous is unworthy of being called an idea at all.

Morality, like art, means drawing a line someplace.

Man is least himself when he talks in his own person. Give him a mask, and he will tell you the truth.

—Oscar Wilde

Notes

Introduction

1. The Motion Picture Production Code of 1930 is reprinted in its entirety as an appendix to Leonard J. Leff and Jerold L. Simmons, *The Dame in the Kimono: Hollywood, Censorship, and the Production Code* (Lexington: University Press of Kentucky, 2001), 285–300. All references to the Code herein will cite page numbers from that appendix.

2. Thomas Babington Macaulay, *The History of England from the Accession of James II*, 5 vols. (Philadelphia: Porter & Coates, 1881), 4:485.

3. Sergei Eisenstein, "Dickens, Griffith, and the Film Today," *Film Form: Essays in Film Theory* (New York: Harcourt Brace Jovanovich, 1949). In this essay, Eisenstein compares Dickens's use of detailed description with Griffith's use of the close-up, Dickens's atmosphere with Griffith's cinematographic effects, and Dickens's style of slightly exaggerating his character depictions with Griffith's style of directing his actors.

4. Thomas Doherty, *Pre-Code Hollywood: Sex, Immorality, and Insurrection in American Cinema, 1930–1934* (New York: Columbia University Press, 1999), 6; Francis G. Couvares, *Movie Censorship and American Culture* (Washington, DC: Smithsonian Institution Press, 1996), 2.

5. Michel Foucault, *The History of Sexuality, Volume 1: An Introduction*, trans. Robert Hurley (New York: Vintage, 1990), 18.

6. Examples of this type of analysis can be found in collections such as *The Administration of Aesthetics: Censorship, Political Criticism, and the Public Sphere*, ed. Richard Burt (Minneapolis: University of Minnesota Press, 1994); *Censorship and Silencing: Practices of Cultural Regulation*, ed. Robert Post (Los Angeles: Getty Research Institute for the History of Art and the Humanities, 1998); Couvares, *Movie Censorship*; and *Writing and Censorship in Britain*, ed. Paul Hyland and Neil Sammells (London and New York: Routledge, 1992). Examples can also be found in monographs such as William Cohen, *Sex Scandal: The Private Parts of Victorian Fiction* (Durham, NC: Duke University Press, 1996); Lee Grieveson, *Policing Cinema: Movies and Censorship in Early-Twentieth-Century America* (Berkeley: University of California Press, 2004); Annette Kuhn, *Cinema, Censorship, and Sexuality, 1909–1925* (London and New York: Routledge, 1988); and Annabel Patterson, *Censorship*

and Interpretation: The Conditions of Writing and Reading in Early Modern England (Madison: University of Wisconsin Press, 1984).

7. Post, *Censorship and Silencing*, 4.

8. Edward J. Bristow, *Vice and Vigilance: Purity Movements in Britain since 1700* (Dublin: Gill & Macmillan, 1977), 32.

9. *Obscene Publications Act* (1857), 20 & 21 Vict. c. 83.

10. *Regina v. Hicklin* (1868), L.R. 3 Q.B. 360.

11. *Roth v. United States* (1957), 354 U.S. 476.

12. *Mutual Film Corporation v. Industrial Commission of Ohio* (1915), 236 U.S. 230.

13. The reason that religious groups found *The Miracle* to be so offensive was that its plot centered around a vagrant stranger seducing and impregnating a peasant woman by convincing her that he is Saint Joseph, so that she believes she is a second Virgin Mary and her child is another product of immaculate conception.

14. *Joseph Burstyn, Inc. v. Wilson* (1952), 343 U.S. 495.

15. J. A. Sutherland, *Victorian Novelists and Publishers* (Chicago: University of Chicago Press, 1976), 27.

16. George Moore, *Literature at Nurse, or Circulating Morals: A Polemic on Victorian Censorship* (Sussex: Harvester Press, 1976), 18.

17. Quoted in Leff and Simmons, *Dame in the Kimono*, 296, 300.

18. Ibid., 11.

19. Quoted in ibid., 294.

20. John Stuart Mill, *On Liberty and Other Writings*, ed. Stefan Collini (Cambridge: Cambridge University Press, 1989), 8.

21. Jason Joy to James Wingate, 5 February 1931, *Little Caesar* Production Code Administration file, Academy of Motion Picture Arts and Sciences Margaret Herrick Library, Los Angeles, CA (hereafter "PCA file").

22. Joseph Litvak, *Strange Gourmets: Sophistication, Theory, and the Novel* (Durham, NC: Duke University Press, 1997), 14.

23. Quoted in Elizabeth Gaskell, *The Life of Charlotte Brontë* (London: Penguin, 1985), 94.

Chapter 1

A version of chapter 1, published in *PMLA* as "Thackeray, Sturges, and the Scandal of Censorship," is reprinted by permission of the copyright owner, The Modern Language Association of America.

1. Foucault, *History of Sexuality*, 22.

2. Mill, *On Liberty*, 8.

3. W. M. Thackeray, *Vanity Fair*, ed. Peter Shillingsburg (New York: W. W. Norton, 1994), 637. Further references will be given parenthetically in the text by page number.

4. Jason Joy to Will Hays, 17 June 1932, *Reunion in Vienna* PCA file.

5. Sturges is generally credited with being the first true Hollywood "writer/director," though his 1940 debut in that role was quickly replicated by the likes of Orson Welles (who directed and cowrote *Citizen Kane*) and John Huston (who adapted and directed *The Maltese Falcon*), both in 1941.

6. James Agee, *Agee on Film: Criticism and Comment on the Movies* (New York: Modern Library, 2000), 330; Manny Farber and W. S. Poster, "Preston Sturges: Success in the Movies," in *Negative Space: Manny Farber on the Movies* (New York: Praeger, 1971), 91; Siegfried Kracauer, "Preston Sturges or Laughter Betrayed," *Films in Review* 1, no. 1 (February 1950): 47.

7. André Bazin, *The Cinema of Cruelty: From Buñuel to Hitchcock* (New York: Seaver, 1982), 44; François Truffaut, introduction to *Cinema of Cruelty*, xii.

8. Charlotte Brontë, preface to second edition of *Jane Eyre*, ed. Q. D. Leavis (London: Penguin, 1985), 36.

9. N. N. Feltes, *Modes of Production of Victorian Novels* (Chicago: University of Chicago Press, 1986), 35.

10. Catherine Peters, *Thackeray: A Writer's Life* (Gloucestershire: Sutton, 1999), x.

11. Nina Auerbach, *Woman and the Demon: The Life of a Victorian Myth* (Cambridge, MA: Harvard University Press, 1982), 100; Eve Kosofsky Sedgwick, *Between Men: English Literature and Male Homosocial Desire* (New York: Columbia University Press, 1985), 148; Peter L. Shillingsburg, *Pegasus in Harness: Victorian Publishing and W. M. Thackeray* (Charlottesville: University of Virginia Press, 1992), 209.

12. Bosley Crowther, *New York Times,* January 1944; and James Agee, *The Nation,* January 1944, *The Miracle of Morgan's Creek* PCA file.

13. Preston Sturges, *Preston Sturges by Preston Sturges: His Life in His Words* (New York: Simon & Schuster, 1991), 301. (Sturges's "semi-autobiography" is an amalgamation of diary entries, letters, and snippets of an unfinished autobiography that Sturges's final wife cut and pasted together after his death.)

14. Ibid., 300.

15. Ibid., 300, 301.

16. Ibid., 301.

17. W. M. Thackeray to Mrs. Carmichael-Smyth, 2 August 1845, in *The Letters and Private Papers of William Makepeace Thackeray*, ed. Gordon N. Ray, 4 vols. (New York: Octagon, 1980), 2:206–7.

18. W. M. Thackeray to Mark Lemon, 24 February 1847, in *Letters*, 2:282.

19. W. M. Thackerary, *Pendennis*, ed. John Sutherland (Oxford: Oxford University Press, 1994), lvi.

20. Ibid., lvii.

21. W. M. Thackeray to Mrs. Carmichael-Smyth, March 1840, in *Letters*, 1:433.

22. W. M. Thackeray, *Catherine: A Story*, ed. Sheldon Goldfarb (Ann Arbor: University of Michigan Press, 1999), 19.

23. Quoted in Leff and Simmons, *Dame in the Kimono*, 296.

24. Joseph Breen to Luigi Luraschi, 9 October 1940, *The Lady Eve* PCA file.

25. Stanley Cavell, *Pursuits of Happiness: The Hollywood Comedy of Remarriage* (Cambridge, MA: Harvard University Press, 1981), 66.

26. Laura Mulvey introduced the concept of the objectifying male gaze in her seminal essay, "Visual Pleasure and Narrative Cinema," *Screen* 16, no. 3 (Autumn 1975): 6–18.

27. It is interesting to note that this passage is one of the many examples of Thackeray toying with our sense of who is speaking—although the passage clearly marks Becky's comment about wishing to "dance before a booth at a fair" as something that she "said to herself," it is immediately followed by Lord Steyne's reply, "You would do it very well," at which point we are told that Becky "used to tell the great man her *ennuis* and perplexities in her artless way—they amused him" (504). This moment has much in common, incidentally, with a scene from *The Lady Eve* in which Jean starts off by telling Sir Alfred her fantasy of how she will reel Charles in and get him to propose to her for a second time, but after we see the scene that we thought was merely a figment of Jean's imagination, we realize that we have actually been watching what "really" takes place next in the story. By so brashly tinkering with our sense of diegetic reality, both Thackeray and Sturges provide a head-spinning additional layer of artistic ambiguity.

28. Mulvey refers to the "to-be-looked-at-ness" of the objectified female in "Visual Pleasure," 11.

29. Cavell, *Pursuits of Happiness*, 61.

30. Quoted in Preston Sturges, *Five Screenplays by Preston Sturges*, ed. Brian Henderson (Berkeley: University of California Press, 1985), 326.

31. Margaret Oliphant, "Mr. Thackeray and His Novels," *Blackwood's Magazine,* January 1855, in *Thackeray: The Critical Heritage*, ed. Geoffrey Tillotson and Donald Hawes (London: Routledge & Kegan Paul, 1968), 204.

32. Elizabeth Rigby (later, Lady Eastlake), "*Vanity Fair*—and *Jane Eyre*," *Quarterly Review*, December 1848, in Tillotson and Hawes, *Critical Heritage*, 77–78.

33. Rigby, "*Vanity Fair*"; Oliphant, "Mr. Thackeray and His Novels"; John Forster, review in *The Examiner*, 22 July 1848, in Tillotson and Hawes, *Critical Heritage*, 81, 204, 58.

34. Andrew Sarris, "Preston Sturges," in *The National Society of Film Critics on Movie Comedy*, ed. Stuart Byron and Elizabeth Weis (New York: Penguin, 1977), 86; Joe McElhaney, "Fast Talk: Preston Sturges and the Speed of Language," in *Cinema and Modernity*, ed. Murray Pomerance (New Brunswick, NJ: Rutgers University Press, 2006), 278.

35. Bosley Crowther, *New York Times,* 26 February 1941, and unsigned review, *Weekly Variety,* 26 February 1941, *The Lady Eve* PCA file.

36. Quoted in Peter Bailey, *Popular Culture and Performance in the Victorian City* (Cambridge: Cambridge University Press, 1998), 145.

37. Quoted in Leff and Simmons, *Dame in the Kimono*, 289, 288.

38. Ibid., 286.

39. Kevin Brownlow, *Behind the Mask of Innocence* (Berkeley: University of California Press, 1990), 20.

40. Joseph Breen to Luigi Luraschi, 9 October 1940, *The Lady Eve* PCA file.

41. Quoted in Leff and Simmons, *Dame in the Kimono*, 47.

42. Brian Henderson, Introduction to Sturges, *Five Screenplays*, 26.

43. Diane Carson, "To Be Seen but Not Heard: *The Awful Truth*," in *Multiple Voices in Feminist Film Criticism*, ed. Diane Carson, Linda Dittmar, and Janice R. Welsch (Minneapolis: University of Minnesota Press, 1994), 216.

44. Lisa Jadwin, "The Seductiveness of Female Duplicity in *Vanity Fair*," *SEL* 32, no. 4 (Autumn 1992): 679.

45. Rigby, "*Vanity Fair*," in Tillotson and Hawes, *Critical Heritage*, 85–86.

46. Ibid., 85.

47. Quoted in *The Two Thackerays: Anne Thackeray Ritchie's Centenary Biographical Introductions to the Works of William Makepeace Thackeray* (New York: AMS Press, 1988), 42.

48. Roland Barthes, *S/Z* (New York: Hill & Wang, 1974), 145.

Chapter 2

1. Motion Picture Producers and Distributors of America's *Report of the Sub-Committee on Eliminations*, May 14, 1927. Available from MPPDA Digital Archive, Record #341. This report was the original formulation of what came to be known as the "Don'ts and Be Carefuls" list.

2. Lea Jacobs, *The Decline of Sentiment: American Film in the 1920s* (Berkeley: University of California Press, 2008), 2.

3. Jason Joy to James Wingate, 5 February 1931, *Little Caesar* PCA file.

4. Quoted in Leff and Simmons, *Dame in the Kimono*, 297–98.

5. Ibid., 295.

6. Ibid., 294.

7. Quoted in Frank Walsh, *Sin and Censorship: The Catholic Church and the Motion Picture Industry* (New Haven: Yale University Press, 1996), 10.

8. Quoted in Leff and Simmons, *Dame in the Kimono*, 290, 288, 300.

9. For a more thorough discussion of the impact of women's moral reform groups on the history of American censorship, see Alison M. Parker, *Purifying America: Women, Cultural Reform, and Pro-Censorship Activism, 1873–1933* (Urbana and Chicago: University of Illinois Press, 1997).

10. George Cukor, interview by Douglas W. Edwards and David B. Goodstein, in *George Cukor: Interviews*, ed. Robert Emmet Long (Jackson: University Press of Mississippi, 2001), 180.

11. Quoted in Jacobs, *Decline of Sentiment*, 23.

12. Jacobs, *Decline of Sentiment*, 23.

13. Gene D. Phillips, *George Cukor* (Boston: Twayne, 1982), 95.

14. Ibid.

15. Although Cukor was fired from working on *Gone with the Wind* only two weeks into production, he continued to give private acting coaching to Vivien Leigh (and Olivia de Havilland) on weekends throughout the shooting of the film, and both actresses credited him with the power of their performances.

16. Quoted in Patrick McGilligan, *George Cukor: A Double Life* (New York: St. Martin's Press, 1991), 89.

17. George Cukor, interview by John Gillett and David Robinson, in *George Cukor: Interviews*, 11–12.

18. Phillips, *George Cukor*, 74; Edwards and Goodstein, in Long, *George Cukor: Interviews*, 174; quoted in Emanuel Levy, *George Cukor: Master of Elegance* (New York: William Morrow, 1994), 269.

19. Quoted in Phillips, *George Cukor*, 95.

20. Litvak, *Strange Gourmets*, 4.

21. Ibid., 3–4.

22. Ibid., 3.

23. Ibid., 14.

24. Herbert Schlossberg, *The Silent Revolution and the Making of Victorian England* (Columbus: Ohio State University Press, 2000), 1. For similar pre-Victorian histories, see also Ford K. Brown, *Fathers of the Victorians: The Age of Wilberforce* (Cambridge: Cambridge University Press, 1961); and Ben Wilson, *The Making of Victorian Values: Decency and Dissent in Britain, 1789–1837* (London: Penguin, 2007).

25. Anthony Mandal, *Jane Austen and the Popular Novel: The Determined Author* (New York: Palgrave Macmillan, 2007), 38–39.

26. Quoted in Donald Thomas, *A Long Time Burning: The History of Literary Censorship in England* (New York: Frederick A. Praeger, 1969), 186. The first edition of *The Family Shakespeare* was published in 1807, though that edition is now credited to Bowdler's sister Harriet. The second, more widely read edition from 1818 contains Bowdler's own excisions.

27. Quoted in John Wolffe, *The Expansion of Evangelicalism: The Age of Wilberforce, More, Chalmers and Finney* (Nottingham: Inter-Varsity Press, 2006), 152; Thomas Doherty, *Hollywood's Censor: Joseph I. Breen and the Production Code Administration* (New York: Columbia University Press, 2007), 9.

28. A good example of an English conservative's use of the term "sophistication" to describe this threatening difference can be found in a passage written by the quintessential English conservative, Edmund Burke; in contrasting his country's purer, nobler ways with the ways of the profligate French, he boasts, "We preserve the whole of our feelings still native and entire, unsophisticated by pedantry and infidelity. We have real hearts of flesh and blood beating in our bosoms." Quoted in Wilson, *Making of Victorian Values*, 11.

29. Quoted in Lisa Wood, *Modes of Discipline: Women, Conservatism, and the Novel after the French Revolution* (Lewisburg, PA: Bucknell University Press, 2003), 13.

30. Deirdre Le Faye, "Letters," in *Jane Austen in Context*, ed. Janet Todd (Cambridge: Cambridge University Press, 2005), 33.

31. Quoted in *Jane Austen: The Critical Heritage*, ed. B. C. Southam (London: Routledge & Kegan Paul, 1968), 55–56.

32. J. E. Austen-Leigh, *A Memoir of Jane Austen* (Oxford: Clarendon, 1926), 157.

33. Jane Austen to Cassandra Austen, 24 January 1809 and 18 November 1814, in *Jane Austen's Letters*, ed. Deirdre Le Faye (Oxford: Oxford University Press, 1995), 170, 280.

34. Jane Austen to Cassandra Austen, 24 January 1809, 30 January 1809, 11 October 1813, and to Anna Lefroy, 24 November 1814, in *Letters*, 170, 172, 234, 283.

35. Quoted in Deirdre Le Faye, *Jane Austen: A Family Record* (Cambridge: Cambridge University Press, 1989), 233.

36. Virginia Woolf, *The Common Reader* (New York: Harcourt, Brace, 1925), 202.

37. Alistair M. Duckworth, *The Improvement of the Estate: A Study of Jane Austen's Novels* (Baltimore: Johns Hopkins University Press, 1971), 10; Jillian Heydt-Stevenson, *Austen's Unbecoming Conjunctions: Subversive Laughter, Embodied History* (New York: Palgrave Macmillan, 2005), 209.

38. D. A. Miller, *Jane Austen, or The Secret of Style* (Princeton: Princeton University Press, 2003), 2–3.

39. Doherty, *Hollywood's Censor*, 339–40.

40. Maria DiBattista, *Fast Talking Dames* (New Haven: Yale University Press, 2003), 31.

41. Marilyn Butler, *Jane Austen and the War of Ideas* (Oxford: Oxford University Press, 1988), 250.

42. Andrew Sarris, *You Ain't Heard Nothin' Yet: The American Talking Film History and Memory, 1927–1949* (Oxford: Oxford University Press, 1998), 451.

43. Dan Callahan, "George Cukor," *Senses of Cinema* 33 (October–December 2004), par. 21, accessed 21 July 2012, http://sensesofcinema.com/2004/great-directors/cukor/.

44. Kathrina Glitre, *Hollywood Romantic Comedy: States of the Union, 1934–65* (London: Manchester University Press, 2006), 114.

45. Quoted in McGilligan, *George Cukor*, 116.

46. McGilligan, *George Cukor*, 145.

47. Duckworth, *Improvement of the Estate*, 36. For an "Evangelical" reading of *Mansfield Park*, see Mandal, *Jane Austen*, in which he discusses "the degree to which *Mansfield Park* participates in a new concern with moral and domestic issues, one spearheaded by fiction with a decidedly Evangelical cast," 91.

48. Mandal, *Jane Austen*, 102.

49. Jane Austen to John Murray, 1 April 1816, in *Letters*, 313.

50. Quoted in Southam, *Critical Heritage*, 50, 49.

51. Ibid., 50.

52. Jane Austen to Cassandra Austen, 29 January 1813, in *Letters*, 201.

53. Jane Austen, *Mansfield Park*, ed. Tony Tanner (London: Penguin, 1985), 245.

54. Jane Austen to Cassandra Austen, 29 January 1813, in *Letters*, 202.

55. Jane Austen to Cassandra Austen, 4 February 1813, in *Letters*, 203.

56. Jane Austen, *Emma*, ed. Stephen M. Parrish (New York: W. W. Norton, 1993), 1. Further references will be given parenthetically in the text by page number.

57. Claudia Johnson, *Jane Austen: Women, Politics, and the Novel* (Chicago: University of Chicago Press, 1988), 140. Johnson is, it should be noted, describing in this sentence the common response to *Emma* that she intends to work beyond.

58. Carson, "To Be Seen," 216, 213.

59. Johnson, *Jane Austen*, 140.

60. Cavell, *Pursuits of Happiness*, 139.

61. Duckworth, *Improvement of the Estate*, 148.

62. Joseph Breen to L. B. Mayer, 18 June 1940, *The Philadelphia Story* PCA file.

63. Unsigned review of *The Philadelphia Story*, *Variety*, 5 December 1940, *The Philadelphia Story* PCA file.

64. Unsigned review of *The Philadelphia Story*, *The Hollywood Reporter*, 5 December 1940, *The Philadelphia Story* PCA file.

65. Vernon Steele, review of *The Philadelphia Story*, *Pacific Coast Musician*, 7 December 1940, *The Philadelphia Story* PCA file.

66. Lea Jacobs, *The Wages of Sin: Censorship and the Fallen Woman Film, 1928–1942* (Berkeley: University of California Press, 1997), 113.

67. In *The Awful Truth*, in fact, the sexist double standard goes even further: Lucy Warriner (Irene Dunne) must be cleared of the charge of infidelity by the story's end, but must also agree to overlook the blatant infidelity of her husband (Cary Grant) that marks the beginning of the film.

68. John Dussinger, *In the Pride of the Moment: Encounters in Jane Austen's World* (Columbus: Ohio State University Press), 45; Woolf, *Common Reader*, 197.

69. For a lengthy explication of Austen's use of this riddle, see Heydt-Stevenson, *Unbecoming Conjunctions*, 161.

70. Alice Chandler, "A Pair of Fine Eyes: Jane Austen's Treatment of Sex," *Studies in the Novel* 7, no. 1 (1975): 92.

71. Dussinger, *Pride of the Moment*, 45.

72. Quoted in Elaine Jordan, "Pulpit, Stage, and Novel: 'Mansfield Park' and Mrs. Inchbald's 'Lovers' Vows,'" *NOVEL: A Forum on Fiction* 20, no. 2 (Winter 1987): 139.

73. Austen, *Mansfield Park*, 452–53.

74. Butler, *War of Ideas*, 251.

75. D. A. Miller, *Narrative and Its Discontents: Problems of Closure in the Traditional Novel* (Princeton: Princeton University Press, 1981), 10.

76. Joseph Litvak, "Reading Characters: Self, Society, and the Text in *Emma*," *PMLA* 100, no. 5 (October 1985): 772.

Chapter 3

1. Frank Fowell and Frank Palmer, *Censorship in England* (New York: Benjamin Blom, 1969), 12. For other helpful accounts of early English censorship, see also Richard Dutton, *Mastering the Revels: The Regulation and Censorship of English Renaissance Drama* (Iowa City: University of Iowa Press, 1991); or Thomas, *Long Time Burning*.

2. Tony Tanner, "Licence and Licencing: To the Presse or to the Spunge," *Journal of the History of Ideas* 38, no. 1 (January–March 1977): 4.

3. Gregory D. Black, *Hollywood Censored: Morality Codes, Catholics, and the Movies* (Cambridge: Cambridge University Press, 1994), 13.

4. Paul Davis, *The Lives and Times of Ebenezer Scrooge* (New Haven: Yale University Press, 1990), 4.

5. Joss Marsh, *Word Crimes: Blasphemy, Culture, and Literature in Nineteenth-Century England* (Chicago: University of Chicago Press, 1998), 54.

6. Sambudha Sen, "Radical Satire and Respectability: Comic Imagination in Hone, Jerrold, and Dickens," *The Working-Class Intellectual in Eighteenth- and Nineteenth-Century Britain*, ed. Aruna Krishnamurthy (Surrey: Ashgate, 2009), 150.

7. Quoted in Fred Kaplan, *Dickens: A Biography* (Baltimore: Johns Hopkins University Press, 1988), 505.

8. For an engaging discussion of Dickens's approach to improving the social status of literature as compared to Thackeray's approach, see Michael J. Flynn, "*Pendennis, Copperfield*, and the Debate on the 'Dignity of Literature,'" *Dickens Studies Annual* 41 (2010): 151–89.

9. Edgar Johnson, *Charles Dickens: His Tragedy and Triumph* (New York: Viking, 1977), 435.

10. Quoted in John Forster, *Life of Charles Dickens* (Limbricht, Netherlands: Diderot, 2005), 446.

11. Ibid.

12. Charles Dickens, *Martin Chuzzlewit* (Hertfordshire: Wordsworth Classics, 1994), 11; Charles Dickens, *Little Dorrit*, ed. Stephen Wall and Helen Small (London: Penguin, 1998), 475.

13. Charles Dickens, *Our Mutual Friend*, ed. Adrian Poole (London: Penguin, 1997), 131.

14. See, for example, Ruth Bernard Yeazell, "Podsnappery, Sexuality, and the English Novel," *Critical Inquiry* 9, no. 2 (December 1982): 339–57; and Richard Stang's chapter on "The Cheek of the Young Person," in *The Theory of the Novel in England, 1850–1870* (London: Routledge & Paul, 1959).

15. Dickens, *Our Mutual Friend*, 132.

16. Barbara Leckie, "'A Preface Is Written to the Public': Print Censorship, Novel Prefaces, and the Construction of a New Reading Public in Late-Victorian England," *Victorian Literature and Culture* 37 (2009): 447–62.

17. Charles Dickens, *Oliver Twist* (New York: Modern Library, 2001), xxix–xxx.

18. Ibid., xxviii.

19. Ibid., xxx.

20. Tanner, "Licence and Licencing," 14.

21. Dickens, *Oliver Twist*, xxviii, xxvii.

22. These similarities were no coincidence: according to Capra's screenwriter on *Mr. Smith Goes to Washington*, Sidney Buchman, "Capra's great passion was Dickens. As soon as he had some money, he bought some of the rarest and most extraordinary editions of Dickens's work, and he was very proud of his collection." Quoted in Joseph McBride, *Frank Capra: The Catastrophe of Success* (Jackson: University Press of Mississippi, 2011), 414.

23. Capra dates this illness to 1935, just after he swept the Academy Awards, but McBride shows that it really must have occurred in 1934.

24. Frank Capra, *The Name Above the Title: An Autobiography* (New York: Macmillan, 1971), 176.

25. Ibid., 185.

26. McBride, *Frank Capra*, 318.

27. Ibid., 322.

28. Capra, *Name Above the Title*, 34.

29. Ibid., xi.

30. Frank Capra, interview by James R. Silke and Bruce Henstell, in *Frank Capra: Interviews*, ed. Leland Poague (Jackson: University Press of Mississippi, 2004), 89.

31. Capra, *Name Above the Title*, 201.

32. Joseph Breen to Will Hays, 31 January 1939, *Mr. Smith Goes to Washington* PCA file.

33. Joseph Breen to L. B. Mayer, 19 January 1938, *Mr. Smith Goes to Washington* PCA file.

34. Joseph Breen to Harry Cohn, 12 November 1933, *It Happened One Night* PCA file.

35. Richard Maltby, "*It Happened One Night*: The Recreation of the Patriarch," in *Frank Capra: Authorship and the Studio System,* ed. Robert Sklar and Vito Zagarrio (Philadelphia: Temple University Press, 1998), 134.

36. Philip K. Scheuer, "Interview with Frank Capra," in Poague, *Frank Capra: Interviews*, 14.

37. Ibid.

38. Cavell, *Pursuits of Happiness,* 82.

39. Ibid., 82–83.

40. Joseph Breen to Will Hays, 31 January 1939, *Mr. Smith Goes to Washington* PCA file.

41. Unsigned reviews in *Motion Picture Daily*, 14 October 1939, and *Variety*, 11 October 1939, *Mr. Smith Goes to Washington* PCA file.

42. Quoted in Capra, *Name Above the Title*, 382.

43. Davis, *Ebenezer Scrooge,* 164.

44. David Mamet, "Crisis in Happyland," *Sight and Sound* 12, no. 1 (January 2002): 22.

45. Quoted in Michael Patrick Hearn, *The Annotated Christmas Carol* (New York: W. W. Norton, 2004), xxxi.

46. Ibid., xxx.

47. Quoted in Forster, *Charles Dickens*, 215.

48. Capra, *Name Above the Title*, 374.

49. Ibid., 378.

50. The first report of the Children's Employment Commission, issued in 1842, revealed the shocking conditions of child labor in England's coal mines, while the second report (February 1843) examined the even worse conditions of other industries, including the needle sweatshops of London.

51. Charles Dickens to Dr. Southwood Smith, 6 March 1843, in *The Letters of Charles Dickens: The Pilgrim Edition*, ed. Madeline House, Graham Storey, and Kathleen Tillotson, 11 vols. (Oxford: Oxford University Press, 1974), 3:459.

52. Charles Dickens to Dr. Southwood Smith, 10 March 1843, in *Letters*, 3:461.

53. Capra, *Name Above the Title*, 375.

54. Ibid., 374–75. Even though the plot of *Wonderful Life* touches on the fact of World War II only briefly—George Bailey's brother and best friends all get to serve in the war while he is forced to fight the "battle of the homefront" due to his one deaf ear—Charles Wolfe has argued that Jimmy Stewart's well-publicized status as a war veteran necessarily connected George Bailey's story to the trauma of postwar life: "George's nightmare vision of dissociation, of the rupture of the family and of small-town values, can also be read as operating within the spirit of postwar *noir*, where the representation of veteran anguish is frequently not literal." Wolfe, "The Return of Jimmy Stewart: The Publicity Photograph as Text," *Wide Angle* 6, no. 4 (1985): 51.

55. Philip Van Doren Stern, "The Greatest Gift," reprinted in Jeanine Basinger, *The "It's a Wonderful Life" Book* (New York: Knopf, 1986), 95.

56. Margaret Oliphant, "Charles Dickens," *Blackwood's Magazine*, June 1871, in *Charles Dickens: The Critical Heritage*, ed. Philip Collins (London: Routledge & Kegan Paul, 1971), 569.

57. Joseph Breen to William Gordon, 6 March, 29 March, and 28 May 1946, *It's a Wonderful Life* PCA file.

58. Ted O'Shea to Samuel Briskin, cable, 18 March 1947, *It's a Wonderful Life* PCA file.

59. Frank Capra to Ted O'Shea, cable, 19 March 1947, *It's a Wonderful Life* PCA file.

60. Quoted in Stephen Cox, *It's a Wonderful Life: A Memory Book* (Nashville: Cumberland House, 2005), 49.

61. Quoted in Hearn, *Annotated Christmas Carol*, 92. It is also important to realize how much more emphatic the Victorian stage censors were about the use of any religious language; in most early stage versions of the *Carol*, Tiny Tim's famous line had to be changed to "Heaven Bless us, every one!"

62. Charles Dickens, *A Christmas Carol and Other Christmas Writings*, ed. Michael

Slater (London: Penguin, 2000), 33. Further references will be given parenthetically in the text by page number.

63. Quoted in Hearn, *Annotated Christmas Carol*, 116.

64. Davis, *Ebenezer Scrooge*, 61.

65. J. Hillis Miller, "The Genres of *A Christmas Carol*," *The Dickensian* 89, no. 3 (Winter 1993): 204.

66. Mamet, "Crisis in Happyland," 22–23.

67. Audrey Jaffe, "Spectacular Sympathy: Visuality and Ideology in Dickens's *A Christmas Carol*," *PMLA* 109, no. 2 (March 1994): 255.

68. Ibid., 255, 262–63.

69. See, for example, Jacobs, *Wages of Sin;* and Black, *Hollywood Censored*.

70. Robin Wood, "Ideology, Genre, Auteur," in *Film Theory and Criticism: Introductory Readings*, ed. Leo Braudy and Marshall Cohen (Oxford: Oxford University Press, 1999), 673–74.

71. Joseph Breen to William Gordon, 6 March 1946, *It's a Wonderful Life* PCA file.

72. Edmund Wilson, *The Wound and the Bow* (New York: Oxford University Press, 1947), 64.

73. George Pechter, "American Madness," in *Frank Capra: The Man and His Films*, ed. Richard Glatzer and John Raeburn (Ann Arbor: University of Michigan Press, 1975), 181–82.

74. It should be noted, though, that George's "vehement resistance" against Mary's advances is precisely what sets the stage for a scene that is every bit as sexually climactic as the encounter from *The Lady Eve* that I discussed in chapter 1—the scene in which George and Mary share a telephone to talk to Sam Wainwright in New York City as her mother listens in on the extension upstairs. As Ned Schantz has previously observed, this scene is "far more erotic than the typical telephonic duet" at least partially "because of the dependably stimulating effects of maternal disapproval." This increased attraction as a direct result of prohibition is a subject that I explore in greater detail in chapter 4. Schantz, "Telephonic Film," *Film Quarterly* 56, no. 4 (2003): 28.

75. "Frank Capra, interview by Neil Hurley," in Poague, *Frank Capra: Interviews*, 198.

76. This view is most famously expressed in a story told about a little costermonger's girl who, on the day of Dickens's death, allegedly exclaimed, "Dickens dead? Then will Father Christmas die too?" Quoted in Theodore Watts-Dunton, *The Coming of Love* (London: John Lane, 1899), 191.

Chapter 4

1. Charlotte Brontë to W. S. Williams, 12 April 1850, in *Selected Letters of Charlotte Brontë*, ed. Margaret Smith (Oxford: Oxford University Press, 2007), 161–62; Elia Kazan, *Kazan on Kazan*, ed. Jeff Young (London: Faber & Faber, 1999), 36.

2. Sigmund Freud, *The New Introductory Lectures of Psychoanalysis*, ed. James Strachey (New York: W. W. Norton, 1965), 103.

3. Sigmund Freud, *Sexuality and the Psychology of Love*, ed. Philip Rieff (New York: Simon & Schuster, 1997), 57.

4. Havelock Ellis, *Studies in the Psychology of Sex*, 6 vols. (Philadelphia: F. A. Davis, 1908), 1:ix.

5. Ibid., 1:45.

6. Ibid., 3:59.

7. John Lahr, foreword to Elia Kazan, *Kazan on Directing* (New York: Alfred A. Knopf, 2009), xi.

8. Joseph Boone, *Libidinal Currents: Sexuality and the Shaping of Modernism* (Chicago: University of Chicago Press, 1998), 33–34.

9. John Kucich, "Passionate Reserve and Reserved Passion in the Works of Charlotte Brontë," *ELH* 52, no. 4 (Winter 1985): 918.

10. John Kucich, *Repression in Victorian Fiction: Charlotte Brontë, George Eliot, and Charles Dickens* (Berkeley: University of California Press, 1987), 2, 3.

11. Boone, *Libidinal Currents,* 27.

12. John Maynard, *Charlotte Brontë and Sexuality* (Cambridge: Cambridge University Press, 1984), 4.

13. *Baby Doll* is often held up alongside films like Roberto Rossellini's *The Miracle* (1950) and Otto Preminger's *The Moon Is Blue* (1953) to represent the beginning of the legal and commercial downfall of Hays Code censorship that culminated with the introduction of the MPAA's Code-replacing rating system in 1968.

14. Vincent Brook, "Courting Controversy: The Making and Selling of *Baby Doll* and the Demise of the Production Code," *Quarterly Review of Film and Video* 18, no. 4 (2001): 357–58.

15. Elia Kazan, *Elia Kazan: A Life* (New York: Alfred A. Knopf, 1988), 564, 563.

16. Ibid., 436.

17. Ibid., 535–36.

18. Kazan, *Kazan on Kazan*, 91.

19. Though Kazan had, by 1951, already made an indelible directorial mark upon the American theater scene, his earlier films—*A Tree Grows in Brooklyn, Sea of Grass, Boomerang, Panic in the Streets, Pinky*, even *A Gentleman's Agreement*, for which he won the Best Director Oscar in 1948—have not attained the same iconic status as many of his later films.

20. Leslie Stephen, "Charlotte Brontë," *Cornhill Magazine*, December 1877, in *The Brontës: The Critical Heritage*, ed. Miriam Allott (London: Routledge & Kegan Paul, 1974), 415.

21. Charlotte Brontë to George Smith, 30 October 1852, in *Letters*, 208.

22. Robert Southey to Charlotte Brontë, 12 March 1837, in *Letters*, 10.

23. Charlotte Brontë to Robert Southey, 16 March 1837, in *Letters*, 9.

24. Charlotte Brontë to G. H. Lewes, 6 November 1847, in *Letters*, 90.

25. Maynard, *Brontë and Sexuality*, 145–46.

26. Charlotte Brontë to W. S. Williams, 31 December 1847, in *Letters,* 95.

27. An example of this defensiveness on Brontë's part can be found in a letter to W. S. Williams from January 4, 1848, in which she insists that "[i]t would take a great deal to crush me, because I know, in the first place, that my own intentions were correct; that I feel in my heart a deep reverence for Religion, that impiety is very abhorrent to me." In *Letters,* 96.

28. Charlotte Brontë to G. H. Lewes, 12 January 1848, in *Letters,* 98.

29. For the most thorough consideration of the effects of the Legion's postproduction censorship, see Leonard J. Leff, "And Transfer to Cemetery: The *Streetcars Named Desire,*" *Film Quarterly* 55, no. 3 (Spring 2002): 29–38.

30. Ellen Dowling, "The Derailment of *A Streetcar Named Desire,*" *Literature/Film Quarterly* 9, no. 4 (1981): 240.

31. Brenda Murphy, *Tennessee Williams and Elia Kazan, A Collaboration in the Theatre* (Cambridge: Cambridge University Press, 1992), 1.

32. Ibid., 3.

33. Kazan, *Elia Kazan,* 380.

34. Kim Hunter, "*Streetcar* on Film," Disc 2: Special Features, *A Streetcar Named Desire,* special ed. DVD, dir. Elia Kazan (Burbank, CA: Warner Home Video, 2001).

35. Kazan, *Kazan on Directing,* 156–57. Whether or not Kazan fully achieved his goal of taking the focus away from Stanley in the film version is, of course, debatable. Even with the camera "crawling into" Blanche as effectively as it does, Marlon Brando's performance continues to overshadow Vivien Leigh's performance in the annals of classical Hollywood cinema.

36. Kazan, *Elia Kazan,* 384.

37. Ibid.

38. Charlotte Brontë, *Villette,* ed. Mark Lilly (London: Penguin, 1985), 94. Further references will be given parenthetically in the text by page number.

39. "I have already told you," she wrote to W. S. Williams on August 14, 1848, "that I regard Mr. Thackeray as the first of Modern Masters, and as the legitimate High Priest of Truth; I study him accordingly with reverence: he—I see—keeps the mermaid's tail below water, and only hints at the dead men's bones and noxious slime amidst which it wriggles; *but*—his hint is more vivid than other men's elaborate explanations, and never is his satire whetted to so keen an edge as when with quiet mocking irony he modestly recommends to the approbation of the Public his own exemplary discretion and forebearance." In *Letters,* 116.

40. Kate Millett, *Sexual Politics* (New York: Doubleday, 1970), 146.

41. For a fuller consideration of the triangulation of desire, see René Girard's *Deceit, Desire, and the Novel: Self and Other in Literary Structure* (Baltimore: Johns Hopkins University Press, 1966), in which he argues that all great literature portrays the necessarily mimetic character of human desire.

42. Millett, *Sexual Politics,* 146.

43. Sandra M. Gilbert and Susan Gubar, *The Madwoman in the Attic: The Woman*

Writer and the Nineteenth-Century Literary Imagination (New Haven: Yale University Press, 1979), 428.

44. Patricia E. Johnson, "Charlotte Brontë and Desire (to Write): Pleasure, Power, and Prohibition," in *Anxious Power: Reading, Writing, and Ambivalence in Narrative by Women*, ed. Carol J. Singley and Susan Elizabeth Sweeney (Albany: State University of New York Press, 1993), 184.

45. Joseph Breen to Luigi Luraschi, 27 June 1949, *A Streetcar Named Desire* PCA file.

46. Hunter, *Streetcar Named Desire* DVD.

47. "Elia Kazan, interview by Stuart Byron and Martin L. Rubin," in *Elia Kazan: Interviews*, ed. William Baer (Jackson: University Press of Mississippi, 2000), 135.

48. Kazan, *Kazan on Directing*, 158.

49. Quoted in Leff and Simmons, *Dame in the Kimono*, 296–97.

50. John M. Roderick, "From 'Tarantula Arms' to Della Robia Blue," in *Tennessee Williams: A Tribute*, ed. Jac Tharpe (Jackson: University Press of Mississippi, 1977), 118.

51. Elia Kazan to Jack Warner, 6 July 1951, *A Streetcar Named Desire* PCA file.

52. Nancy Tischler, "The Distorted Reality: Tennessee Williams' Self-Portrait," in *Tennessee Williams: A Collection of Critical Essays*, ed. Stephen S. Stanton (New York: Prentice-Hall, 1977), 168.

53. Richard Schickel, *Streetcar Named Desire* DVD.

54. Kazan, *Elia Kazan*, 435.

55. Elia Kazan to Joseph Breen, 18 May 1951, *A Streetcar Named Desire* PCA file.

56. Gaskell, *Life of Charlotte Brontë*, 484.

57. To name a few such figurative sea storms: The unidentified misfortunes of Lucy's childhood are described as a "heavy tempest" that demolishes the vessel on which she and her family are traveling, so that "the ship was lost, the crew perished" (94). At the peak of Lucy's nervous breakdown, she imagines a cup of "suffering" being forced to her lips that is "drawn from no well, but filled up seething from a bottomless and boundless sea" (231). When Lucy must wait in agonizing suspense for M. Paul to come say goodbye to her before departing for the West Indies, she describes the hours as "pass[ing] like drift cloud—like the rack scudding before a storm" (542).

58. Charlotte Brontë to W. S. Williams, 6 November 1852, in *Letters*, 211.

59. Sigmund Freud, *The Interpretation of Dreams*, trans. A. A. Brill (New York: Modern Library, 1994), 52.

60. Ibid.

Postscript

1. Ari Adut, "A Theory of Scandal: Victorians, Homosexuality, and the Fall of Oscar Wilde," *American Journal of Sociology* 111, no. 1 (July 2005): 214; Marybeth Hamilton, "Goodness Had Nothing to Do with It: Censoring Mae West," in Couvares, *Movie Censorship*, 187.

2. Peter Raby, ed., *The Cambridge Companion to Oscar Wilde* (Cambridge: Cambridge University Press, 1997), 146.

3. Hamilton, "Censoring Mae West," in Couvares, *Movie Censorship*, 200.

4. Quoted in Marybeth Hamilton, *When I'm Bad, I'm Better: Mae West, Sex, and American Entertainment* (New York: HarperCollins, 1995), 201.

5. Joseph Breen, interoffice memo, 10 February 1936, *Klondike Annie* PCA file.

6. Leff and Simmons, *Dame in the Kimono*, 51.

7. Richard Ellman, *Oscar Wilde* (New York: Vintage, 1988), 153.

8. Quoted in Stuart Mason, *Oscar Wilde: Art and Morality* (New York: Haskell, 1971), 200.

9. Quoted in Ellman, *Oscar Wilde*, 323. The most famous example of a critic who did this was Walter Pater.

10. Ibid., 477–78.

Bibliography

Adut, Ari. "A Theory of Scandal: Victorians, Homosexuality, and the Fall of Oscar Wilde." *American Journal of Sociology* III, no. 1 (July 2005): 213–50.

Agee, James. *Agee on Film: Criticism and Comment on the Movies.* New York: Modern Library, 2000.

Allott, Miriam, ed. *The Brontës: The Critical Heritage.* London: Routledge & Kegan Paul, 1974.

Auerbach, Nina. *Woman and the Demon: The Life of a Victorian Myth.* Cambridge, MA: Harvard University Press, 1982.

Austen, Jane. *Emma.* Edited by Stephen M. Parrish. New York: W. W. Norton, 1993.

———. *Jane Austen's Letters.* Edited by Deirdre Le Faye. Oxford: Oxford University Press, 1995.

———. *Mansfield Park.* Edited by Tony Tanner. London: Penguin Books, 1985.

Austen-Leigh, J. E. *A Memoir of Jane Austen.* Oxford: Clarendon, 1926.

Baer, William, ed. *Elia Kazan: Interviews.* Jackson: University Press of Mississippi, 2000.

Bailey, Peter. *Popular Culture and Performance in the Victorian City.* Cambridge: Cambridge University Press, 1998.

Barthes, Roland. *S/Z.* New York: Hill & Wang, 1974.

Bazin, André. *The Cinema of Cruelty: From Buñuel to Hitchcock.* Introduction by François Truffaut. New York: Seaver, 1982.

Bernard Yeazell, Ruth. "Podsnappery, Sexuality, and the English Novel." *Critical Inquiry* 9, no. 2 (December 1982): 339–57.

Black, Gregory D. *Hollywood Censored: Morality Codes, Catholics, and the Movies.* Cambridge: Cambridge University Press, 1994.

Boone, Joseph. *Libidinal Currents: Sexuality and the Shaping of Modernism.* Chicago: University of Chicago Press, 1998.

Bristow, Edward J. *Vice and Vigilance: Purity Movements in Britain since 1700.* Dublin: Gill & Macmillan, 1977.

Brontë, Charlotte. *Jane Eyre.* Edited by Q. D. Leavis. London: Penguin, 1985.

———. *Selected Letters of Charlotte Brontë.* Edited by Margaret Smith. Oxford: Oxford University Press, 2007.

————. *Villette.* Edited by Mark Lilly. London: Penguin, 1985.

Brook, Vincent. "Courting Controversy: The Making and Selling of *Baby Doll* and the Demise of the Production Code." *Quarterly Review of Film and Video* 18, no. 4 (2001): 347–60.

Brown, Ford K. *Fathers of the Victorians: The Age of Wilberforce.* Cambridge: Cambridge University Press, 1961.

Brownlow, Kevin. *Behind the Mask of Innocence.* Berkeley: University of California Press, 1990.

Burt, Richard, ed. *The Administration of Aesthetics: Censorship, Political Criticism, and the Public Sphere.* Minneapolis: University of Minnesota Press, 1994.

Butler, Marilyn. *Jane Austen and the War of Ideas.* Oxford: Oxford University Press, 1988.

Callahan, Dan. "George Cukor." *Senses of Cinema* 33 (October–December 2004): n.p., accessed 21 July 2012, http://sensesofcinema.com/2004/great-directors/cukor/.

Capra, Frank. *The Name Above the Title: An Autobiography.* New York: Macmillan, 1971.

Carson, Diane. "To Be Seen but Not Heard: *The Awful Truth.*" In *Multiple Voices in Feminist Film Criticism*, edited by Diane Carson, Linda Dittmar, and Janice R. Welsch, 213–25. Minneapolis: University of Minnesota Press, 1994.

Cavell, Stanley. *Pursuits of Happiness: The Hollywood Comedy of Remarriage.* Cambridge, MA: Harvard University Press, 1981.

Chandler, Alice. "A Pair of Fine Eyes: Jane Austen's Treatment of Sex." *Studies in the Novel* 7, no. 1 (1975): 88–103.

Cohen, William. *Sex Scandal: The Private Parts of Victorian Fiction.* Durham, NC: Duke University Press, 1996.

Collins, Philip, ed. *Charles Dickens: The Critical Heritage.* London: Routledge & Kegan Paul, 1971.

Couvares, Francis G., ed. *Movie Censorship and American Culture.* Washington, DC: Smithsonian Institution Press, 1996.

Cox, Stephen. *It's a Wonderful Life: A Memory Book.* Nashville: Cumberland House, 2003.

Davis, Paul. *The Lives and Times of Ebenezer Scrooge.* New Haven: Yale University Press, 1990.

DiBattista, Maria. *Fast Talking Dames.* New Haven: Yale University Press, 2003.

Dickens, Charles. *A Christmas Carol and Other Christmas Writings.* Edited by Michael Slater. London: Penguin, 2003.

————. *The Letters of Charles Dickens: The Pilgrim Edition.* Edited by Madeline House, Graham Storey, and Kathleen Tillotson. 11 vols. Oxford: Oxford University Press, 1974.

————. *Little Dorrit.* Edited by Stephen Wall and Helen Small. London: Penguin Classics, 1998.

————. *Martin Chuzzlewit.* Hertfordshire: Wordsworth Classics, 1994.

————. *Oliver Twist*. New York: Modern Library, 2001.

————. *Our Mutual Friend*. Edited by Adrian Poole. London: Penguin, 1997.

Doherty, Thomas. *Hollywood's Censor: Joseph I. Breen and the Production Code Administration*. New York: Columbia University Press, 2007.

————. *Pre-Code Hollywood: Sex, Immorality, and Insurrection in American Cinema, 1930–1934*. New York: Columbia University Press, 1999.

Dowling, Ellen. "The Derailment of *A Streetcar Named Desire*." *Literature/Film Quarterly* 9, no. 4 (1981): 233–40.

Duckworth, Alistair M. *The Improvement of the Estate: A Study of Jane Austen's Novels*. Baltimore: Johns Hopkins University Press, 1971.

Dussinger, John. *In the Pride of the Moment: Encounters in Jane Austen's World*. Columbus: Ohio State University Press, 1990.

Dutton, Richard. *Mastering the Revels: The Regulation and Censorship of English Renaissance Drama*. Iowa City: University of Iowa Press, 1991.

Eisenstein, Sergei. "Dickens, Griffith, and the Film Today." In *Film Form: Essays in Film Theory*. New York: Harcourt Brace Jovanovich, 1949.

Ellis, Havelock. *Studies in the Psychology of Sex*. 6 vols. Philadelphia: F. A. Davis, 1908.

Ellman, Richard. *Oscar Wilde*. New York: Vintage, 1988.

Farber, Manny. *Negative Space: Manny Farber on the Movies*. New York: Praeger, 1971.

Feltes, N. N. *Modes of Production of Victorian Novels*. Chicago: University of Chicago Press, 1986.

Flynn, Michael J. "*Pendennis, Copperfield*, and the Debate on the 'Dignity of Literature.'" *Dickens Studies Annual* 41 (2010): 151–89.

Forster, John. *Life of Charles Dickens*. Limbricht, Netherlands: Diderot, 2005.

Foucault, Michel. *The History of Sexuality*. Volume 1, *An Introduction*. Translated by Robert Hurley. New York: Vintage, 1990.

Fowell, Frank, and Frank Palmer. *Censorship in England*. New York: Benjamin Blom, 1969.

Freud, Sigmund. *The Interpretation of Dreams*. Translated by A. A. Brill. New York: Modern Library, 1978.

————. *The New Introductory Lectures of Psychoanalysis*. Edited by James Strachey. New York: W. W. Norton, 1965.

————. *Sexuality and the Psychology of Love*. Edited by Philip Rieff. New York: Simon & Schuster, 1997.

Gaskell, Elizabeth. *The Life of Charlotte Brontë*. London: Penguin, 1985.

Gilbert, Sandra M., and Susan Gubar. *The Madwoman in the Attic: The Woman Writer and the Nineteenth-Century Literary Imagination*. New Haven: Yale University Press, 1979.

Girard, René. *Deceit, Desire, and the Novel: Self and Other in Literary Structure*. Baltimore: Johns Hopkins University Press, 1966.

Glitre, Kathrina. *Hollywood Romantic Comedy: States of the Union, 1934–65*. London: Manchester University Press, 2006.

Grieveson, Lee. *Policing Cinema: Movies and Censorship in Early-Twentieth-Century America.* Berkeley: University of California, 2004.

Hamilton, Marybeth. *When I'm Bad, I'm Better: Mae West, Sex, and American Entertainment.* New York: HarperCollins, 1995.

Hearn, Michael Patrick. *The Annotated Christmas Carol.* New York: W. W. Norton, 2004.

Heydt-Stevenson, Jillian. *Austen's Unbecoming Conjunctions: Subversive Laughter, Embodied History.* New York: Palgrave Macmillan, 2005.

Hyland, Paul, and Neil Sammells, eds. *Writing and Censorship in Britain.* London and New York: Routledge, 1992.

It's a Wonderful Life. DVD. Directed by Frank Capra. 1946; Los Angeles: Paramount, 2006.

Jacobs, Lea. *The Decline of Sentiment: American Film in the 1920s.* Berkeley: University of California Press, 2008.

———. *The Wages of Sin: Censorship and the Fallen Woman Film, 1928–1942.* Berkeley: University of California Press, 1997.

Jadwin, Lisa. "The Seductiveness of Female Duplicity in *Vanity Fair.*" *SEL* 32, no. 4 (Autumn 1992): 663–87.

Jaffe, Audrey. "Spectacular Sympathy: Visuality and Ideology in Dickens' *A Christmas Carol.*" *PMLA* 109, no. 2 (March 1994): 254–65.

Johnson, Claudia. *Jane Austen: Women, Politics, and the Novel.* Chicago: University of Chicago Press, 1988.

Johnson, Edgar. *Charles Dickens: His Tragedy and Triumph.* New York: Viking, 1977.

Johnson, Patricia E. "Charlotte Brontë and Desire (to Write): Pleasure, Power, and Prohibition." In *Anxious Power: Reading, Writing, and Ambivalence in Narrative by Women,* edited by Carol J. Singley and Susan Elizabeth Sweeney. Albany: State University of New York Press, 1993.

Jordan, Elaine. "Pulpit, Stage, and Novel: 'Mansfield Park' and Mrs. Inchbald's 'Lovers' Vows.'" *NOVEL: A Forum on Fiction* 20, no. 2 (Winter 1987): 138–48.

Kaplan, Fred. *Dickens: A Biography.* Baltimore: Johns Hopkins University Press, 1988.

Kazan, Elia. *Elia Kazan: A Life.* New York: Alfred A. Knopf, 1988.

———. *Kazan on Directing.* New York: Alfred A. Knopf, 2009.

———. *Kazan on Kazan.* Edited by Jeff Young. London: Faber & Faber, 1999.

Kosofsky Sedgwick, Eve. *Between Men: English Literature and Male Homosocial Desire.* New York: Columbia University Press, 1985.

Kracauer, Siegfried. "Preston Sturges or Laughter Betrayed." *Films in Review* 1, no. 1 (February 1950): 43–47.

Kucich, John. "Passionate Reserve and Reserved Passion in the Works of Charlotte Brontë." *ELH* 52, no. 4 (Winter 1985): 913–37.

———. *Repression in Victorian Fiction: Charlotte Brontë, George Eliot, and Charles Dickens.* Berkeley: University of California Press, 1987.

Kuhn, Annette. *Cinema, Censorship, and Sexuality, 1909–1925.* London and New York: Routledge, 1988.

The Lady Eve. DVD. Directed by Preston Sturges. 1941; New York: Criterion Collection, 2001.

Leckie, Barbara. "'A Preface Is Written to the Public': Print Censorship, Novel Prefaces, and the Construction of a New Reading Public in Late-Victorian England." *Victorian Literature and Culture* 37 (2009): 447–62.

Le Faye, Deirdre. *Jane Austen: A Family Record*. Cambridge: Cambridge University Press, 1989.

———. "Letters." In *Jane Austen in Context*, edited by Janet Todd. Cambridge: Cambridge University Press, 2005.

Leff, Leonard J. "And Transfer to Cemetery: The *Streetcars Named Desire*." *Film Quarterly* 55, no. 3 (Spring 2002): 29–38.

Leff, Leonard J., and Jerold L. Simmons. *The Dame in the Kimono: Hollywood, Censorship, and the Production Code*. Lexington: University Press of Kentucky, 2001.

Levy, Emanuel. *George Cukor: Master of Elegance*. New York: William Morrow, 1994.

Litvak, Joseph. "Reading Characters: Self, Society, and the Text in *Emma*." *PMLA* 100, no. 5 (October 1985): 763–73.

———. *Strange Gourmets: Sophistication, Theory, and the Novel*. Durham, NC: Duke University Press, 1997.

Long, Robert Emmet, ed. *George Cukor: Interviews*. Jackson: University Press of Mississippi, 2001.

Macaulay, Thomas Babington. *The History of England from the Accession of James II*. 5 vols. Philadelphia: Porter & Coates, 1881.

Maltby, Richard. "*It Happened One Night*: The Recreation of the Patriarch." In *Frank Capra: Authorship and the Studio System*, edited by Robert Sklar and Vito Zagarrio. Philadelphia: Temple University Press, 1998.

Mamet, David. "Crisis in Happyland." *Sight and Sound* 12, no. 1 (January 2002): 22–23.

Mandal, Anthony. *Jane Austen and the Popular Novel: The Determined Author*. New York: Palgrave Macmillan, 2007.

Marcus, Steven. *The Other Victorians: A Study of Sexuality and Pornography in Mid-Nineteenth-Century England*. New York: Bantam Books, 1967.

Marsh, Joss. *Word Crimes: Blasphemy, Culture, and Literature in Nineteenth-Century England*. Chicago: University of Chicago Press, 1998.

Mason, Stuart. *Oscar Wilde: Art and Morality*. New York: Haskell, 1971.

Maynard, John. *Charlotte Brontë and Sexuality*. Cambridge: Cambridge University Press, 1984.

McBride, Joseph. *Frank Capra: The Catastrophe of Success*. Jackson: University Press of Mississippi, 2011.

McElhaney, Joe. "Fast Talk: Preston Sturges and the Speed of Language." In *Cinema and Modernity*, edited by Murray Pomerance, 273–94. New Brunswick, NJ: Rutgers University Press, 2006.

McGilligan, Patrick. *George Cukor: A Double Life*. New York: St. Martin's Press, 1991.

Mill, John Stuart. *On Liberty and Other Writings.* Edited by Stefan Collini. Cambridge: Cambridge University Press, 1989.

Miller, D. A. *Jane Austen, or The Secret of Style.* Princeton: Princeton University Press, 2003.

———. *Narrative and Its Discontents: Problems of Closure in the Traditional Novel.* Princeton: Princeton University Press, 1981.

Miller, J. Hillis. "The Genres of *A Christmas Carol.*" *The Dickensian* 89, no. 3 (Winter 1993): 193–206.

Millett, Kate. *Sexual Politics.* New York: Doubleday, 1969.

The Miracle of Morgan's Creek. DVD. Directed by Preston Sturges. 1944; Los Angeles: Paramount, 2005.

Moore, George. *Literature at Nurse, or Circulating Morals: A Polemic on Victorian Censorship.* Sussex: Harvester Press, 1976.

Motion Picture Producers and Distributors of America's "Report of the Sub-Committee on Eliminations." May 14, 1927. Available from MPPDA Digital Archive, Record #341.

Mr. Deeds Goes to Town. DVD. Directed by Frank Capra. 1936; Los Angeles: Sony Pictures, 2008.

Mr. Smith Goes to Washington. DVD. Directed by Frank Capra. 1939; Los Angeles: Sony Pictures, 2000.

Mulvey, Laura. "Visual Pleasure and Narrative Cinema." *Screen* 16, no. 3 (Autumn 1975): 6–18.

Murphy, Brenda. *Tennessee Williams and Elia Kazan: A Collaboration in the Theatre.* Cambridge: Cambridge University Press, 1992.

Parker, Alison M. *Purifying America: Women, Cultural Reform, and Pro-Censorship Activism, 1873–1933.* Urbana and Chicago: University of Illinois Press, 1997.

Patterson, Annabel. *Censorship and Interpretation: The Conditions of Writing and Reading in Early Modern England.* Madison: University of Wisconsin Press, 1984.

Pechter, George. "American Madness." In *Frank Capra: The Man and His Films,* edited by Richard Glatzer and John Raeburn. Ann Arbor: University of Michigan Press, 1975.

Peters, Catherine. *Thackeray: A Writer's Life.* Gloucestershire: Sutton, 1999.

The Philadelphia Story. DVD. Directed by George Cukor. 1940; Burbank: Warner Home Video, 2000.

Phillips, Gene D. *George Cukor.* Boston: Twayne, 1982.

Poague, Leland, ed. *Frank Capra: Interviews.* Jackson: University Press of Mississippi, 2004.

Post, Robert, ed. *Censorship and Silencing: Practices of Cultural Regulation.* Los Angeles: Getty Research Institute for the History of Art and the Humanities, 1998.

Production Code Administration files. Academy of Motion Picture Arts and Sciences Margaret Herrick Library, Los Angeles, CA.

Raby, Peter, ed. *The Cambridge Companion to Oscar Wilde.* Cambridge: Cambridge University Press, 1997.

Roderick, John M. "From 'Tarantula Arms' to Della Robia Blue." In *Tennessee Williams: A Tribute*, edited by Jac Tharpe. Jackson: University Press of Mississippi, 1977.

Sarris, Andrew. "Preston Sturges." In *The National Society of Film Critics on Movie Comedy*, edited by Stuart Byron and Elizabeth Weis. New York: Penguin, 1977.

———. *You Ain't Heard Nothin' Yet: The American Talking Film History and Memory, 1927–1949*. Oxford: Oxford University Press, 1998.

Schantz, Ned. "Telephonic Film." *Film Quarterly* 56, no. 4 (Summer 2003): 23–35.

Schlossberg, Herbert. *The Silent Revolution and the Making of Victorian England*. Columbus: Ohio State University Press, 2000.

Sen, Sambudha. "Radical Satire and Respectability: Comic Imagination in Hone, Jerrold, and Dickens." In *The Working-Class Intellectual in Eighteenth- and Nineteenth-Century Britain*, edited by Aruna Krishnamurthy. Surrey: Ashgate, 2009.

Shillingsburg, Peter L. *Pegasus in Harness: Victorian Publishing and W. M. Thackeray*. Charlottesville: University of Virginia Press, 1992.

Southam, B. C., ed. *Jane Austen: The Critical Heritage*. London: Routledge & Kegan Paul, 1968.

Stang, Richard. *The Theory of the Novel in England, 1850–1870*. London: Routledge & Paul, 1959.

A Streetcar Named Desire. Special Edition DVD. Directed by Elia Kazan. 1951; Burbank: Warner Home Video, 2006.

Sturges, Preston. *Five Screenplays by Preston Sturges*. Edited by Brian Henderson. Berkeley: University of California Press, 1985.

———. *Preston Sturges by Preston Sturges: His Life in His Words*. New York: Simon & Schuster, 1991.

Sutherland, J. A. *Victorian Novelists and Publishers*. Chicago: University of Chicago Press, 1976.

Tanner, Tony. "Licence and Licencing: To the Presse or to the Spunge." *Journal of the History of Ideas* 38, no. 1 (January–March 1977): 3–18.

Thackeray, William Makepeace. *Catherine: A Story*. Edited by Sheldon Goldfarb. Ann Arbor: University of Michigan Press, 1999.

———. *The Letters and Private Papers of William Makepeace Thackeray*. Edited by Gordon N. Ray. 4 vols. New York: Octagon, 1980.

———. *Pendennis*. Edited by John Sutherland. Oxford: Oxford University Press, 1994.

———. *Roundabout Papers*. Edited by John Edwin Wells. New York: Harcourt, Brace, 1925.

———. *Vanity Fair*. Edited by Peter Shillingsburg. New York: W. W. Norton, 1994.

Thackeray Ritchie, Anne. *The Two Thackerays: Anne Thackeray Ritchie's Centenary Biographical Introductions to the Works of William Makepeace Thackeray*. New York: AMS Press, 1988.

Thomas, Donald. *A Long Time Burning: The History of Literary Censorship in England*. New York: Frederick A. Praeger, 1969.

Tillotson, Geoffrey, and Donald Hawes, eds. *Thackeray: The Critical Heritage*. London: Routledge & Kegan Paul, 1968.

Tischler, Nancy. "The Distorted Reality: Tennessee Williams' Self-Portrait." In *Tennessee Williams: A Collection of Critical Essays*, edited by Stephen S. Stanton. New York: Prentice-Hall, 1977.

Van Doren Stern, Philip. "The Greatest Gift." Reprinted in Jeanine Basinger, *The "It's a Wonderful Life" Book*. New York: Knopf, 1986.

Walsh, Frank. *Sin and Censorship: The Catholic Church and the Motion Picture Industry*. New Haven: Yale University Press, 1996.

Watts-Dunton, Theodore. *The Coming of Love*. London: John Lane, 1899.

Wilson, Ben. *The Making of Victorian Values: Decency and Dissent in Britain, 1789–1837*. London: Penguin, 2007.

Wilson, Edmund. *The Wound and the Bow*. New York: Oxford University Press, 1947.

Wolfe, Charles. "The Return of Jimmy Stewart: The Publicity Photograph as Text." *Wide Angle* 6, no. 4 (1985): 44–52.

Wolffe, John. *The Expansion of Evangelicalism: The Age of Wilberforce, More, Chalmers and Finney*. Nottingham: Inter-Varsity Press, 2006.

Wood, Lisa. *Modes of Discipline: Women, Conservatism, and the Novel after the French Revolution*. Lewisburg, PA: Bucknell University Press, 2003.

Wood, Robin. "Ideology, Genre, Auteur." In *Film Theory and Criticism: Introductory Readings*, edited by Leo Braudy and Marshall Cohen. Oxford: Oxford University Press, 1999.

Woolf, Virginia. *The Common Reader*. New York: Harcourt, Brace, 1925.

Index

THE CULTURAL LIVES OF LAW

Austin Sarat, Editor

The Cultural Lives of Law series brings insights and approaches from cultural studies to law and tries to secure for law a place in cultural analysis. Books in the series focus on the production, interpretation, consumption, and circulation of legal meanings. They take up the challenges posed as boundaries collapse between as well as within cultures, and as the circulation of legal meanings becomes more fluid. They also attend to the ways law's power in cultural production is renewed and resisted.